ENGLISH in Common 3

Teacher's Resource Book with ActiveTeach

Araminta Crace
with Nick Witherick, Alison Bewsher, and John Peebles

Series Consultants
María Victoria Saumell and Sarah Louisa Birchley

ALWAYS LEARNING

PEARSON

English in Common 6
Teacher's Resource Book

Pearson Education, 10 Bank Street, White Plains, NY 10606

Staff credits: The editorial, design, production, and manufacturing people who make up the *English in Common 6* team are Margaret Antonini, Allen Ascher, Rhea Banker, Eleanor Kirby Barnes, Mike Boyle, Tracey Cataldo, Aerin Csigay, Mindy DePalma, Dave Dickey, Chris Edmonds, Charlie Green, Mike Kemper, Jessica Miller-Smith, Loretta Steeves, and Leigh Stolle.

This series is dedicated to Charlie Green. Without Charlie's knowledge of pedagogy, strong work ethic, sense of humor, patience, perseverance, and creativity, *English in Common* would never have existed.

Cover design: Tracey Cataldo

Cover photo: © qushe/shutterstock.com

Text design: Tracey Cataldo

Text composition: TSI Graphics

Text font: MetaPlus

ISBN 13: 978-0-13-267897-1

ISBN 10: 0-13-267897-7

Library of Congress Cataloging-in-Publication Data

Bygrave, Jonathan

English in common. Book 1 / Jonathan Bygrave.

p. cm.

ISBN 0-13-247003-9—ISBN 0-13-262725-6—ISBN 0-13-262727-2—ISBN 0-13-262728-0—ISBN 0-13-262729-9—ISBN 0-13-262731-0

1. English language—Textbooks for foreign speakers. 2. English language—Grammar. 3. English language—Spoken English.

PE1128.B865 2011

428.24--dc23

2011024736

Illustrated by Abel Ippólito.

Printed in the United States of America
1 2 3 4 5 6 7 8 9 10—V001—16 15 14 13 12

Contents

Teacher's Introduction

Teaching Notes

Extension Activities

ENGLISH 6
in Common
with ActiveBook
PEARSON

English in Common is a six-level course that helps adult and young-adult English learners develop effective communication skills that correspond to the Common European Framework of Reference for Languages (CEFR). Every level of *English in Common* is correlated to a level of the CEFR, and each lesson is formulated around a specific CAN DO objective.

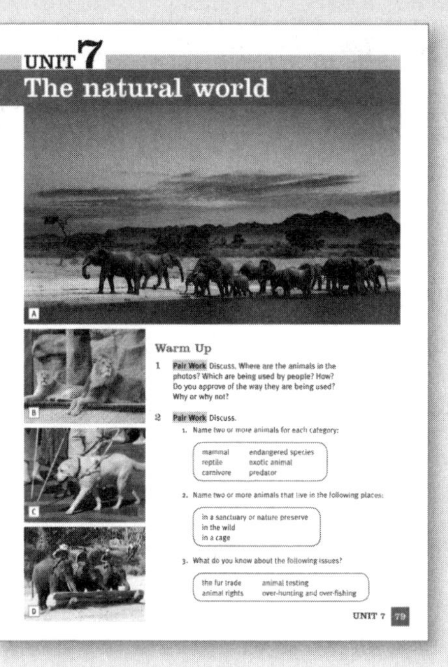

English in Common 6 has ten units. Each unit has twelve pages.

UNIT 7
The natural world
Warm Up
UNIT 7 79

There are three three-page lessons in each unit.

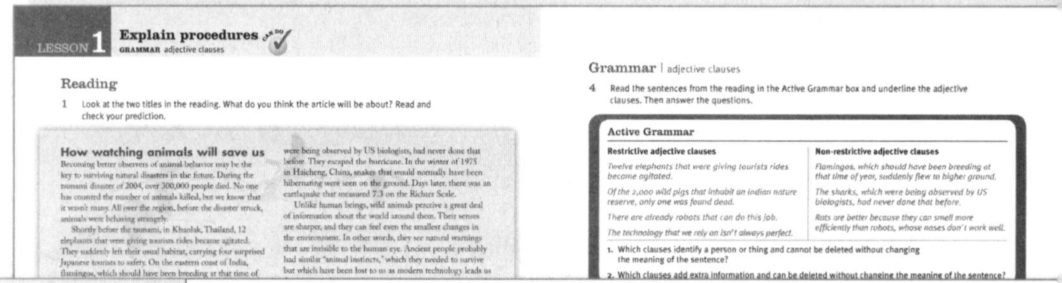

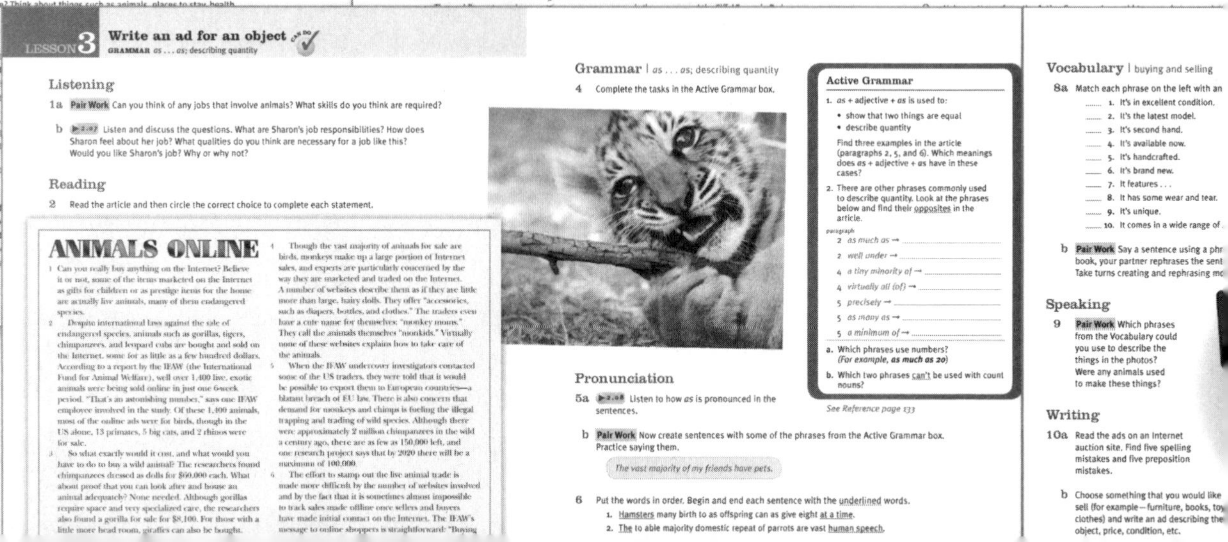

LESSON 1 Explain procedures
GRAMMAR adjective clauses
Reading
How watching animals will save us
Grammar | adjective clauses
Active Grammar

LESSON 2 Make inferences based on extended prose
GRAMMAR verbs followed by infinitives or gerunds: meaning
Vocabulary | descriptive language
Grammar | verbs followed by infinitives or gerunds: meaning
Active Grammar
Speaking
Listening

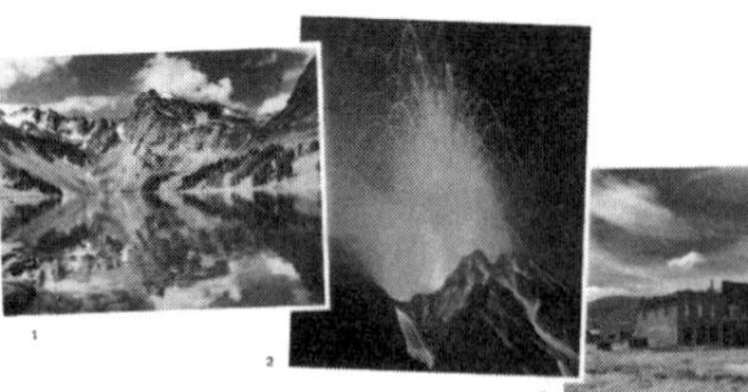

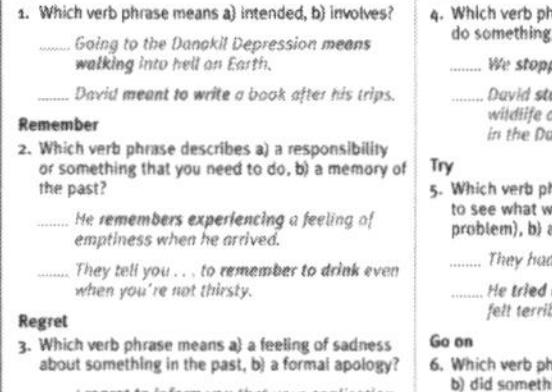

LESSON 3 Write an ad for an object
GRAMMAR as . . . as; describing quantity
Listening
Reading
ANIMALS ONLINE
Grammar | as . . . as; describing quantity
Active Grammar
Pronunciation
Vocabulary | buying and selling
Speaking
Writing

A Unit Wrap Up ends each unit.

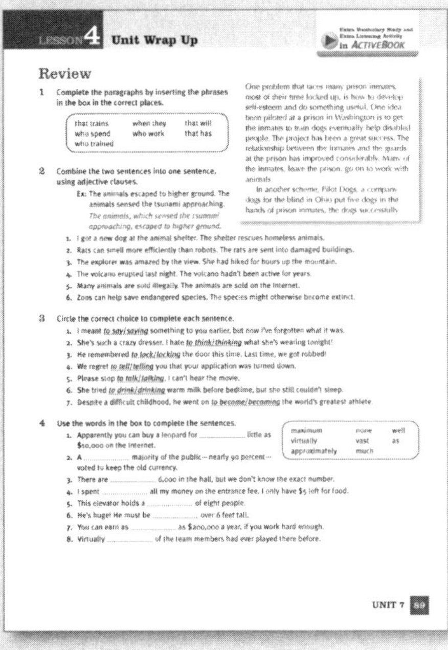

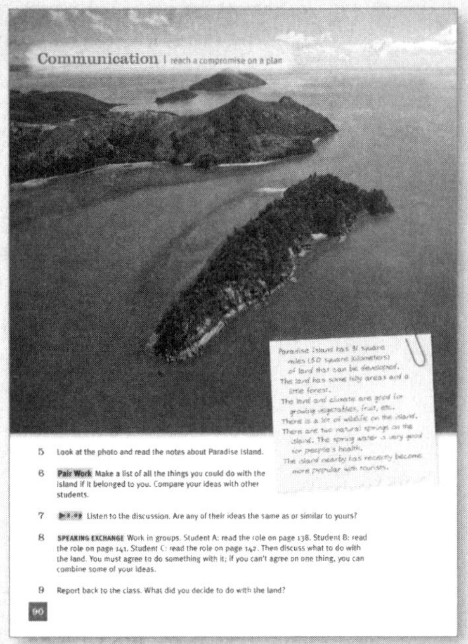

Back of Student Book

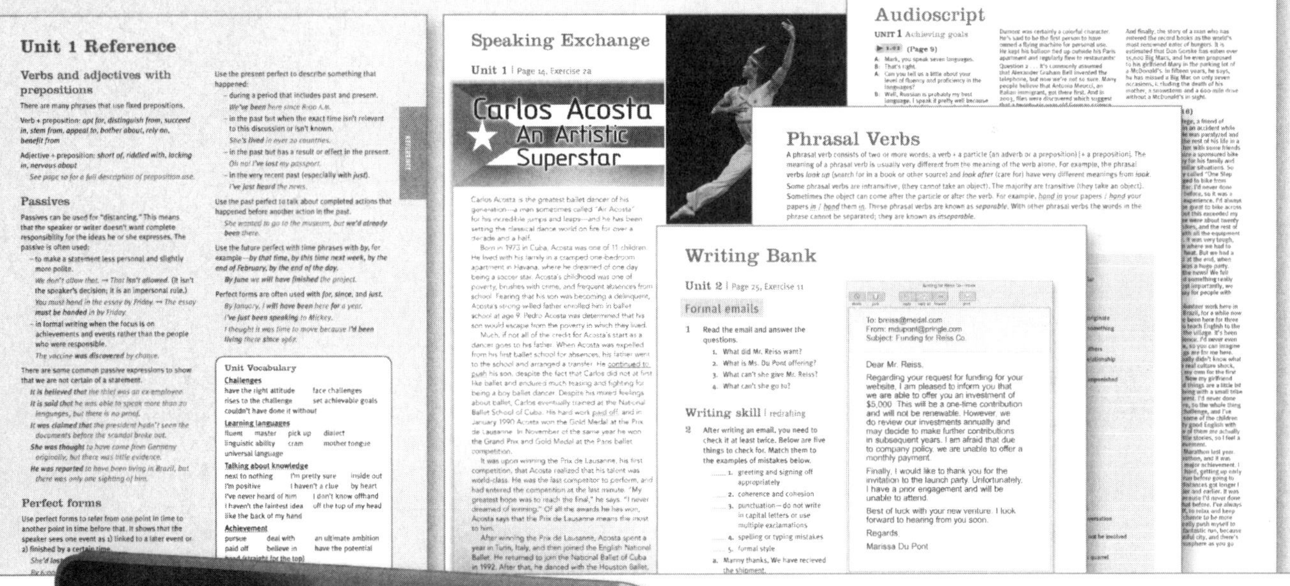

- Each Student Book contains an ***ActiveBook***, which provides the Student Book in digital format. *ActiveBook* also includes the complete Audio Program and Extra Listening activities.
- An optional online **MyEnglishLab** provides the opportunity for extra practice anytime, anywhere.
- The Teacher's Resource Book contains teaching notes, photocopiable extension activities, and an ***ActiveTeach***, which provides a digital Student Book enhanced by interactive whiteboard software. *ActiveTeach* also includes the videos and video activities, as well as the complete Test Bank.

	READING/WRITING	LISTENING	COMMUNICATION/EXTRA VOCABULARY STUDY
	Reading texts: • an article about polyglots • articles about two incredible athletes • a personality quiz **Writing task:** write a news report based on a picture	**Listening texts:** • an interview with a polyglot • a radio show about "famous firsts" • news stories • descriptions of personal achievements • analysis of answers to a personality quiz	**Communication:** take a personality quiz **Extra Vocabulary Study in *ActiveBook*:** prefixes
	Reading texts: • an article about Wikipedia • formal emails • descriptions of travel destinations **Writing tasks:** • write recommendations for travelers to your country • write a formal email • write a description of a favorite place	**Listening texts:** • descriptions of life abroad • a debate over the value of the Internet • descriptions of two clubs to which people belong	**Communication:** collaborate on a plan **Extra Vocabulary Study in *ActiveBook*:** phrasal verbs
	Reading texts: • an article about famous hoaxes • a biography of Groucho Marx **Writing task:** write a description of someone	**Listening texts:** • descriptions of favorite fictional characters • an abridged biography of Groucho Marx • a joke	**Communication:** tell a story **Extra Vocabulary Study in *ActiveBook*:** metaphors
	Reading texts: • an article on scientifically generated "superpowers" • an article on child geniuses • descriptions of new technology **Writing task:** summarize a story from a listening	**Listening texts:** • news stories • a conversation about superheroes • an interview with the creator of Spider Man • telephone conversations about future plans • an interview about child geniuses • discussions about discoveries and inventions	**Communication:** make an argument for research funding **Extra Vocabulary Study in *ActiveBook*:** two-part expressions
	Reading texts: • an article about a unique business model • true "riches to rags" stories • an article about famous philanthropists • an article about *Fortune* Magazine's 100 Best Companies to Work For **Writing task:** write a paragraph supporting an opinion	**Listening texts:** • advice on choosing a business partner • an interview with the CEO of a successful company • a discussion about a hypothetical business situation	**Communication:** negotiate **Extra Vocabulary Study in *ActiveBook*:** idioms 1
	Reading texts: • an article on architecture as a symbol of power • an article about the power of charisma **Writing tasks:** • write about two important pieces of architecture • write an autobiographical statement	**Listening texts:** • descriptions of important architectural structures • an interview about the influence of teens on technology • conversations about limits on teenagers	**Communication:** evaluate personal characteristics **Extra Vocabulary Study in *ActiveBook*:** idioms 2
	Reading texts: • an article on using animals to save human lives • an article about illegal online animal sales **Writing tasks:** • explain procedures in your home • write an ad for an object	**Listening texts:** • advice on choosing and caring for pets • a description of a travel adventure • a description of an unusual job • a discussion about how to develop a piece of land	**Communication:** reach a compromise on a plan **Extra Vocabulary Study in *ActiveBook*:** suffixes
	Reading texts: • opinions on necessary future inventions • an "online" advice column **Writing tasks:** • write an essay on a problem or issue	**Listening texts:** • descriptions of imaginary inventions • explanations of career choices • conversations about problems with machines	**Communication:** summarize opinions on issues **Extra Vocabulary Study in *ActiveBook*:** academic English
	Reading texts: • an article about famous visionaries • an article about fine art theft • advice for aspiring travel writers and photographers **Writing tasks:** • write about thoughts and actions inspired by a photo • write a story based on a hypothetical situation	**Listening texts:** • an interview about geniuses' "aha" moments • conversations about works of art • histories of two important inventors	**Communication:** collaborate on a proposal **Extra Vocabulary Study in *ActiveBook*:** confusing words
	Reading texts: • an article about a blind photographer • a book review • an excerpt from a novel **Writing task:** write about a childhood memory	**Listening texts:** • an interview about optimism and pessimism • deductions about feelings in the past • recollections of childhood • explanations of strong opinions	**Communication:** express strong feelings about an issue **Extra Vocabulary Study in *ActiveBook*:** phrasal verbs and particles

Introduction

Teaching and learning are unpredictable experiences. Learners can be energized and engaged in one lesson and then tired or demotivated the next. The goal of *English in Common* is twofold—first, to set new standards through its transparency of purpose, interest level, and teachability; second, to address the reality of unpredictable teaching situations that are experienced every day.

Finding direction and purpose

In order to stay motivated, learners need to know what they are learning, why they are learning it, and how it can be applied outside the classroom. Clear goals and objectives are crucial to this process. *English in Common* meets these needs by beginning each input lesson with a clearly stated Can Do learning objective and grammar focus. The Can Do objectives give a direction and purpose for learning. They ensure that students not only know what they are learning, but also why, and how they will be able to use it.

Engaging learners' interest

Maintaining motivation through engagement is equally important for successful language learning. *English in Common* engages learners' interest by offering a new twist to familiar topics—topics that reflect students' needs and interests. This guarantees that students will always have something to say about the content of the lesson. Students have frequent opportunities to exchange ideas and opinions and engage with the material on a personal level. Activities have been designed to be as realistic as possible so learners can see how the language they are learning can be applied outside the classroom.

Developing active learners

Effective learning also requires active participation. *English in Common* encourages students to become active participants in their own learning. By using a discovery approach to learning, *English in Common* guides students to observe structures in context and then use their own knowledge to figure out language use and form. Similarly, the series' approach to listening and reading texts develops a variety of skills and strategies that further cultivate learners' ability to cope with authentic material independently.

Student Book Structure

Each unit of the Student Book follows a consistent structure that makes it easy to use. The units are structured as follows:

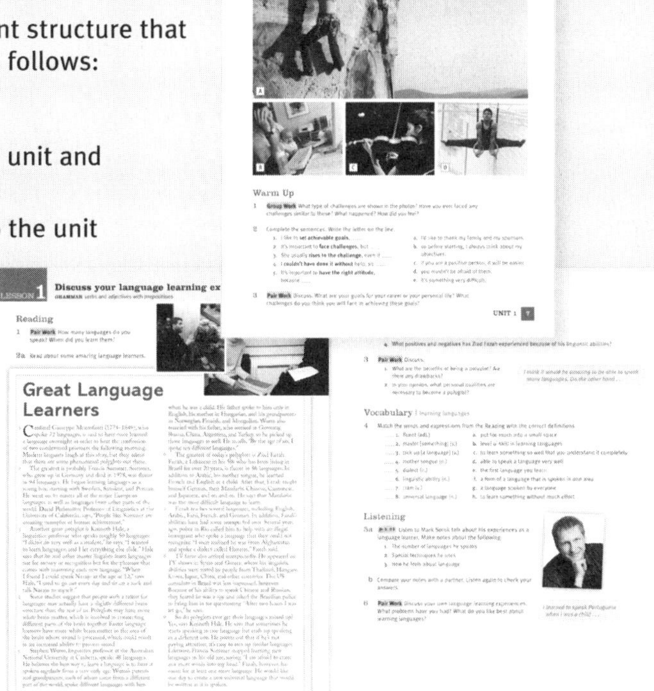

Warm Up

- Acts as a springboard into the topic of the unit and engages students' interest
- Introduces essential vocabulary related to the unit

Input Lessons (Lessons 1–3)

- Offers thematically linked lessons with interesting angles on the unit topic
- Based on a Can Do objective and grammar focus
- Contains listening texts and a substantial reading element for rich input
- Includes grammar, vocabulary, and skills work
- Develops students' communicative competence through How To boxes, in line with the CEFR

Unit Wrap Up (Lesson 4)

- Offers review through a range of exercises and a realistic free communication activity that consolidates the unit grammar and vocabulary
- Can be used to check progress, enabling teachers to identify areas that need further practice
- Provides a measurable goal or outcome for speaking

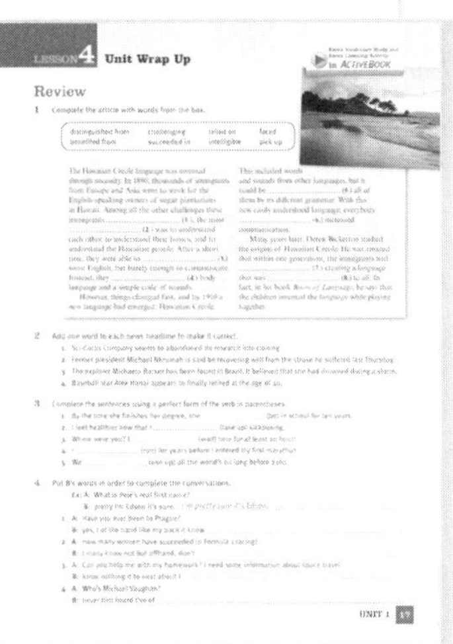

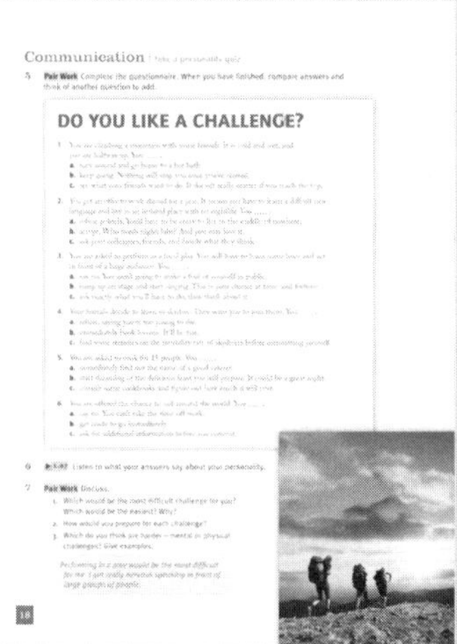

Back of Student Book

- **Reference** – Summarizes and reinforces the unit grammar and vocabulary
- **Speaking Exchange** – concrete stimulus for conversation activities
- **Writing Bank** – mini-lessons for key writing skills
- **Phrasal Verbs** – reference for 60 of the most commonly used phrasal verbs in American English
- **Audioscript** – for all listening activities in the Student Book

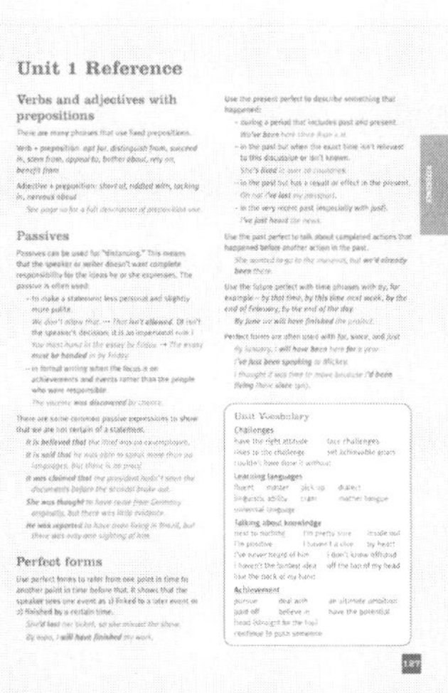

Teaching Approaches

Active Grammar

English in Common takes a "guided discovery" approach to grammar that invites learners to think about grammar examples and work out the rules for themselves.

- **Clear presentation and analysis**
  Each lesson has a clear grammar aim that is stated at the beginning of the lesson. New language items are presented in context through reading and/or listening. Then grammar rules are analyzed and explained through the Active Grammar boxes in the lessons.

Active Grammar

Often we use a reporting verb to *paraphrase* the meaning:

"Let's go home." → *She* ***thinks*** *we should leave.*

"Why don't we discuss it with everyone?" → *He* ***suggested*** *that we talk about it with everyone.*

"It was my mistake." → *He* ***admitted*** *that it was his fault.*

Match reporting verbs with similar meanings. Are there any differences in meaning or formality?

A	B
____ 1. admit	a. maintain
____ 2. remember	b. imply
____ 3. tell	c. respond
____ 4. answer	d. confess
____ 5. suggest	e. recollect
____ 6. threaten	f. inform
____ 7. insist	g. warn

See Reference page 134

- **Varied, regular practice**
  Once learners have grasped the rules, all new language is practiced in various ways so that learners are able to use the grammar with confidence. Practice activities include form-based exercises designed to help students manipulate new structures, as well as more meaningful, personalized practice. Additional grammar practice exercises can be found in the Unit Wrap Up lessons at the end of each unit and in the Workbooks. The Teacher's Resource Books also contain an extensive bank of photocopiable grammar activities designed to practice the language in freer, more communicative contexts.
- **Accessible reference material**
  In addition to the explanations in the Active Grammar boxes, a Reference page at the end of each unit summarizes the rules in greater detail and provides extra information and examples.

Vocabulary

English in Common recognizes the central role that vocabulary plays in successful communication. The emphasis is on providing learners with high-frequency, useful vocabulary that is regularly practiced and reviewed. New vocabulary is presented and practiced in a variety of different ways:

- Warm Up pages contain essential vocabulary related to the unit topic
- Reading and listening texts offer vocabulary in context
- Vocabulary sections and related exercises feature word combinations
- Extra Vocabulary Study that systematically extends student knowledge of lexical items such as collocations, word families, etc.
- Additional vocabulary practice is provided in the Unit Wrap Up lessons, the Workbooks, and printable vocabulary worksheets in the Teacher's Resource Book.

Vocabulary | expressing quantity

7a Complete the phrases from the listening, using the words in the box.

1. as ____________ as (a surprisingly large number)
2. a little ____________ more (a little more)
3. a great ____________ of energy (a lot of energy)
4. ____________ of benefits (a lot of benefits)
5. not ____________ of an expert (not really an expert)
6. for the ____________ part (generally)
7. the vast ____________ (most of)
8. quite a ____________ employees (a large number)
9. only a ____________ of people (very few people)

Speaking

The key aim for most learners is spoken fluency. *English in Common* supports fluency by providing:

- Interesting discussion topics that offer learners something to talk about
- Tasks that motivate learners to communicate
- Clear models that provide support for getting started
- How To boxes that teach key discourse strategies

How To:

Respond to hypothetical questions

positively	***It's highly likely*** *I'd agree.* *I* ***would probably*** *agree to that.* *I* ***would consider*** *doing that.* *I* ***suppose*** *I* ***might*** *do that.*
negatively	*I* ***probably wouldn't*** *accept.* ***It's unlikely*** *I'd be able to do that.* ***There's no way*** *I'd do that.*

All lessons feature pair work and group work speaking activities. Communication Activities at the end of each unit engage learners in a variety of problem-solving tasks and involve learners in a number of different skills—including speaking. In addition, the Teacher's Resource Book contains printable interactive activities that promote speaking practice.

Listening

Listening is one of the most important and difficult skills to master. *English in Common* pays particular attention to developing confidence in this area. Listenings range in length and type from short conversations and announcements to longer conversations, interviews, and excerpts from radio shows. Tasks range from simple "Listen and check your answers" activities to more challenging ones such as listening for gist, details, and making inferences. The recorded material features a variety of native-speaker and non-native speaker accents. Extra Listening in the *ActiveBook* at the back of each Student Book provides further practice understanding the spoken word.

Reading

There is a wide variety of readings in *English in Common* extending from simple forms and advertisements to articles from newspapers and magazines to short excerpts from novels. The length and complexity of reading texts increases from level to level. Readings have been chosen for their intrinsic interest and their use of the target grammar and vocabulary. Many readings have been adapted from a variety of authentic, real-life sources (magazines, websites, etc.), and related tasks have been carefully selected to develop learner confidence in dealing with them. Activities include comprehension and vocabulary work as well as practicing different reading sub-skills such as prediction and reading for gist. There are also a number of "jigsaw" readings in which learners read separate material and then work together to share the information.

Writing

As interest in globally-recognized standards and testing increases, writing is becoming an increasingly important skill. *English in Common* acknowledges this by including regular writing tasks in each unit. These carefully structured exercises and examples are designed to ensure that learners actually carry out the tasks. Models of emails, formal and informal letters, reports, and essays are provided in the Writing Bank in the back of the Student Book. Also included are additional advice and guidance on punctuation, spelling, and paragraph structure and useful phrases that model appropriate language for the genre.

Useful Phrases

Apologizing	• *I would like to apologize for the delay.*
Giving good or bad news	• *I am pleased to inform you that . . .* • *I regret to inform you that . . .*
Making a request	• *We would be grateful if you could . . .*
Responding to a request	• *We would be happy to . . .* • *I am afraid we are unable to . . .*
Complaining	• *I am writing to complain about . . .*
Responding to an invitation	• *We would be very happy to come to . . .* • *I am afraid I will be unable to attend.*

The Complete Course Package

Each level of *English in Common* consists of:

Student Book with *ActiveBook*

English in Common Student Books are divided into either ten or twelve units and have enough material for approximately 60 to 90 hours of instruction. Each Student Book has a bound-in *ActiveBook*, which contains a digital Student Book with the entire audio program, Extra Listening practice and activities, and a printable Language Portfolio to help students keep a record of their progress.

Workbook

The *English in Common* Workbook contains further practice of language areas covered in the Student Book. Split editions with a bound-in workbook are also available.

MyEnglishLab

Student Books are also available with an online MyEnglishLab that offers personalized, interactive practice, and an easy-to-use learning management system with an automatic gradebook.

Audio Program

The *English in Common* Audio Program includes all the listening and pronunciation material from the Student Book, as well as the audio for the Extra Listening and the Test Bank.

Teacher's Resource Book with *ActiveTeach*

The *English in Common* Teacher's Resource Book provides:

Teaching Notes – Detailed lesson plans that correlate to the relevant CEFR standards

Extension Activities – Photocopiable worksheets for grammar, vocabulary, and speaking with Teaching Notes

ActiveTeach

ActiveTeach contains a wide range of resources for lesson planning and in-class presentation. Everything you need is on one disc:

- **Digital Student Book** for projection
- **Interactive whiteboard tools** to write, highlight, zoom in and out of each Student Book page
- **Audio Program** with on-page, clickable MP3 files
- **Video Program** with videos, video activity worksheets, transcripts, and Teaching Notes
- **Extra Listening Activities** with audio, activity worksheets, answer key, and audioscripts (also provided on the Student *ActiveBook* for students' independent use)
- **Test Bank** with editable Progress Tests and a Placement Test with guidelines

How to Use *ActiveTeach*

Insert the disc into a computer to open the digital Student Book. *ActiveTeach* can be used with a laptop connected to a projector OR with an interactive whiteboard. You can also insert the disc into a DVD player to play the video alone.

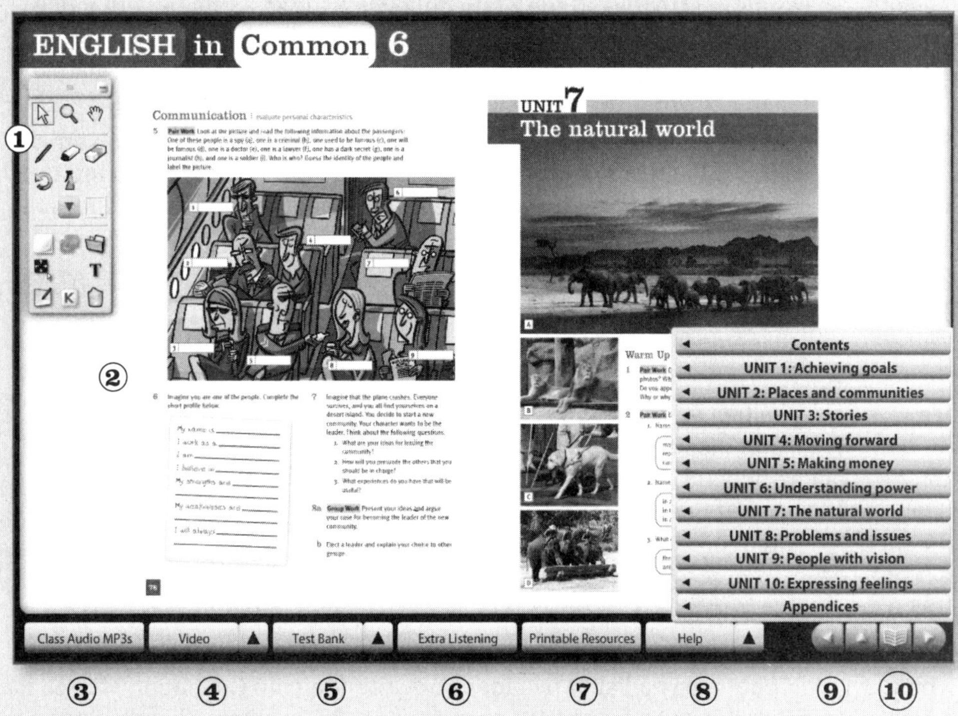

① Use the IWB tools to zoom in or out, write, highlight, create notes, and more.

② Click on an audio icon to open the audio player.

③ Download MP3 audio files to your computer or to an MP3 player.

④ Open the video player.

⑤ Choose and print ready-made tests or adapt them to your own teaching situation.

⑥ Play Extra Listening audio and print Extra Listening activity worksheets.

⑦ Choose from a variety of printable resources including video worksheets, Extra Vocabulary Study, workbook answer key, and the Language Portfolio.

⑧ Use the Help Button to run a video demonstration on How to Use *ActiveTeach*.

⑨ Use the arrows to navigate forward and backward.

⑩ Choose a unit or lesson.

Getting Started

Warm-up Suggestions

Warm-up activities help to focus learners' attention, review previously taught material, or introduce a new topic. Fun, movement, music, and visuals are important ingredients. Below are some ideas for easy-to-use warm-up activities. None of the following suggestions require much preparation. Consider playing classic board games and competitive activities such as Hang Man, Bingo, Trivial Pursuit, Tic Tac Toe, Scrabble, etc. Popular TV quiz shows provide useful formats for quizzes because students are familiar with them and can focus on content and language.

Name game 1 Students stand in a circle. To model, introduce yourself by taking a step toward the middle and saying, "My name is Irene, and I like Indian food." OR "My name is Fred, and I like baseball." Then a student steps toward the middle, repeats your sentence and introduces himself or herself. The next student repeats both sentences.

Name game 2 Students sit or stand in a circle or U shape. Say, "My name is [your name]." A student says, "This is [your name], and my name is John." Another student says, "This is [your name], and this is John, and my name is Sara." Go around the class. At the end of the game, you have to say all the names.

Play ball Practice exercises can be more fun if you stand in a circle and a student throws the ball to the next person. Use a soft medium-size ball. Short question-and-answer exercises, vocabulary review, etc., can be done like this. Start off by asking a question and throwing the ball to a student who has to answer the question. That student then asks the next question and throws the ball to another student and so on.

Walkabout This is similar to musical chairs. Play some music and ask students to walk around the classroom. When you stop the music, they stop and talk to the person standing nearest to them. This is a good way to get learners moving around and talking to others.

Find someone who . . . Either photocopy a list of five ideas or write them on the board. This can be used to introduce any topic and is good for practicing questions. For example: "Find someone who likes Shakira." One student asks another, "Do you like Shakira?" Students circulate and ask one another questions. Ask them to find at least three people for each idea or to find a different person for each idea. Clarify how to use negatives before the game, such as: "Find someone who doesn't like chocolate." In this case, the affirmative question is still used, "Do you like chocolate?" but only a negative answer counts.

Card games Always have a pack of cards with you. Take out the cards as necessary to form groups or pairs. Have each student pick a card and form groups accordingly (odd numbers and even numbers, hearts and diamonds, etc.). Additionally, you can create your own cards with words, pictures, phrases, etc. You can use almost any structure such as synonyms, antonyms, or irregular verbs to group students.

How to Use the Test Bank

These tests are included:

***English in Common* Placement Test**—to place students at the appropriate levels; the score guidelines for level placement are provided with the placement answer key

Unit Tests—at the end of every unit of the Student Book

Review Tests—one for the first half of the Student Book and one for the last half

A Final Test—cumulative for the entire Student Book

The Unit, Review, and Final tests can be printed as is, or they can be edited and adapted to suit your teaching situation using the Microsoft® Word files provided. Here are some ideas:

- Delete or add exercises to make the test shorter or longer
- Delete exercises for which you didn't include the content
- Add exercises to cover extra content you introduced
- Edit exercises to make them harder or easier
- Edit the format of exercises to match other exams
- Personalize the content with local information to bring the exercises to life
- Use the audioscripts to create additional listening exercises, for example, fill ins, error correction, or multiple-choice questions
- Add the name of your institution to the top of the test

Series Consultants

María Victoria Saumell

María Victoria Saumell holds a degree in Literary and Technical Translation and a Diploma, with Distinction, in the Theory and Methodology of TESOL. She is co-author of "Preparing for the Teaching Knowledge Test (TKT)," a module of the Longman online multimedia teacher-training program, *Teacher Development Interactive*. In addition, she is author of *Meeting Point*, a teacher's guide to digital tools, as well as the author of and tutor for *New Learning Environments*, an online teacher-training course for the Masters in ELT program at Universidad de la Sabana in Colombia. Ms. Saumell has taught English in private schools for the past twenty years and is currently the Overall Coordinator of the EFL department at Instituto Francisco de Asis in Buenos Aires, Argentina. She is a frequent presenter at professional development conferences and is an expert on the integration of new technologies for language learning.

Sarah Louisa Birchley

Sarah Louisa Birchley has been teaching in Japan for over ten years, including working as a researcher at the Foreign Language Research Institute of Gunma Prefectural Women's University. She is currently Assistant Professor in the Faculty of Business Administration at Toyo Gakuen University and has presented at international conferences throughout Asia, Australia, and the US. Ms. Birchley is an active member of the Japan Association for Language Teaching (JALT) and has served as their international Conference Program Chair and, most recently, Conference Manager. She is also coordinator of the JALT Business English Special Interest Group and a member of the Japan Business Communication Association. Ms. Birchley has an MA in Education from the University of Bath and is currently in the final stages of her Doctorate of Education.

English in Common and International Standards

The chart below shows how the different levels of *English in Common* relate to international standards and exams.

	CEFR	Cambridge Exams	TOEFL iBT	TOEIC
English in Common 1	A1	Foundation for KET		110–280
English in Common 2	A2	KET	26–40	280–400
English in Common 3	B1	PET	40–54	400–540
English in Common 4		PCE	54–72	540–710
English in Common 5	B2	PCE	72–92	710–800
English in Common 6	C1	CAE	92–100	800+

UNIT 1

Achieving goals

Unit Overview

Warm Up Lesson	
LESSON 1	**CAN DO** discuss your language learning experiences **GRAMMAR** verbs and adjectives with prepositions **VOCABULARY** learning languages
LESSON 2	**CAN DO** say how much you know or don't know **GRAMMAR** passives **VOCABULARY** talking about knowledge
LESSON 3	**CAN DO** talk about your achievements **GRAMMAR** perfect forms **VOCABULARY** achievement
LESSON 4	**Unit Wrap Up** **Review** reinforce lessons 1–3 **Communication** take a personality quiz
Grammar and Vocabulary Reference Charts	

OPTIONAL LANGUAGE PORTFOLIO

The *English in Common* Language Portfolio is designed to:

- help learners think about their objectives and reflect on how they learn best
- motivate learners by acknowledging their progress
- provide learners with a record of achievement that they can show others.

It consists of three sections:

1. *Personal Profile*
2. *Self-Assessment*
3. *Achievement Portfolio.*

Download the Language Portfolio from your *ActiveTeach* disc (at the back of this Teacher's Resource Book), or have students download it from their *ActiveBook* discs (at the back of their Student Books). Ask students to fill out the *Personal Profile.*

Teaching Resources

- **Workbook** pp. 4–11
- **Class Audio** CD1 Tracks 2–7
- ***ActiveBook*** Digital Student Book pages with complete unit audio plus Extra Listening Activity and Extra Vocabulary Study
- ***ActiveTeach*** Interactive whiteboard (IWB) software with video, Test Bank, and test audio

Warm Up p. 7

OPTIONAL WARM UP

Write the word *challenge* on the board. Have students work with a partner to write a definition of the word. Then ask students to share their definitions with the rest of the class.

Write the following questions on the board for the students to discuss in pairs:

- What challenges did you face as a child or teenager?
- What challenges do you face now as an adult?
- What was the last challenge you faced? Were you successful?

Elicit answers from different pairs.

1 Ask students to focus on the photos. Elicit from the class the types of challenges illustrated in each one. Students can then tell their group partners if they have ever faced challenges like the ones shown and how they felt.

2 Direct students to match the clauses in items 1–5 to the clauses in a–e. Ask students to check their answers with a partner. Check answers with the class and make sure that students understand the meaning of the expressions in bold.

Answers: 1. b **2.** d **3.** e **4.** a **5.** c

3 Ask students to discuss the questions with a partner. Encourage them to use the phrases from Exercise 2 where possible. Monitor the conversations carefully for errors. Elicit answers from the class and write any errors the students have made on the board. Ask different students to correct the errors. Finally, draw students' attention to any interesting language they used in the conversations and congratulate them on its use.

EXTEND THE WARM UP

Focus students on the four photos on page 7 again. Have pairs of students rank the challenges (1–4) in order of difficulty for them. Then direct students to work with a new partner and tell the order they have chosen, explaining their reasons. Elicit feedback from different pairs, and then encourage the class as a whole to try to agree on an order. This may start a debate as to whether a physical, mental, or emotional challenge is the most difficult.

LESSON 1 pp. 8–10

CAN DO discuss your language learning experiences
GRAMMAR verbs and adjectives with prepositions
VOCABULARY learning languages

Summary: In this lesson, students read an article about people who speak many languages (polyglots). They go on to look at vocabulary from the reading related to learning languages. They also listen to someone describing their experiences as a language learner. Students then look at prepositions that collocate with different verbs and adjectives.

Note: A polyglot is a person who has a high degree of proficiency in several languages. For different reasons, it can be very difficult to calculate accurately how many languages a person speaks. Perhaps most importantly, it is very difficult to define what it actually means to speak a language. For example, a four-year-old Spanish girl would usually be considered to speak Spanish fluently, but may not have as accurate a command of the subjunctive as a foreign student of the language would. There have been many famous people who have been credited with being polyglots. James Joyce, the author of *Ulysses*, reputedly spoke 13 languages, including Danish, Dutch, French and Irish. J.R.R. Tolkien, the author of *The Lord of the Rings*, apparently also knew 13 languages. Pope John Paul II learned as many as 11 languages in his lifetime.

OPTIONAL WARM UP
For homework prior to the lesson, ask students to do some research on languages, using the Internet or an encyclopedia. Direct students to find interesting facts about, for example, which language is spoken by the most or least people, the language spoken in a less well-known country, etc. Students should bring their facts to the next class and work with a partner to create a quiz from their facts. Have students exchange and complete quizzes. Elicit feedback by asking which pair got the highest score and which quiz was the most difficult.

Reading

1 Ask students to discuss the questions with a partner. Monitor conversations and take note of any important errors. Keep these errors to correct after Exercise 3. Discuss the students' ideas as a class.

2a Have students read the article. Tell them not to worry about any words or expressions they don't know, as you will deal with any difficult vocabulary later.

b Direct students to look back at the reading to find answers to the questions. Then have them compare their answers with a partner. Check the answers, and the paragraphs they are found in, with the class.

Answers: 1. Because they enjoy it; "the pleasure that comes with mastering each new language." (paragraph 3)
2. They may have more white brain matter in the area of the brain where sound is processed, which could result in an increased ability to process sound. (paragraph 4)
3. Getting their languages mixed up. (paragraph 9)
4. Positives: He has appeared on television, and he was able to help the police to identify the nationality of a man. Negatives: He was suspected of being a spy because he spoke Chinese and Russian. (paragraphs 7 and 8)

Ask students if there are any words or phrases from the reading that they don't understand. Encourage students to answer each others' questions or to consult an English-English dictionary before you explain the vocabulary to the class.

3 Have students discuss the questions with a partner. Monitor the conversations carefully for errors and any interesting language the students use. Elicit answers from different pairs and discuss the students' ideas as a class. Finally, write any errors from the students' discussions in Exercises 1 and 3 on the board. Look at the errors with the class and encourage different students to correct them. Draw students' attention to any interesting language that they have used and praise them on its use.

Vocabulary

4 Instruct students to cover definitions a–h. Have students work with a partner to discuss the meaning of the words and expressions in items 1–8. They can look back at the reading if necessary and try to work out the meaning from the context. Then have students uncover the definitions and match them to the words and expressions on the left. Ask students to compare their answers with another partner. Check answers with the whole class.

Answers: 1. d **2.** c **3.** h **4.** e **5.** f **6.** b **7.** a **8.** g

Listening

OPTIONAL WARM UP
Call on students to tell the class which languages they have learned. Make a list on the board. Ask follow-up questions, such as *When did you begin learning? Is/Was it a difficult language to learn? Do other members of your family speak the language?*

5a Focus students' attention on the topics in items 1–3. Play audio 1.02. As students listen to Mark Sorok talking about his experiences as a language learner, have them make notes about each of the topics.

b Give students time to compare their notes with a partner. Play audio 1.02 again. Have students listen again and check their answers with their partners. Check answers with the whole class.

Answers: 1. Number of languages: seven **2.** Special techniques: memory training, watching movies in their original language, sticking lists of words around the house **3.** How he feels about language: he loves languages

6 Ask students to look at the topics in Exercise 5a again. Tell them to make notes about these topics, focusing on their own experiences as language learners. Ask students to exchange notes with a partner. Elicit information from different pairs. Then ask students to tell the class about their partner's language learning experiences. Decide with the class who has had some of the most interesting language learning experiences.

Grammar

OPTIONAL WARM UP

Write the following verbs from the article on page 8 on the board: *laugh, come, work*. Have students work in groups of three to think of prepositions that can collocate with each verb. Then ask students to share their ideas with another group. Elicit ideas from different groups and write the collocations on the board. Now have students scan paragraphs 1–5 of the article quickly to check which prepositions collocate with the verbs. Finally, discuss with the class how they might be able to keep a record in their notebooks of words and the prepositions that are sometimes used with them.

7 Ask students to cover the captions on the left. Direct students to look at the pictures and discuss what messages each conveys. Tell students to uncover the captions and match them with the pictures.

Answers: 1. B **2.** A

8 Focus students' attention on the Active Grammar box. Ask them to answer questions 1 and 2. Check answers with the whole class. Then have students rewrite sentence 2 in Exercise 7 so that the preposition is followed by a gerund. Have students compare their sentences with a partner. Check the sentences students have written and write the correct sentence on the board. (*Tanya tended to rely on translating when she learned new words.*)

Answers: 1. verb + preposition = sentence 2; adjective + preposition = sentence 1 **2. 1.** opportunities **2.** translation

Direct students to the Reference section on page 127 and give them time to read the different fixed phrases. Ask students to work with a partner to add other examples of fixed phrases that use *verb + preposition* and *adjective + preposition*. Monitor the class and check the examples students are writing. Write some of the examples on the board and check as a class.

9 Direct students to complete sentences 1–10 with the correct prepositions from the box. Tell students that if there are any expressions they haven't seen before, they can look them up in their dictionaries. Check answers with the whole class.

Answers: 1. in **2.** for **3.** from **4.** in **5.** with **6.** from **7.** to **8.** with **9.** about **10.** from

OPTIONAL PRESENTATION

If you prefer a more deductive approach, use the complete grammar charts and explanations on the Reference page to present the concepts. (page 127)

Speaking

10a Have students work with a partner to discuss questions 1–10 in Exercise 9. They should answer the questions for themselves and give reasons for their answers. Monitor the conversations and take note of important errors.

b Ask various students to tell the class what they have found out about their partners. Write any important errors you have heard on the board and ask different students to correct them.

OPTIONAL EXTENSION

Ask students to think of five study techniques that they think are the best ways to improve their English. Students should compare their ideas with a partner and explain why they think the methods they have chosen are best. Then have students compare ideas with another pair. Elicit feedback from different pairs and discuss as a class which of the methods are the most practical and why.

NOTES

LESSON 2 pp. 11–13

CAN DO say how much you know or don't know
GRAMMAR passives
VOCABULARY talking about knowledge

Summary: In this lesson, students look at expressions for saying how much you know or don't know about things. Students take a quiz about the first people to do important things and then look at passive constructions. Then they listen to radio news headlines before going on to write their own news report.

Note: Some famous firsts: First movie to earn one billion dollars worldwide: *Titanic*, released in 1997. First webmail service: Hotmail, launched in 1996. First music video on MTV: *Video Killed the Radio Star* by The Buggles, broadcast on August 1, 1981.

OPTIONAL WARM UP

Make sure that students are familiar with the concept of a "famous first," giving examples if necessary. Students decide what they consider to be the most important "famous first" in history. Ask students to work in groups of four to share their ideas and justify their choices. Each group should try to reach agreement about what the most important "famous first" is. Rearrange students into new groups of four to share their ideas. Ask the class to try to agree on the three most important "famous firsts" in history.

Vocabulary

1a Instruct students to complete sentences 1–12 with words from the box. Then have students compare answers with a partner. Check answers with the class.

Answers: **1.** clue **2.** head **3.** sure *or* certain **4.** of **5.** hand **6.** know **7.** heart **8.** out **9.** nothing **10.** idea **11.** sure *or* certain **12.** certain *or* positive *or* sure

b Have students decide whether the expressions in bold in Exercise 1a mean *I know* or *I don't know.* After they have marked their answers, ask them to compare answers with a partner. Finally, check answers with the class.

Answers:
Meanings: *I'm pretty sure* means *I'm fairly certain. I don't know off the top of my head* and *I don't know offhand* are similar. They mean *I can't tell you the answer now (without looking for the relevant information).* We use *I've never heard of . . .* when we don't recognize the name of the thing mentioned (it could be a person, an object, a place, etc). We use *next to nothing* when we recognize the name of the subject but know almost nothing about it/him/her. We use this expression in response to a *What do you know about . . . ?* question, or in the expression *I know next to nothing about it. I know it like the back of my hand, I know it by heart* and *I know it inside out* mean *I know it extremely well. I know it like the back of my hand* is often used to talk about a place, while *I know it inside out* is often used to talk about a subject. *I know it by heart* is used for something we have memorized, perhaps a poem or a speech.
I know: *I'm pretty sure / certain, I know it like the back of my hand, I know it by heart, I know it inside out, I'm fairly sure / certain, I'm positive / certain / sure it is*
I don't know: *I haven't a clue, I don't know off the top of my head, I've never heard of him, I don't know offhand, I know next to nothing (about) . . . , I haven't the faintest idea*

Speaking

2 Have students ask a partner how much they know or don't know about the topics in the box. Encourage students to use the language from the Vocabulary presentation. Monitor the conversations for use of the expressions. Elicit feedback from the class and discuss which of the expressions they used in their conversations.

OPTIONAL EXTENSION

Ask students to think about what they know or don't know about other students in the class. They should write down one thing they think they know and one thing they don't know about five other students in the class. Then have students mingle and talk about how much they know or don't know using the expressions from the Vocabulary.

Listening

3 Have students read the quiz questions with a partner and choose what they think are the correct answers. Encourage students to use the expressions from Exercise 1a while discussing the quiz. Then ask students to compare answers with another pair. Elicit answers from the class.

4 Tell students that they are going to listen to a radio show to check their answers. Play audio 1.03. Students listen and check their answers.

Answers: **1.** a or b **2.** b or c **3.** a or possibly b **4.** Probably a **5.** b **6.** b **7.** c **8.** c

Encourage students to discuss the answers after listening. Are there any answers that surprised them? Any that they disagree with?

Grammar

OPTIONAL WARM UP
Ask students to share with a partner what they can remember about Ziad Fazah from the article on page 8. Discuss answers as a class, then write the following sentence on the board: *People from different countries tested his linguistic abilities on TV programs.* Under this sentence write: *His linguistic abilities . . .* Ask a student to complete the second sentence so that it has the same meaning as the first sentence. If the student cannot produce the correct answer, write it on the board: *His linguistic abilities were tested by people from different countries.* Ask students what the difference between the two sentences is (Sentence 1 is active, sentence 2 is passive). Have students discuss with a partner how the passive is formed and why it is used in English. Focus students on the pronunciation of the weak form of were: /wər/. Draw students' attention to the use of *by* to include the agent, or "doer," in a passive sentence.

5 Focus students on the Active Grammar box and give them time to read it and choose the correct answer to item 1.

Answer: **1.** a

Direct students to the Reference section on page 127. Give students time to read the notes. Check that students are familiar with the form of the passive in English: the verb *be* + past participle.

6 Direct students to complete the sentences. Make sure that students use passives and the verb in bold. Remind them to pay attention to verb tense. After students have completed the exercise, have them compare answers with a partner. Check answers and write the sentences on the board.

Answers: **1.** seems as **2.** is thought to have **3.** is asserted **4.** was claimed **5.** are believed to have **6.** was reported **7.** is (now) believed

OPTIONAL PRESENTATION
If you prefer a more deductive approach, use the complete grammar charts and explanations on the Reference page to present the concepts. (page 127)

Listening

OPTIONAL WARM UP
With a monolingual class, ask students to tell you what is happening in the news in their country at the moment. With a multilingual class, students can tell a partner what is happening in the news in their countries. Elicit feedback from different pairs.

7a Tell students that they are going to hear some radio news headlines about different achievements. Play audio 1.04 and ask students to take notes about the achievements mentioned. Then have students compare their notes with a partner.

Answers: Achievements mentioned: The breeding of clones of wild cats. An Australian teenager has become the youngest person to sail solo around the world. Don Gorske has entered the record books for having eaten over 15,000 Big Macs in his life.

b Have students retell the stories to their partner and discuss their opinions of whether the stories are important or not. If necessary, you may wish to have students look at the audioscript on page 148 to check the accuracy of their summaries.

Speaking

8 Direct students to discuss the questions with a partner. Monitor conversations for errors. Elicit answers from different pairs. Write errors you have heard on the board and ask students to correct them.

Writing

9a Ask students to choose one of the pictures. Tell students that they are going to write a news report based on the picture they have chosen. Before students start writing, review the passive constructions for distancing and write them on the board. Monitor what students are writing, helping where necessary. Make sure that students include passive constructions in their bulletins.

b Give students time to practice reading their news bulletins with their group partners. As you monitor, encourage students to concentrate on their stress patterns. You may then wish to have students read their reports to the rest of the class. These could be recorded on audio or video for later evaluation.

LESSON 3 pp. 14–16

CAN DO talk about your achievements
GRAMMAR perfect forms
VOCABULARY achievement

Summary: In this lesson, students discuss which sports are typically dominated by men and which by women. Then they read about a female race-car driver and a male ballet dancer and exchange information about what they have read. Students listen to people who have achieved difficult things and through this context study perfect verb forms. Finally, they discuss their greatest achievement.

OPTIONAL WARM UP

Ask students to make a list of four activities that they do well and four activities that they do badly. Then have them share their lists with a partner and explain why they are good or bad at the activities.

Reading

1 Ask students to discuss the questions with a partner. Monitor conversations for errors. Compare answers as a class and write any important errors you have heard on the board. Try to elicit the correct forms from the students before correcting them yourself. Discuss the dangers of sexual stereotyping with the class.

2a Divide the class into two groups, A and B. Students A read the article on page 15. Students B read the article on page 137. While reading, students make notes in the chart. If students have any questions about vocabulary, tell them they will be addressed later in the lesson.

When students have finished completing the chart, they can check what they have written with other members of their group.

Answers:
What is/was their ambition?
Figueiredo: To be a great driver
Acosta: To reach the final of the Prix de Lausanne
To what extent have they achieved it?
Figueiredo: She is competing in the IZOD IndyCar series
Acosta: He won the Grand Prix and the Gold Medal at the Paris Ballet and went on to be a great dancer
What challenges have they faced?
Figueiredo: Chauvinism, money problems, time constraints when she was studying
Acosta: Prejudice (boys don't do ballet), fighting and teasing from boys at school. He was brought up in a rough suburb in Havana.
Who has helped them achieve their ambitions? How?
Figueiredo: Her father—he has both encouraged and financed her ambition. Nô—her mechanic and mentor. He believes in her.
Acosta: His father—enrolled him in ballet school. When the school threw Carlos out, his father arranged a transfer and pushed him to stay with ballet as a good career.

b Pair students so that Students A are working with Students B. Direct students to exchange information about their articles (from looking at their notes, not the articles). Encourage students to decide if there are similarities between the two stories and then discuss the similarities as a class.

3 Organize students into small groups to discuss the questions. Rearrange students so that they are working with different students. Ask them to report what they have discussed to their new groups. Monitor the conversations for important errors and interesting language. Then compare ideas as a class. Write important errors you have heard on the board and encourage students to correct them. Finally, write examples of interesting language students have used and congratulate them on its use.

Vocabulary

4a Focus students' attention on the words and expressions in items 1–8. You may wish to have students discuss with a partner the meaning of the vocabulary. Encourage students to use the context of the articles to help work out the meaning of the vocabulary. Then ask different students to explain the meaning of the words and expressions to the rest of the class.

OPTIONAL VARIATION

Instruct students to keep their books closed. Write the main words from Exercise 4a (*head*, *pursue*, *deal with*, etc.) in a column on the left-hand side of the board. Write the expressions in parentheses (*straight for the top*, etc.) in a separate column on the right-hand side of the board in a different order. Direct students to work with a partner to match the main words with the expressions in the right-hand column. To check answers, ask one student from each pair to come to the board to connect the words and expressions. Then ask students to write an example sentence for each word or expression. Students compare sentences with a partner. Monitor and note any good examples. Write these on the board.

b Have students complete sentences 1–8 using the words and expressions from Exercise 4a. You may want to have students compare their answers with a partner. Check answers with the whole class.

Answers: 1. had the potential **2.** deal with **3.** pursued **4.** believe in **5.** ultimate ambition **6.** push **7.** paid off **8.** headed (straight)

Listening

5 Have students discuss the questions with a partner. Monitor conversations and take note of errors and interesting language students use.

OPTIONAL VARIATION

Brainstorm as a class some activities that are difficult. Write students' ideas on the board. Then organize students into groups of three. Tell students to rank the activities in order of difficulty but that they do not have to agree with the other students in their group. They should try to convince the other students of their point of view. Give students a few minutes to think about what they are going to say, then let them start the discussion. Monitor the different groups closely, listening especially for any expressions for disagreeing that the students use. Then compare ideas as a class.

6 Tell students that they are going to listen to different people talking about the things they have achieved. Have students read the two questions to focus their attention. Play audio 1.05. Direct students to answer the questions.

Give students time to compare their answers with a partner. Play audio 1.05 again. Check answers with the class.

Answers: 1. Speaker 1: Raised money for a good cause by helping to organize and taking part in a long-distance bicycle ride. Speaker 2: Is doing volunteer work teaching English to children in a remote village. Speaker 3: Ran a marathon. **2.** Speaker 1: It was very tough cycling, especially in Spain against the heat. Speaker 2: He'd never left the U.S. before. It was a real culture shock initially. Speaker 3: She had to train really hard; she'd never done any training like that before.

Grammar

7 Direct students' attention to the Active Grammar box. Give students time to read the notes in the box. Instruct students to match the examples on the left to the timelines on the right. Then have students compare their answers with a partner. Check answers with the class.

Answers: 1. b **2.** c **3.** a

Direct students to the Reference section on page 127. Give them time to read the notes. Ask: *If the speaker uses a perfect form, what two possible ways does the speaker see the event?* (Linked to a later event or finished by a certain time.) *What words do we often use perfect forms with? (For, since, and just.)*

8a Focus students' attention on the sentences. Instruct them to circle the correct choice to complete the sentences. Check answers with the whole class.

Answers: 1. Jake, this is my friend Amy, whom I've **known** forever. (*I've been knowing* is incorrect—we don't use the progressive form with a stative verb.) **2.** I asked what had **happened**, but nobody could tell me. (*Had been happened* is incorrect—we need the active, not the passive form here.) **3.** I chose this school because **I'd heard** it was the best. (Need to use a past participle to form the past perfect tense.) **4.** Before I came to the US, **I'd** never been abroad. (The past perfect is used to talk about something that happened before another action in the past.) **5.** I'm so exhausted. **I've** been working really hard. (*I'm so . . . I'd been* is incorrect—we can only use the past perfect with another past tense.) **7.** By the time she retires, she'll **have been working** there for more than 50 years. (*she'll had been working* is incorrect—the future perfect continuous is formed with *will have been* + present participle)

b Play audio 1.06 so that students can check their answers.

You may wish to have students practice saying the sentences with a partner. Ask different students to say the sentences for the rest of the class.

OPTIONAL PRESENTATION

If you prefer a more deductive approach, use the complete grammar charts and explanations on the Reference page to present the concepts. (page 127)

Speaking

9 Focus students' attention on the How To box. Discuss the meaning of any expressions with which students are unfamiliar.

Give students time to think about what they consider to be their greatest achievement. Have them make notes using the language in the How To box. Ask them to think about how they can use perfect verb forms in their story. Then have students tell their partner about their achievement. Monitor the language used and take note of errors.

When all students have finished talking about their achievements, write important errors on the board. Have students correct the errors with a partner. Draw the class's attention to any interesting language used and the correct use of language from the How To box.

NOTES

LESSON **4** pp. 17–18

Unit Wrap Up
Review reinforce lessons 1–3
Communication take a personality quiz

Summary: In this lesson, students review the unit's language. Then they take a personality quiz to see if they are the type of person who likes challenges or not.

Review

1

Answers: 1. faced **2.** challenging **3.** pick up **4.** relied on **5.** distinguished from **6.** benefited from **7.** succeeded in **8.** intelligible

2

Answers: 1. Sci-Corps Company seems to **have** abandoned its research into cloning. **2.** Former President Michael Nkrumah is said **to** be recovering well from the stroke he suffered last Thursday. **3.** The explorer Michaela Barker has been found in Brazil. It **was** believed that she had drowned during a storm. **4.** Baseball star Alex Hanai appears to **have** finally retired at the age of 40.

3

Answers: 1. will have been **2.** have taken up **3.** 've been waiting **4.** 'd been running **5.** 'll have used up

4

Answers: 1. Yes, I know it like the back of my hand. **2.** I don't know offhand, but not many. **3.** I know next to nothing about it. **4.** I've never heard of him.

OPTIONAL EXTRA LISTENING

These audio tracks, activities, and audioscripts are available on both the *ActiveBook* CD-ROM at the back of each Student Book and on the *ActiveTeach* DVD at the back of this Teacher's Resource Book. The audio can also be found on the Audio Program CD. The audioscripts can also be found at the back of the Workbook. These listening activities can be completed in class or done as homework.

Communication

take a personality quiz

OPTIONAL WARM UP

Write the following questions on the board: 1. *In what types of magazines can you find quizzes?* 2. *Do you ever take the quizzes in magazines? Why or why not?* Have students discuss the questions with their partners and whether they believe the results of quizzes in magazines. Elicit responses from different pairs and tell students they are going to take a quiz.

5 Have students take the quiz individually by choosing an answer for each question. Monitor to check that students understand the vocabulary in the questionnaire. If there are any unknown words, encourage them to answer each others' questions before you explain the words to them.

When the students have finished answering the questions, instruct them to share their answers with a partner and explain why they have chosen them. Ask different pairs to share their answers.

Have pairs add another question to the questionnaire. Help students as necessary and check the questions students are writing. Encourage students to decide what each of the answers would "reveal" about the personality of a person doing the questionnaire.

Students can ask classmates the extra question they have written and tell them what their answers mean about their personality.

6 Play audio 1.07 for students to hear what their answers say about their personality. You may wish to have students then discuss with a partner if they agree or disagree with the "results."

7 Have students discuss the questions with a new partner. Monitor the conversations for important errors and any interesting language students use.

Discuss answers as a class. Finally, write any important errors on the board. Have students correct the errors with a partner. Elicit feedback from different pairs and write the correct forms on the board.

Notes for using the CEF

The Common European Framework (CEF), a reference document for language teaching professionals, was produced by the council of Europe as a means of ensuring parity in terms of language teaching and language qualifications across Europe. It has since increasingly become an accepted standard for English learners throughout the world. It can be downloaded as a PDF file fro free from www.coe.int from the section on Language Policy. There is also a link to the site from the *English in Common* website: www.PearsonELT.com/EnglishinCommon.

The CEF recommends that language learners use a portfolio to document, reflect on, and demonstrate their progress. *English in Common* has a Language Portfolio, which can be downloaded from your *ActiveTeach* disc (at the back of this Teacher's Resource Book) or from the *ActiveBook* disc (at the back of each Student Book). Suggested tasks are provided at the beginning of every unit on the Unit Overview page.

CEF REFERENCES

Lesson 1 CAN DO: discuss your language learning experiences
CEF C1 descriptor: Can easily follow and contribute to complex interactions between third parties in group discussion even on abstract, complex unfamiliar topics. (CEF page 77)

Lesson 2 CAN DO: say how much you know or don't know
CEF C1 descriptor: Can select an appropriate formulation from a broad range of language to express him/herself clearly, without having to restrict what he/she wants to say. (CEF page 110)

Lesson 3 CAN DO: talk about your achievements
CEF B2 descriptor: Can plan what is to be said and the means to say it, considering the effect on the recipient/s. (CEF page 64)

Additional Resources

Activity Worksheets and Teaching Notes—Unit 1

Photocopiable worksheets for this unit can be found on pages 103–108 and Teaching Notes can be found on pages 163–164 of this Teacher's Resource Book. They consist of games and other interactive activities for: Vocabulary, Grammar, and Speaking.

Extra Listening Activity—Unit 1

This activity is designed to provide students with additional opportunities to listen to and practice comprehension of spoken English. The audio can be accessed by clicking the Extra Listening folder in both the Student's *ActiveBook* (for independent student use) and in the Teacher's *ActiveTeach* (for classroom use). The audio is also provided at the end of the Audio Program CD. An activity worksheet can also be printed out from either the *ActiveBook* or *ActiveTeach*.

Extra Listening Unit 1—Audioscript

M1: Good evening listeners. This is Mark Johnson, reporting from a base camp on the slopes of Mt. Everest, the world's tallest mountain at eight thousand eight hundred fifty meters, which is around 29,000 feet. There's no chairlift to the top, so if you want to reach the peak, both your body and your bank account had better be in very good shape! I've learned that a guided trek for four to seven people can cost up to 80,000 dollars per person! Why is it so expensive? Well, the price includes a lead guide at 25,000 dollars, 2 assistant guides at 10,000 dollars each, 3–4 cooks at three thousand five hundred dollars each, a doctor at 4,000 dollars, high quality oxygen at 30,000 dollars, 150 yaks to transport equipment, and much more! Not to mention very pricey climbing permits and fees from the government of Nepal, and a garbage and human waste disposal fee of 4,000 dollars paid to the Sagarmatha National Park.

Today, I'm talking to a young mountaineer, Sunny Lee, a 30-year-old Korean-American climber. Sunny, I understand that this is the fifth of the fourteen tallest summits that you are attempting to climb. Why have you chosen Everest, and how have you raised the money to pay for the expedition?

F1: Well, first, of course, I couldn't have gotten here without a lot of help. As you said, climbing is a very expensive sport. I'd like to thank my parents, my sponsors, and my many supporters. I've also been very lucky in raising funds—a TV production company is filming this climb, which covers most of the cost. Why am I here? Well, I've always wanted to climb Everest—like most people say, "Because it is there!"

M1: What inspired you to take up this dangerous sport?

F1: A Korean mountaineer, Oh Eun-Sun sun has been my inspiration—she's a fantastic climber, the number two woman in the world. I've learned a lot from her example.

M1: Like what?

F1: Well, mostly to be very careful. I never climb alone, for example—I don't want any accidents to happen. And I like to set attainable goals, so before starting, every detail of the climb is planned very carefully. My team knows where we'll be stopping each night, and what supplies we'll need. Base camps are set up in advance. Of course, Sherpa guides always climb alongside us.

M1: What is your happiest climbing memory?

F1: It's hard to say. There have been many wonderful times, but maybe the best was when I reached the top of the first mountain I climbed. It was Mt. Hallasan, in Korea. It's small compared to Everest, but I felt as if the world was at my feet.

M1: What are your plans for the future? How long will you continue climbing?

F1: I don't really know. I don't climb mountains to set records; I climb because I love the challenge. I'd like to keep climbing for a few more years, but I'd also like to spend more time with my family . . .

Tests

A **Unit 1 Test** is provided in the Test Bank as a Word file on the *ActiveTeach* disc. It includes discrete sections on: Grammar, Vocabulary, Reading, and Writing. An Answer Key is also provided. If you wish, this test can be easily modified to suit the particular needs of your class.

Extra Vocabulary: Prefixes

Extra Vocabulary activities for this unit can be found in both the Student's *ActiveBook* and in the Teacher's *ActiveTeach*, along with an answer key.

UNIT 2
Places and communities

Unit Overview

Warm Up Lesson	
LESSON 1	**CAN DO** give advice and make recommendations about places **GRAMMAR** gerund and infinitive review **VOCABULARY** recommending places
LESSON 2	**CAN DO** use features of formal and informal language **GRAMMAR** comparisons
LESSON 3	**CAN DO** describe a place **GRAMMAR** adjectives **VOCABULARY** adjectives to describe places
LESSON 4	**Unit Wrap Up** **Review** reinforce lessons 1–3 **Communication** collaborate on a plan
Grammar and Vocabulary Reference Charts	

OPTIONAL LANGUAGE PORTFOLIO

(located in both the *ActiveBook* at the back of the Student Book and in the *ActiveTeach* at the back of this Teacher's Resource Book)

Have students review any materials (written or oral) that they created during this unit. Encourage them to select material to add to the *Achievement Portfolio* section of their Language Portfolios. These works will provide a physical representation of each student's progress over the course of the term. Also ask students to update any information in their *Personal Profiles*.

Teaching Resources

- **Workbook** pp. 12–19
- **Class Audio** CD1 Tracks 8–10
- ***ActiveBook*** Digital Student Book pages with complete unit audio plus Extra Listening Activity and Extra Vocabulary Study
- ***ActiveTeach*** Interactive whiteboard (IWB) software with video, Test Bank, and test audio

Warm Up

p. 19

OPTIONAL WARM UP

Ask students to think back to when they were children and to write notes about the community in which they lived. To help, you could write the following prompts on the board: *house or apartment*, *family*, *area*, *school*. Have students share what they have written with a partner and discuss the positive and negative aspects of the community in which they lived. Elicit responses from the whole class.

1 Focus students' attention on the photos of the different communities. Have students discuss with a partner what type of community is shown in each of the photos. They should then decide on the positive and negative aspects of each of the communities. Monitor the conversations for errors, which you can correct after Exercise 2b. Compare ideas as a class and write students' ideas on the board.

Have students work with a different partner and discuss which of the communities they would like to be a part of and which they would not like to be a part of and their reasons. Elicit responses from different pairs.

2a Instruct students to unscramble the underlined words. Review definitions as necessary.

Answers: 1. cost of living **2.** mild **3.** freedom **4.** healthcare **5.** standard of living **6.** crime rate **7.** unemployment **8.** air pollution **9.** cultural **10.** nightlife

Direct students to mark the sentences with a + if they are positive and with a — if they are negative. Then discuss why they think the sentences are positive or negative.

b Have students work in groups of three or four to discuss the questions.

EXTEND THE WARM UP

Ask students to think about the place where they live or where they are from. Have them describe the place they live to their partners, using as much of the vocabulary from Exercise 2a as possible. Then discuss as a class and compare the different places students live in or are from.

LESSON 1 pp. 20–22

CAN DO give advice and make recommendations about places
GRAMMAR gerund and infinitive review

Summary: In this lesson, students listen to different people discussing their experiences of living abroad. Then they review the use of gerunds and infinitives before looking at cultural awareness and at ways of saying things in a polite way. The lesson concludes with students writing a "web page" containing advice to visitors of their country.

OPTIONAL WARM UP

Ask students to make a list of all the things they think foreigners might find difficult if they came to visit or to live in their country. In a monolingual class, have students make the list in pairs. Elicit ideas from different pairs. In a multilingual class, have students make the list then share it with a partner from a different country.

Listening

1 Ask students to discuss the questions in pairs. Monitor conversations for errors. Then discuss the questions as a class. Write errors you have heard on the board and ask students to correct them.

2a Focus students' attention on the chart and give them time to read the questions. Play audio 1.08. Direct students to complete the chart with information about the three speakers.

Have students compare answers with a partner. Play audio 1.08 again so students can check their answers. Then check answers with the whole class.

OPTIONAL VARIATION

Play audio 1.08 first with students' books closed. Then ask students to tell you some things that they can recall from the listening. Finally, have students read the chart in Exercise 2a and then listen again for the answers.

Answers:

	Speaker 1	Speaker 2	Speaker 3
1	Canada	Austria	Japan
2	starting a business	working as a teaching assistant	work as an English language teacher
3	beautiful city, beaches, mountains, food, friendly people	long weekends, skiing, ice skating, scenery, people	the people, the completely different lifestyle
4	Starting a business when Canada's economy wasn't doing well was difficult.	The food—Austrians tend to eat a lot of meat, which was difficult because she is vegetarian.	She couldn't read Japanese, so everyday things (like shopping) were an adventure for her.
5	the open spaces, the vastness, and the friendly people	the scenery, going to the mountains after school, skiing or swimming in the lakes	the people

b Play the audio again and instruct students to listen for which of the speakers (1, 2, or 3) said the things in items 1–8.

c Play audio 1.08 again and have students check their answers.

Answers: 1. Speaker 3 **2.** Speaker 1 **3.** Speaker 3 **4.** Speaker 2 **5.** Speaker 3 **6.** Speaker 1 **7.** Speaker 2 **8.** Speaker 3

3 Focus students' attention on the questions. Have students discuss the questions in small groups. Monitor conversations for errors and interesting language. Then discuss the questions with the whole class.

OPTIONAL EXTENSION

In a monolingual class, have students work with a partner to decide on the five things they would miss the most about their country if they went to live abroad. Then have students share their ideas with another pair. In a multilingual class, direct students to write a list of the five things they would miss most, then share it with a partner from another country, explaining why they would miss it. Then elicit responses from the class as a whole.

Grammar

OPTIONAL WARM UP

Write the following sentences with blanks (taken from the listening on page 20) on the board: *You can take a bus and go ______ in the mountains forty minutes later. I was studying German so I wanted ______ a year in a German-speaking country.* Ask students to discuss what words could go in the blanks and what form the words should be in. Write the words students suggest in the blanks. Tell students to check their answers by looking at the audioscript on page 150. Ask why the verbs are in these forms. Elicit that when a verb is followed by another verb, the second verb is either an infinitive or *a* gerund.

4 Instruct students to complete the sentences with a gerund or an infinitive. Then have them compare their answers with a partner. Check answers with the class.

Answers: 2. to eat **3.** living **4.** offending **5.** standing **6.** to miss out **7.** traveling **8.** to paying **9.** to try **10.** to see **11.** going **12.** to visit

5 Direct students to write the words in bold from Exercise 4 in the spaces in the Active Grammar box. Check answers.

Answers:
Verb + gerund: imagine, avoid, don't mind, can't stand, recommend
Verb + infinitive: can't afford, want
Verb + object + infinitive: encourage, urge, persuade
Verb + preposition + gerund: think of, object to

Direct students to the Reference section on page 128.

6 Tell students to rewrite the sentences using the verbs in bold. Tell students that they may need to change the form of the verb. Make sure students begin each sentence with *I* or *I'm*. Check answers with the class.

Answers: 1. I can't afford to go to the theater. **2.** I advise you to go to the museum on Sunday. **3.** I encourage people to use the parks more. **4.** I recommend buying tickets early. **5.** I avoid taking the train. **6.** I'm thinking of going to Thailand in February.

OPTIONAL PRESENTATION

If you prefer a more deductive approach, use the complete grammar charts and explanations on the Reference page to present the concepts. (page 128)

7 You may wish to go over the expressions in the How To box before students complete the activity. See if students can think of any more expressions to add. Then have students tell their partner about a place they have visited and make recommendations. Students can then switch partners and exchange recommendations again.

Speaking

8 Have students discuss the questions in small groups. Then discuss the questions as a class. Write errors you have heard on the board and encourage students to self-correct.

9 Direct students to complete the "polite" sentences with words from the box. Check answers.

Answers: 1. mind **2.** please **3.** think **4.** was **5.** wondering **6.** possible **7.** were

10a Instruct students to think about a time when they unintentionally offended someone from another culture or were offended themselves. Have them take notes on the questions. Then have students tell a partner about their experience. Encourage students to ask questions.

b You may wish to do this part of the activity as a whole class or in small groups. Ask students to summarize their partner's experience and explain whether they would have made the same mistake.

11 Have students work in small groups to compile a "cultural awareness guide." Encourage them to use the experiences from Exercise 10. When students have finished, ask them to share their guides with the class. Students may wish to "publish" the guides and print them out for the class.

Writing

12 Instruct students to make lists of any information they wish to include in their "web pages." You may wish to have students work in groups for this activity. Encourage them to think of as much as they can—what visitors shouldn't miss and what they should avoid. Have students share their finished "web pages" with the class.

LESSON 2 pp. 23–25

CAN DO use features of formal and informal language
GRAMMAR comparisons

Summary: In this lesson, students listen to two people talking about the Internet. Through this context, students review ways of making comparisons. Then they read an article about Wikipedia before looking at features of formal and informal writing styles. Finally, students write a formal email.

Note: Wikipedia is a free web-based encyclopedia created in 2001. It allows any visitor to the site to freely edit its content. Currently it has millions of articles in 281 languages. There has been some controversy about how reliable the contents of Wikipedia are. Because it is possible for anyone to edit the content of the encyclopedia, some think it is open to vandalism and that it can be inconsistent. To consult Wikipedia, see www.wikipedia.org.

OPTIONAL WARM UP

Write *Internet* on the board. Give students two minutes to write down as many words as they can think of connected to the Internet. Have students compare their words with a partner and explain why they are connected to the Internet. Elicit ideas from the class and write the words on the board to check the spelling.

Listening

1 Have students discuss the questions with a partner. Then discuss the questions with the whole class.

OPTIONAL VARIATION

Divide the class into two groups, A and B. Tell Group A that they think the Internet is a good thing. Tell Group B that they think the Internet is a bad thing. Give students five minutes in their groups to think of reasons to support their view. Pair off students so that Students A are working with Students B. Students should try and convince their partner of their point of view. When they have finished, compare ideas as a class.

2 Tell students that they are going to hear two people discussing the questions from Exercise 1. Play audio 1.09 and ask students to decide which issues the people are discussing. Then have students discuss whether their own ideas are similar to the ideas of the people on the recording.

Answers: They discuss the value of communication by email, whether information found on the Internet is reliable, and whether purchasing things on the Internet is safe.

3 Give students time to read phrases 1–11. Tell students that they are going to listen to the discussion again and that this time they should check the phrases they hear. Play audio 1.09 again and have students check the phrases.

Answers: Phrases heard are: 1, 3, 5, 6, 7, 8.

Grammar

OPTIONAL WARM UP

Write *New York City* on the board. Give students one minute to think of ways that their hometown or city is different from New York. Elicit responses from different students and take note of any comparative language that students use. Write this comparative language on the board and discuss its form and use.

4 Focus students' attention on the Active Grammar box. Have students write the phrases from Exercise 3 in the correct place in the box. Then have them compare answers with a partner. Check answers with the class.

Answers: 1. A big difference: so much . . . (than), far . . . (than), not nearly as . . . as, It's considerably . . .
2. A little difference: It's not quite as . . . as . . . , It's slightly . . . , (It's) almost the same as, a little bit . . . (than)
3. No difference: It's the same as
4. *The* + comparative + *the* + comparative: the less we . . . , the less we . . . ; the more we . . . , the more we . . .

Direct students to the Reference section on page 128.

5 Focus students' attention on sentences 1–6. Direct students to complete the sentences with phrases from the Active Grammar box. Check answers with the class.

Answers: 1. so much easier, far easier, considerably easier, slightly easier, *or* a little bit easier **2.** not nearly *or* not quite as **3.** so much faster, far faster, considerably faster, slightly faster, *or* a little bit faster **4.** the more **5.** so much riskier, far riskier, considerably riskier, slightly riskier, *or* a little bit riskier **6.** not nearly as reliable *or* not quite as reliable

OPTIONAL PRESENTATION

If you prefer a more deductive approach, use the complete grammar charts and explanations on the Reference page to present the concepts. (page 128)

Speaking

6 Tell students to look at the sentences in Exercise 5 again. Students should decide if they agree or disagree with each statement and then discuss with their partner. Monitor the conversations for important errors. Compare responses as a class.

Reading

7 Write *Wikipedia* on the board. Have students discuss with a partner if they know what it is or have ever used it, and if so why they have used it. If students haven't heard of it, ask them to predict what it might be. Then discuss students' ideas and experiences as a class.

8 Have students read the article. Circulate to address any comprehension issues.

Direct students to read questions 1–6 and then read the article again to find the answers. Check answers.

Answers: 1. It's an online free encyclopedia that anyone can edit. **2.** It's a piece of software that you can use to set up a website that anyone can edit. **3.** He's the founder of Wikipedia. **4.** Users who delete, deface and push one-sided views on Wikipedia. **5.** Some people say you can't trust it because the people who edit it aren't reliable authorities. **6.** They like the collaborative nature of it and the fact that all kinds of viewpoints are offered.

9 Write *Formal* and *Informal* on the board at the top of two columns. Divide students into two groups. Each group takes one of the styles and makes a list of features of that style of writing. Elicit and write students' ideas on the board in the correct column and discuss them as a class.

Have students read the article on page 24 again quickly and decide if it is formal or informal in style. (The text is informal. It contains colloquialisms, spoken English, humor, etc.)

Focus students' attention on the headings and examples in the How To box. Ask students to find other examples in the article for each heading.

Finally, have students answer questions 1–2. Check answers with the class.

Answers: 1. Informal vocabulary: Believe it or not (paragraph 3), all these great people (paragraph 4) **Spoken English style:** Anyway, . . . (paragraph 4), Ah, fun (paragraph 5), well, . . . (paragraph 7) **Omitted words:** Quitting his job to start . . . ? (paragraph 5), Simply amazing (paragraph 5) **Humor:** "Oh my gosh," they write, "you've got a major security flaw." (paragraph 1) **2.** full verb forms: formal, lots of phrasal verbs: informal, sentences beginning with *and* or *but*: informal, repeated use of the passive: formal

OPTIONAL EXTENSION

Have students work with a partner to compare an entry from Wikipedia with an entry from a traditional encyclopedia. While doing so, encourage students to use the expressions for comparing things from Exercise 3 on page 23.

10 Direct students to read the two formal emails. Have them replace words and phrases that are too informal with words or phrases from the box. Then have students compare answers with a partner. Check answers.

Answers:
Dear Mr. Fry,
. . . A dinner in the evening, to which you are invited, will **follow. Could you please confirm your attendance** by November 4th. **We would be grateful if you could** bring copies of the sample contract. **Don't hesitate to** contact us if you have any questions.

Dear Ms. Johnson,
Thank you very much for the invitation to come to the meeting on November 15th **concerning** the plan to start a new website, and thank you also for the agenda. I **will be very happy to attend.**
As **requested,** I will bring copies of the sample contract. Unfortunately I **will be unable to attend** the dinner because of **a previous arrangement.**
I look forward to seeing you there.

Writing

11a Refer students to the Writing bank on page 144. Give them time to do the exercises. Monitor and help as necessary. Then have students compare answers with a partner.

Answers: 1: 1. Funding for a new website **2.** $5,000 **3.** a monthly payment **4.** the launch party
2: 1. e **2.** d **3.** b **4.** a **5.** c

b Have students write the formal email using the information in the box. Make sure students pay particular attention to the following: greeting and signing off, coherence and cohesion, punctuation, spelling, and style. Have students then exchange emails with a partner and write comments on their partner's use of a formal writing style.

LESSON 3 pp. 26–28

CAN DO describe a place
GRAMMAR adjectives
VOCABULARY adjectives to describe places

Summary: In this lesson, students read descriptions of three vacation destinations. Then they go on to look at adjectives to describe places. Students finish the lesson by writing a short paragraph about their favorite places.

Note: Cali, Colombia is situated approximately 3,281-feet (1,000-meters) above sea level, and because it is close to the equator it doesn't experience major climate changes. It is the third largest city in Colombia, with over two million inhabitants, many of them recent immigrants from poor rural areas. It can be a dangerous city because of drug-related violence. Cape Town is the third biggest city in South Africa and is a very popular destination with tourists who go there in part for its Mediterranean-style climate. It was home to many leaders of the anti-apartheid movement, and Nelson Mandela made his first public speech there after being released from prison. It can be a dangerous city as it has one of the world's highest homicide rates. Koh Chang is the third largest island in Thailand. Its name means *Elephant Island*, for the shape of the island, though elephants are not native to the island. Koh Chang is known for its waterfalls, coral reefs, and rainforests. There are eight villages on the island.

OPTIONAL WARM UP

Write the following countries on the board: *Colombia, Thailand,* and *South Africa*. Organize students into three groups. Direct each group to choose one of the countries and brainstorm everything they know about it. You may wish to write the following prompts on the board to help: *weather, food, customs, people*. Then have students form new groups and share information with their new group. Elicit feedback from the different groups.

Reading

1 Focus students' attention on the three photos of the different places. Have students discuss the questions with a partner. Monitor the conversations and take note of any important errors.

After students have had time to discuss the questions with their partners, have a discussion as a class. Finally, write any important errors you have heard on the board and ask students to correct them with a partner. Check the correct forms with the class and write them on the board.

2 Have students read the descriptions. Instruct students to take notes while they read. Tell students not to worry about any words and expressions they don't understand at this stage, because you will be dealing with them later.

When students have finished taking notes, ask the class to describe the places in their own words. Encourage students to add information. Ask if there are any words or phrases in the text that students do not know the meaning of. Encourage students to explain the meanings to each other or consult an English-English dictionary before explaining the words and expressions yourself.

3 Organize students into groups of three or four to discuss the questions. Monitor the conversations for errors and any interesting language the students use.

Then discuss the questions with the whole class. Write any errors you have heard on the board. Encourage students to give you the correct forms and write them on the board. Finally, draw students' attention to any interesting language they have used and congratulate them on its use.

OPTIONAL EXTENSION

Tell students that for homework you want them to find out as much as possible about one of the places they have read about on the Internet or using any other resources they can think of. In the following class, students can then give a presentation on the place they chose. Encourage students to be aware of engaging their audience, maintaining eye contact, the use of visuals, and varying their tone of voice.

Vocabulary

OPTIONAL WARM UP

In a monolingual class, give students a few minutes to think of a place in their country and adjectives they would use to describe it. Have students describe the place to a partner, who tries to guess the place that is being described. In a multilingual class, students can describe famous cities or places in the world for their partners to guess.

4 Direct students to look through the readings on pages 26 and 27 to find the words defined in items 1–10. You may wish to have students do this activity with a partner. Monitor carefully to check that the students have found the correct words. Check answers with the whole class.

Answers: 1. unspoiled **2.** diverse **3.** vast **4.** run down **5.** stunning **6.** packed **7.** tranquil (tranquility) **8.** off the beaten track **9.** bustling **10.** magnificent

5 Focus students' attention on sentences 1–8. Direct students to complete the sentences with words from Exercise 4. Then have students compare their answers with a partner. Check answers as a class.

Answers: 1. run down **2.** off the beaten track **3.** packed **4.** diverse **5.** vast **6.** tranquil **7.** unspoiled **8.** magnificent

6 Have students think of different places that fit the descriptions a–e. Then ask them to compare their ideas with a partner.

Ask students to switch partners and share their ideas with their new partners. Then discuss the places the students have chosen to fit the descriptions as a class.

Writing

7a Have students decide on a favorite place and make notes about it. Make sure that they have made notes about the atmosphere, the landscape, things to see and do there, and the food that you can eat there.

Give students time to write a paragraph of about 100–150 words about their favorite place, using their notes. Monitor and help where necessary, encouraging students to include the vocabulary from Exercise 4 in their writing.

b Have students form groups and share their paragraphs. Encourage them to ask questions about what they have read to get more information.

OPTIONAL VARIATION

When students write their paragraphs, tell them to leave a wide margin down the right-hand side of the page. After writing, students can exchange their paragraphs with a partner. Their partners read the paragraphs and write comments and questions in the margin. These comments and questions can be about the structure or the content of the paragraph. Encourage students to write positive comments wherever possible. Monitor carefully to check the comments. Have students then give the paragraphs back to their partners. If students think they can improve their paragraphs based on the comments and questions, they can revise them. Finally, ask students to read the revised versions of the paragraphs to the class.

OPTIONAL EXTENSION

After students have shared their paragraphs with the class, decide as a class which of the places would be best for a group vacation. Then have students form small groups to plan the vacation. Write the following topics on the board: *transportation, accommodations, food, shopping, sightseeing*. Have students work with their groups to plan the vacation, discussing the areas on the board. When students have finished planning, have students form different groups and share the information about the vacations they have planned. You can then ask each group to decide which vacation sounds the best and why.

LESSON 4 pp. 29–30

Unit Wrap Up
Review reinforce lessons 1–3
Communication collaborate on a plan

Summary: In this lesson, students review the unit's language. Then they read a description of a club and listen to two people describing clubs that they belong to. Students then plan their own club and present their ideas to the rest of the class.

Review

1

Answers: 1. to consult **2.** spending **3.** to buy **4.** applying **5.** to paying **6.** to go **7.** living **8.** taking **9.** to hearing **10.** to wear

2

Answers: 1. Paraguay is **not** as large as Brazil—Brazil is much larger. **2.** Switzerland is the **same** as it always has been: safe, clean, and expensive. **3.** The more cars we use, the **more** polluted our environment becomes. **4.** Poland **isn't** quite as cold as Norway, but its climate is similar in the northeast. **5.** France is a little bit larger **than** Spain. **6.** China is far **more** populated than Greenland. **7.** Traveling by train is considerably **more** comfortable than traveling by bus.

3

Answers: Sentences should be numbered in the following order: 1, 9, 3, 5, 7, 4, 2, 8, 10, 6

OPTIONAL EXTRA LISTENING

These audio tracks, activities, and audioscripts are available on both the *ActiveBook* CD-ROM at the back of each Student Book and on the *ActiveTeach* DVD at the back of this Teacher's Resource Book. The audio can also be found on the Audio Program CD. The audioscripts can also be found at the back of the Workbook. These listening activities can be completed in class or done as homework.

Communication

collaborate on a plan

OPTIONAL WARM UP

Ask students to make a list of all the clubs or organizations they have been a member of. They can then share their lists with a partner, explaining the type of clubs and organizations they belonged to and how important they were to them. Elicit responses from different pairs.

4a Have students read the article about the club. Ask them to decide if the club is silly, funny, or a good idea, and discuss with a partner. Ask students if there are any words or phrases they don't understand in the article. Encourage them to answer each others' questions before asking you.

b Ask students to think about a presentation they could give if they were joining the Not Terribly Good Club. Have them share their presentation idea with a partner and then with the class.

OPTIONAL EXTENSION

Have students prepare their presentations and present them to the rest of the class. When all students have made their presentations, the class can decide whose presentation was the best.

5 Ask students to look at the headings and predict what type of thing each club does and the type of people who might be members. Play audio 1.10 and have students take notes on what they hear. Check answers with the class.

Answers: Alumni Club: 1. The main purpose of the club: to keep in touch with old friends, have reunions **2.** Other things that it does: gets involved in charity events **3.** Type of meeting: party **4.** Who can be a member: anyone who went to the same school **Ballroom Dancing Club: 1.** Number and type of people in the club: 30, a lot of beginners **2.** When and where it meets: once a week, in a school gym **3.** Things they have learned: waltz, foxtrot, Latin dances like the jive and the tango

6a Have students work in groups of 3 or 4 to discuss the questions. Monitor conversations and help the groups as necessary.

b Invite students to present their ideas to the rest of the class. When all the groups have presented their ideas, ask students to decide which of the clubs they would be interested in joining. Point out some errors you have heard and call on different students to correct them. Finally, congratulate students on interesting ideas or language they have used in the lesson.

Notes for using the CEF

The Common European Framework (CEF), a reference document for language teaching professionals, was produced by the council of Europe as a means of ensuring parity in terms of language teaching and language qualifications across Europe. It has since increasingly become an accepted standard for English learners throughout the world. It can be downloaded as a PDF file fro free from www.coe.int from the section on Language Policy. There is also a link to the site from the *English in Common* website: www.PearsonELT.com/EnglishinCommon.

The CEF recommends that language learners use a portfolio to document, reflect on, and demonstrate their progress. *English in Common* has a Language Portfolio, which can be downloaded from your *ActiveTeach* disc (at the back of this Teacher's Resource Book) or from the *ActiveBook* disc (at the back of each Student Book). Suggested tasks are provided at the beginning of every unit on the Unit Overview page.

CEF REFERENCES

Lesson 1 CAN DO: give advice and make recommendations about places
CEF C1 descriptor: Can express him/herself with clarity and precision, relating to the addressee flexibly and effectively. (CEF page 83)

Lesson 2 CAN DO: Use features of formal and informal language
CEF C1 descriptor: Can recognize a wide range of idiomatic expressions and colloquialisms, appreciating register shifts. (CEF page 122)

Lesson 3 CAN DO: describe a place
CEF C1 descriptor: Can write clear, detailed, well-structured and developed descriptions and imaginative texts in an assured, personal, natural style appropriate to the reader in mind. (CEF page 62)

Additional Resources

Activity Worksheets and Teaching Notes—Unit 2

Photocopiable worksheets for this unit can be found on pages 109–113 and Teaching Notes can be found on pages 165–166 of this Teacher's Resource Book. They consist of games and other interactive activities for: Vocabulary, Grammar, and Speaking.

Extra Listening Activity—Unit 2

This activity is designed to provide students with additional opportunities to listen to and practice comprehension of spoken English. The audio can be accessed by clicking the Extra Listening folder in both the Student's *ActiveBook* (for independent student use) and in the Teacher's *ActiveTeach* (for classroom use). The audio is also provided at the end of the Audio Program CD. An activity worksheet can also be printed out from either the *ActiveBook* or *ActiveTeach*.

Extra Listening Unit 2—Audioscript

M1: So how was your trip around the world? You were gone for over three months.

F1: Did you have a great time?

F2: YES! I loved the sights, of course, but the best part was meeting people. We became couchsurfers and sometimes stayed in people's homes—free!

M1: Couchsurfers.? What's that? I've never heard of it before.

F2: Well, the actual name of the organization is couchsurfers dot org. It's a volunteer network of people who open their homes for a few nights to visitors. You may have a bedroom, or sleep on the couch in the living room. Your hosts set rules, like whether you can use their kitchen or washing machine. It's a fantastic way to make international friends.

M2: It wasn't always as comfortable as staying in a hotel, but it was wonderful to see how people live. All of our hosts were glad to talk to us. Some also showed us around, and some included us in day-to-day chores like shopping and cooking.

F2: And of course, they know great local restaurants and local sights that we would never find on our own.

F1: You know, I just read a really interesting article in *Travel and Leisure* magazine about cultural mistakes that people make on their vacations.

F2: I think we made a lot of them!

M1: Like what?

F2: Well, there was the time I used my left hand to eat couscous in Azerbaijan. Everyone looked at me so strangely. I didn't have a clue what I was doing wrong.

M2: Yeah, later we found out why . . . our hostess whispered to her, "That's the bathroom hand."

M1: F1: Uh oh!

F2: I was so embarrassed.

M2: Yeah, well what about in Japan when I put my arm around Noriko's shoulder? She gave me a very funny look. I learned not to do that again.

F2: Yeah, but contrast that to our time in Brazil when I was introduced to Silvia's boyfriend. I was giving him my hand to shake, when he kissed me three times! That felt weird—but nice!

M1: I guess you just have to observe what locals do. Different cultures have different personal space comfort levels

F2: Yeah, and I also became aware of some unconscious habits Americans have.

M1: Like what?

F2: Like smiling at strangers! We think it's friendly, but French people think we're insincere.

M2: But, you know, even within the same country, it's possible to offend people. Do you remember when we were in the Midwest, visiting our cousins?

F1: What did you do wrong?

M2: Well, Midwesterners usually say, "Hello" or "Good morning" when they pass someone on the street, even a stranger. New Yorkers are more apt to just walk on by without a greeting. We discovered that Midwesterners see that as being rude.

F1: That's true! New Yorkers can be a little less than friendly!

M2: Oh, I forgot, you're from the Midwest, too!

F2: Well, the more we travel, the more we have to learn! We're already starting to plan our next trip . . .

Video
Who Writes on Wikipedia?

Students watch a *Good Morning America* news segment that investigates whether companies and individuals are manipulating entries on the popular online encyclopedia for their own benefit. This video segment can be played on the Teacher's *ActiveTeach* disc and projected for classroom viewing or the disc can be played on any DVD player. Teaching notes and video scripts are also provided on the *ActiveTeach* disc.

Tests

A **Unit 2 Test** is provided in the Test Bank as a Word file on the *ActiveTeach* disc. It includes discrete sections on: Grammar, Vocabulary, Reading, and Writing. An Answer Key is also provided. If you wish, this test can be easily modified to suit the particular needs of your class.

Extra Vocabulary: Phrasal verbs

Extra Vocabulary activities for this unit can be found in both the Student's *ActiveBook* and in the Teacher's *ActiveTeach*, along with an answer key.

UNIT 3
Stories

Unit Overview

Warm Up Lesson	
LESSON 1	**CAN DO** tell an anecdote **GRAMMAR** review of past forms **VOCABULARY** synonyms
LESSON 2	**CAN DO** describe a person in detail **GRAMMAR** compound adjectives **VOCABULARY** books
LESSON 3	**CAN DO** tell a joke **GRAMMAR** phrases with participles and gerunds **VOCABULARY** humor
LESSON 4	**Unit Wrap Up** **Review** reinforce lessons 1–3 **Communication** tell a story
Grammar and Vocabulary Reference Charts	

OPTIONAL LANGUAGE PORTFOLIO

(located in both the *ActiveBook* at the back of the Student Book and in the *ActiveTeach* at the back of this Teacher's Resource Book)

Have students review any materials (written or oral) that they created during this unit. Encourage them to select material to add to the *Achievement Portfolio* section of their Language Portfolios. These works will provide a physical representation of each student's progress over the course of the term. Also ask students to update any information in their *Personal Profiles.*

Teaching Resources

- **Workbook** pp. 20–27
- **Class Audio** CD1 Tracks 11–14
- ***ActiveBook*** Digital Student Book pages with complete unit audio plus Extra Listening Activity and Extra Vocabulary Study
- ***ActiveTeach*** Interactive whiteboard (IWB) software with video, Test Bank, and test audio

Warm Up p. 31

OPTIONAL WARM UP

Organize students into pairs, A and B. Direct Students A to open the book and describe two of the pictures on page 31 to B. B draws the pictures as A describes them. Tell Students B that they don't have to draw a perfect picture and that a representation will be adequate. When all of the pictures have been described, Students B can open their books and compare their drawings with the pictures on page 31. Students B can also check any details that Students A did not describe to them, and compare what they had imagined the picture to be like with the real picture.

1 Focus students' attention on the pictures. Have students discuss with a partner what type of story each of the pictures illustrates. Students can also discuss if they ever tell stories and if they are good at storytelling. As a class, ask students to discuss what makes a good storyteller.

2 Ask students to think of examples for each of the story types. You may then have them form small groups to compare their examples. Finally, compare examples as a class and ask students to explain their examples.

3 Have students work with a partner to check that they know the meaning of the phrases in bold. Encourage students to help each other with the vocabulary or to use an English-English dictionary. Help and answer their questions as necessary. Then call on students to explain the meanings of the phrases.

Finally, have students answer the questions with their partner. Monitor the conversations and take note of errors. Elicit answers from the class. Write the errors on the board and ask students to correct them before writing the correct forms on the board.

EXTEND THE WARM UP

Have students look at the pictures again with a partner and decide what happens next in each of the stories. Encourage them to be imaginative and use humor if they can. Then have students share their ideas with new partners. Finally, compare ideas as a class and decide who had the best ideas for what happened next in the stories.

LESSON 1 pp. 32–34

CAN DO tell an anecdote
GRAMMAR review of past forms
VOCABULARY synonyms

Summary: In this lesson, students read about some famous hoaxes. Through this context they look at past verb forms. Students then tell a story about something that has happened to them. They look at synonyms, and finish the lesson by completing a crossword puzzle using words from the Reading.

Note: April Fool's Day (April 1) is the day in the United States when people play tricks on each other. Radio and TV stations often include hoax news stories to try to fool listeners and viewers. Many cultures have similar days when people play tricks on each other. In France on April 1 people often try to attach a paper fish to other people's backs. In Spanish-speaking countries tricks are played on December 28, the day of the Holy Innocents. Sometimes people create hoaxes not because of a special day but to make money. In 1983, the German magazine *Stern* reportedly paid 10 million marks for the diaries of Adolf Hitler. The diaries turned out to be a fake (this story is included in the photocopiable worksheets section, page 114). For more examples of famous hoaxes and April Fool's Day tricks, see: www.museumofhoaxes.com.

OPTIONAL WARM UP
Write *April Fool's Day* on the board and ask students if they know what it is. If some students know, tell them to explain to the rest of the class. If none of the students know, explain what it is. Ask students to discuss if such a day exists in their culture. In a monolingual class, students can tell you about their country. In a multilingual class, students of different nationalities can tell a partner about the days in their country. Encourage students to ask follow-up questions to find out more information before you compare responses as a class.

Reading

1 Ask students to look at the photos and discuss questions 1–2 with a partner. Elicit answers from different groups and discuss students' ideas with the whole class.

2 Have students read the article to find the answers to the questions in Exercise 1. You might want to give a time limit, for example five minutes. Tell students not to worry about any words or phrases they don't understand at this stage, as you will deal with them later.

Next, instruct students to read the questions that follow the article. You can choose to discuss the answers as a class or to have students discuss them in small groups. Monitor the group conversations for important errors. Call on different groups for answers and discuss the students' ideas as a class. Alternatively, you may wish to have students work on their own and write their answers.

Grammar

OPTIONAL WARM UP
Write the following sentences with blanks (taken from the article on page 32) on the board:
1. In 1971, while he _____ _____ (work) as a government minister, Manuel Elizalde _____ (announce) a great discovery.
2 They explained that they _____ _____ _____ (pretend) all along; Elizalde _____ _____ (pay) them to act like a Stone Age tribe.

Ask students to fill in the blanks with the correct forms of the verbs. When they have completed the sentences, elicit answers from the class and write the correct forms on the board. Ask students to identify the tenses used to fill the spaces (past continuous, simple past, past perfect continuous, and past perfect). Discuss why we use each of these tenses and write the tenses next to the sentences on the board.

3a Direct students back to the first paragraph of the article on page 32. Monitor and answer students' questions where necessary.

Answers: 1. simple past: *Elizalde announced a great discovery* past continuous: *while he was working as a government minister* past perfect: *He had found a Stone Age tribe* past perfect continuous: *This . . . tribe . . . had been living this way . . .*

b You may wish to have students discuss the differences in meaning with a partner.

Answers: 1a means Elizalde had left the country before the truth came out. **1b** means Elizalde was in the country at the time the truth came out, and then he left immediately. Here 1a is more appropriate; the truth came out after Elizalde had left the country. **2a** uses the continuous to emphasize duration (the long period of time). **2b** is also possible but doesn't emphasize duration as strongly as 2a. **3a** and **3b** are similar in meaning.

4 Have students complete the rules in the Active Grammar box. Direct them to look back at the sentences they found in Exercise 3a to help them.

Answers: 1. chronological **2.** progress **3.** before **4.** length

Direct students to the Reference section on page 129.

5a Direct students to read the paragraphs and to complete them with the correct form of the verb in parentheses. Check answers with the whole class.

Answers: **1.** were picking **2.** called **3.** had published **4.** admitted **5.** had been joking

b Play audio 1.11 and allow students to check their answers.

OPTIONAL PRESENTATION
If you prefer a more deductive approach, use the complete grammar charts and explanations on the Reference page to present the concepts. (page 129)

OPTIONAL EXTENSION
If students have access to the Internet, ask them to find out more information about famous hoaxes for homework. In the following lesson, ask students to share anything they have found out with the rest of the class. They can also discuss if they think that these hoaxes are believable or not and which one is the most amusing.

Speaking

6a Ask students to think of an event in their lives that they can tell a story about. If necessary, brainstorm as a class to come up with some general categories, such as a travel adventure, something frightening, how you met your spouse, etc. Tell students to think about questions 1–4 when preparing their stories and also to think about how they can include past verb forms. Encourage them to write notes to help them organize their thoughts. Monitor and help where necessary.

When students have finished preparing how to tell the real events of the story, tell students to invent two or three false details to include in the story. Tell them it is important that they include these details in a natural way, and give them time to think about how to include the false details.

b Have students tell their stories to a partner. Tell students listening to the stories to think of questions they can ask to try to guess which of the details are not true. Monitor conversations carefully for use of past verb forms. When students have finished telling the stories, their partners should ask questions to try and discover the invented parts of the story.

Check if the students have been able to discover the invented details. Write errors students have made while using past verb forms on the board and ask the class to correct them. Draw students' attention to their correct use of verb forms and congratulate them on their use.

Vocabulary

7a Ask students to read the newspaper excerpts and to think of synonyms for the underlined words and phrases. Encourage students to use the context to guess the meaning of any unknown words. Elicit answers from different students.

b Instruct students to match the words in the box to the underlined words and phrases that have similar meanings.

Answers: **1.** prevent **2.** combat **3.** settle **4.** keep track **5.** drastic measures **6.** claims **7.** detained **8.** arises **9.** loaded **10.** placing **11.** considered **12.** talks **13.** deal with **14.** led to **15.** purchased **16.** initiated

8 Have students work with a partner to complete the crossword. Tell students that all of the answers are from the article about hoaxes on page 32. After completing the puzzle, students can compare their answers with another pair. Check answers with the class.

Answers: **1.** (across) pretending (down) prominent **2.** isolated **3.** fictitious **4.** vital **5.** liberated **6.** extended **7.** destroy **8.** tragic **9.** hoax **10.** fooled

OPTIONAL EXTENSION
Ask students to retell a story that has recently been in the news to a partner. A variation of this activity is to instruct students to add some fictitious details to the story and have their partner determine which parts of the story are false.

NOTES

LESSON 2 pp. 35–37

CAN DO describe a person in detail
GRAMMAR compound adjectives
VOCABULARY books

Summary: In this lesson, students look at vocabulary for describing books. Then they listen to people describing characters from books before reading some book excerpts. They go on to look at compound adjectives. Finally, students describe someone they know well to the rest of the class.

OPTIONAL WARM UP

Ask students to discuss with a partner when and where they like to read books, magazines, e-readers, or newspapers. Ask if they sometimes read in situations like the ones shown on page 35. Elicit responses from different pairs.

Vocabulary

1 Ask students to discuss the questions with a partner. Monitor conversations for any interesting language that students use. Then discuss as a class. You may wish to elicit students' favorite books and make a "recommended reading list" on the board.

OPTIONAL EXTENSION

Write the following prompts on the board: *books, music, luxuries, tools.* Tell students that they are going to be on a desert island with a partner for a year and can bring only three of each of the things on the board to the island. Ask students to individually decide on three things for each category then try, with a partner, to agree on what to take to the island. Then discuss choices as a class.

2 Tell students to cover the right-hand column. Ask them to think of other ways to say each sentence in the left-hand column. Check answers with the class and write possible sentences on the board.

Ask students which of the expressions is negative. (*The characters are one-dimensional.*) Then have students uncover the right-hand column and complete the exercise. Students can compare their answers with a partner. Check answers with the class.

Answers: 1. b **2.** e **3.** c **4.** g **5.** h **6.** d **7.** a **8.** f

3 Have students work in groups to discuss books that they have read, using the vocabulary from Exercise 2. Encourage students to write down books that they may want to read, based on their classmates' comments.

Listening

4a Focus students' attention on questions 1–5 in the chart. Give them time to read them and check understanding.

Tell students that they are going to listen to three people discussing these questions. Play audio 1.12. Direct students to make notes in the chart as they listen. They can then compare notes with a partner.

b Play audio 1.12 again and have students check their answers and fill in any missing information. Check answers with the class.

Answers:
Speaker 1: 1. Linda Hammerick **2.** She is strong, and she can empathize with others. **3.** having long, dark hair **4.** strong-minded **5.** She overcomes her medical condition and her difficult relationship with her mother and grandmother.
Speaker 2: 1. Elizabeth Bennett **2.** She takes control of her own life, she is very modern for her time. **3.** pretty tall with a lively face and dark hair **4.** lively, feisty, talks back to men, takes control of her own life **5.** Women had little control over what happened to them in marriage, people thought she was socially unacceptable.
Speaker 3: 1. The old man from *The Old Man and the Sea* **2.** reminds the speaker of his father, does things to the best of his ability **3.** fairly old, big strong hands that were cut and bruised, a little bit of grey hair **4.** wise, took pride in his job, did his best **5.** He was down on his luck in the story, hadn't caught anything for a long time, had little opportunity in life.

5 Ask students to think about their own favorite fictional character from a book. Give them a few minutes to think about how they would answer the questions in Exercise 4a.

Then have students tell a partner about their character. Monitor for any important errors. Elicit responses from the class, then write the errors you have heard on the board and ask different students to correct them.

For homework, you may wish to ask students to use their notes to write a full description of the character. They can then read their character descriptions to the rest of the class or hand them in.

OPTIONAL VARIATION

If students can't think of a favorite character from a book, they can describe a favorite character from a movie or a television show.

Reading

6 Ask students to read the excerpts and match them to the questions. If there are any words or expressions in the excerpts that students don't understand, explain that you will address them later. Have students compare their answers with a partner. Check answers with the whole class.

Answers: 1. excerpt 5 **2.** excerpt 3 **3.** excerpt 2 **4.** excerpt 1 **5.** excerpt 4

7 Direct students to discuss the questions in small groups. Some of the vocabulary might be challenging, so encourage students to figure out the meaning from the context before using a dictionary or asking you. Elicit answers from different groups.

Grammar

OPTIONAL WARM UP

Ask students to reread the excerpts in Exercise 6 and to look at the words in bold. Have them work in pairs to decide what these words have in common. (They are all compound adjectives.) Then ask students to discuss if they know of any characteristics of compound words. Discuss as a class.

8 Focus students' attention on the Active Grammar box. Have them answer the questions in items 1 and 3 in the box. Then have students compare their answers with a partner. Check answers with the whole class.

Answers: 1. a. self-conscious, hot-headed **b.** weather-beaten, far-seeing, hollow-cheeked, fast-moving, washed-out **3.** works hard = hard-working keeps an open mind = open-minded looks good = good-looking thinks freely = free-thinking loves fun = fun-loving

Direct students to the Reference section on page 129.

9 Have students work with a partner to discuss the meaning of the compound adjectives in bold. Check answers by asking different pairs the meanings.

Possible Answers: 1. single-minded: determined *or* never gives up **2.** self-sufficient: doesn't rely on other people *or* looks after herself **3.** thick-skinned: doesn't get upset when criticized *or* doesn't take criticism personally **4.** kind-hearted: good to other people *or* generous **5.** stand-offish: not friendly *or* doesn't talk to other people **6.** career-orientated: always thinks about his career *or* does a lot of things to enhance his career **7.** level-headed: calm (in good and bad situations) *or* not too excitable **8.** absent-minded: forgetful

OPTIONAL PRESENTATION

If you prefer a more deductive approach, use the complete grammar charts and explanations on the Reference page to present the concepts. (page 129)

Writing

10a Tell students that they are going to describe someone they know well. Have them focus on the How To box and ask them to make notes about first impressions, physical details, and character. Encourage students to use the expressions from the box and compound adjectives where possible when making their notes. It may be a good idea to ask students to describe someone who is unusual in some way, either physically or in character.

b Have students describe their person to others in their groups. Take note of any errors in using compound words. Ask students to decide if any of the descriptions are of the same person and if any sound similar. Write any errors in compound adjectives on the board and call on students to correct them.

NOTES

LESSON 3 pp. 38–40

CAN DO tell a joke
GRAMMAR phrases with participles and gerunds
VOCABULARY humor

Summary: In this lesson, students read an abridged biography of Groucho Marx. Through this context they look at phrases with participles and gerunds. Students go on to look at vocabulary connected with humor. Then they listen to someone telling a joke before finishing the lesson by telling a joke themselves.

Note: Groucho Marx was an American comedian who appeared in many films both as a member of the Marx Brothers and on his own. He also appeared on American radio and TV shows. He was recognizable for his trademark greasepaint moustache, bushy eyebrows, and cigar, as well as for his witty remarks both off- and on-screen. In 1974 he was awarded a special Academy Award for his and his brothers' services to the film industry. Groucho Marx died in 1977. See www.marx-brothers.org for more information.

OPTIONAL WARM UP

Show students the picture of Groucho Marx on page 38. Ask students to discuss what they know about him with a partner. If they have never seen Groucho Marx before, they can guess who he is, what is he famous for, and in what period he was most famous. Then elicit information from the class.

Reading

1 Ask students to discuss the questions with a partner. Discuss with the class and decide who the most popular comedians are.

2 Tell students that they are going to learn about Groucho Marx, the comedian in the picture. Tell students that they are going to read the biography in sections. At the end of each section, they will read three possible answers to a question. They should guess the answer for each question. They will then go to the relevant next section, as instructed, to find out if they were correct. Monitor to check that students are reading the sections in the correct order.

Answers: 1. a **2.** c **3.** b **4.** b **5.** a **6.** c **7.** a

3 Tell students that they are going to hear someone describing Groucho Marx's life but that there will be some mistakes in the description. Play audio 1.13. Have students take note of any mistakes the speaker makes. Then have students compare their answers with a partner. Play audio 1.13 again for students to check their answers.

Answers: It wasn't during a radio show that they started making jokes. It was on stage. The boys' mother died and the Great Depression began in 1929, not 1926. Thalberg helped them get into the movie business, not television. Their last film was *The Big Store*, not *A Day at the Races*. He was in his eighties, not his nineties.

Grammar

OPTIONAL WARM UP

Write the following grammatically incorrect sentences on the board:
1. *Desperately attempted to win some money, Groucho met Irving Thalberg during a card game.* 2. *Thalberg, impressing with his new friend's act, helped the Marx Brothers to get established in the movie business.*
Elicit the correct forms of the verbs from the class (*attempting* and *impressed*). Tell students that one of these forms is called the present participle and one the past participle and ask them to identify them (present participle: *attempting*, past participle: *impressed*). Explain that we often use participles to add extra information to the idea in the sentence. Refer students to the Active Grammar box for more information about participle clauses and gerunds.

4 Direct students back to Exercise 2 to find the examples called for in the Active Grammar box. Then have students compare their answers with a partner. Check answers with the class.

Answers: 1. past participle–Thalberg, impressed with his . . . . present participle–Desperately attempting to win . . . **2.** Having been no more than a moderate success . . . **3.** After hitting the heights . . . **4.** Growing up with a comedian . . .

Direct students to the Reference section on page 129.

5 Direct students to complete the sentences with participles or gerunds. Check answers with the class and write the correct forms of the verbs on the board.

Answers: 1. telling **2.** Working **3.** Made **4.** Telling **5.** being **6.** watching

6 Ask students to read the statements in Exercise 5 and decide whether they agree or disagree with them. Then have students compare their answers with a partner and discuss why they agree or disagree with the statements. Monitor the conversations for important errors.

Open the discussion to the whole class. Point out any errors that you heard and elicit the correct answers from the class.

OPTIONAL PRESENTATION

If you prefer a more deductive approach, use the complete grammar charts and explanations on the Reference page to present the concepts. (page 129)

Vocabulary

7 Tell students to cover the left-hand column. Focus students' attention on the words in the right-hand column. Ask students if they have seen these words before and what they think they mean. Encourage students to use an English-English dictionary to look up any unknown words. Then have students match the types of humor to the definitions. Students can check any words that they are not sure of in their dictionaries. Students can compare their answers with their partners. Finally, check answers with the whole class.

Answers: 1. e **2.** a **3.** c **4.** d **5.** b **6.** f **7.** g **8.** h

8 Have students discuss the questions with a partner. Monitor the conversations carefully for errors.

In a monolingual class, students can discuss the questions in small groups before you discuss as a class. In a multilingual class, pair students so that they are working with someone of another nationality. Get feedback by asking students from different countries to talk about the humor of their country.

Listening

9a Direct students to cover the reading. Tell them that they are going to listen to someone telling a joke. Play audio 1.14. If necessary, students can take notes while listening. After listening, discuss the joke as a class or in pairs. Ask students to explain whether they find the joke funny or not.

b Ask students why they think the speaker pauses at certain moments. (To give dramatic effect and to keep the listeners interested.) Direct students to uncover the text. Play audio 1.14 again. As they listen and read, have them mark the places in the joke where the person telling the joke pauses.

OPTIONAL EXTENSION

Get students to practice telling the joke to a partner, pausing at the right moments. Invite various students to tell the joke in front of the class, as long as they feel comfortable doing so.

Speaking

10a Organize students into groups of three. Tell them that they are going to tell a joke to their partners. Refer Student A to page 139, Student B to page 141, and Student C to page 142. Give students time to read through their jokes two or three times. Tell them to try to memorize their jokes if possible. Monitor to check that students understand all the words and expressions in their jokes and help them where necessary. Encourage students to think about the best places to pause while telling the joke.

b Have students tell their jokes to the other students in their group. Monitor carefully to see if they pause at important moments while telling the joke and for any errors. Encourage students to decide which joke was the funniest and also who was the best at telling the joke. Finally, write important errors on the board and call on students to correct them. Congratulate students on telling the jokes, as it is not an easy skill in a foreign language.

OPTIONAL EXTENSION

Tell students that they are going to prepare to tell their own jokes, either in their own language or in English. Tell them to write the joke down and mark where they think the best place would be to pause while telling the joke. Collect the jokes and make sure that there is nothing unsuitable or offensive. Also check the jokes for errors. Hand back the jokes in the following lesson and ask students to tell their jokes to the rest of the class, reminding them to be aware of pausing for dramatic effect.

NOTES

LESSON **4** pp. 41–42

Unit Wrap Up
Review reinforce lessons 1–3
Communication tell a story

Summary: In this lesson, students review the unit's language. Then they read the opening sentences of some pieces of fiction. Finally, they discuss in small groups how the story could continue and tell their stories.

Review

1

Answers: 1. decided **2.** claimed **3.** hadn't **4.** saw **5.** received **6.** included **7.** had forgotten

2

Answers: 1. Doing things for other people is life's biggest pleasure. **2.** Anyone wishing to take the exam must register in June. **3.** Most of the jewelry stolen from the store . . . **4.** Feeling sleepy, Luisa went to bed. **5.** When swimming, you must wear a bathing cap. **6.** Having been famous for years, he finally wanted some peace and quiet. **7.** Censored in their own country, they decided to . . . **8.** Waking up early, David went for a run.

3

Answers: 1. avid **2.** page-turner **3.** black humor **4.** hooked **5.** readable **6.** one-dimensional **7.** based **8.** gripping **9.** couldn't put it down **10.** best-seller **11.** puns **12.** irony

OPTIONAL EXTRA LISTENING

These audio tracks, activities, and audioscripts are available on both the *ActiveBook* CD-ROM at the back of each Student Book and on the *ActiveTeach* DVD at the back of this Teacher's Resource Book. The audio can also be found on the Audio Program CD. The audioscripts can also be found at the back of the Workbook. These listening activities can be completed in class or done as homework.

Communication

tell a story

OPTIONAL WARM UP

Ask students to discuss what they think makes a good opening sentence of a story. Discuss ideas as a class.

4a Have students work in groups of three or four. Focus their attention on the opening sentences to the pieces of fiction. Have students read them and discuss the questions in their groups. Monitor the conversations for interesting language. Then discuss the students' ideas as a class.

b In their groups, have students choose one of the openings and discuss how the story could continue. Give students time to prepare their ideas and take notes. Students should decide who will tell each part of the story and then practice telling the stories in their groups.

c Have students tell their stories to another group. Monitor the stories and take note of interesting language. Then decide as a class which pair or group has told the most interesting and unusual story. Draw students' attention to any interesting language that they have used while telling the stories and congratulate them on its use.

OPTIONAL EXTENSION

For homework, ask students to write their stories. In the following lesson, collect the stories and photocopy them. Hold a competition for the best story, which the students themselves can judge. You could divide the competition into categories such as *best humorous story, best dramatic story, best use of dialog,* etc.

OPTIONAL EXTENSION

Tell students to choose one of the novels whose opening is on page 42. Using the Internet or a library, students should try to find out what happened next in the book. They can bring their findings to the following class and compare their ideas from Exercise 4b with what really happened next in the story.

Notes for using the CEF

The Common European Framework (CEF), a reference document for language teaching professionals, was produced by the council of Europe as a means of ensuring parity in terms of language teaching and language qualifications across Europe. It has since increasingly become an accepted standard for English learners throughout the world. It can be downloaded as a PDF file fro free from www.coe.int from the section on Language Policy. There is also a link to the site from the *English in Common* website: www.PearsonELT.com/EnglishinCommon.

The CEF recommends that language learners use a portfolio to document, reflect on, and demonstrate their progress. *English in Common* has a Language Portfolio, which can be downloaded from your *ActiveTeach* disc (at the back of this Teacher's Resource Book) or from the *ActiveBook* disc (at the back of each Student Book). Suggested tasks are provided at the beginning of every unit on the Unit Overview page.

CEF REFERENCES

Lesson 1 CAN DO: tell an anecdote
CEF C1 descriptor: Can give elaborate descriptions and narratives, integrating sub-themes, developing particular points and rounding off with an appropriate conclusion. (CEF page 125)

Lesson 2 CAN DO: describe a person in detail
CEF C1 descriptor: Can write clear, detailed, well-structured and developed descriptions and imaginative texts in an assured, personal, natural style appropriate to the reader in mind. (CEF page 62)

Lesson 3 CAN DO: tell a joke
CEF C1 descriptor: Can use language flexibly and effectively for social purposes, including emotional, allusive and joking usage. (CEF page 76)

Additional Resources

Activity Worksheets and Teaching Notes—Unit 3

Photocopiable worksheets for this unit can be found on pages 114–119 and Teaching Notes can be found on pages 167–168 of this Teacher's Resource Book. They consist of games and other interactive activities for: Vocabulary, Grammar, and Speaking.

Extra Listening Activity—Unit 3

This activity is designed to provide students with additional opportunities to listen to and practice comprehension of spoken English. The audio can be accessed by clicking the Extra Listening folder in both the Student's *ActiveBook* (for independent student use) and in the Teacher's *ActiveTeach* (for classroom use). The audio is also provided at the end of the Audio Program CD. An activity worksheet can also be printed out from either the *ActiveBook* or *ActiveTeach*.

Extra Listening Unit 3—Audioscript

M1: Good evening, everyone. I hope you're enjoying your time camping at our beautiful National Forest here in Minnesota. Our program tonight, around the campfire, will be story-telling. Now, how many of you have heard of Paul Bunyan?

Voices: I have.
No, who is he?
Was he a real person?

M1: Was he a real person? Hmm. Well, most people say he was "larger than life." I guess you'll see if you agree after you hear a few of my stories. Here goes:
Well, Paul was born right around here. He was a VERY big baby—and he grew so fast that one week after he was born, he had to wear his father's clothes! By the time he was one, his mother sewed wagon wheels on his shirts for buttons, and boy did he have a big appetite. It is said that he ate 40 bowls of oatmeal every morning for breakfast! He got to be so tall and wide that he wasn't comfortable in a house, except maybe to sleep. It was natural that he became a lumberjack, with the great outdoors for his home.

Voices: I guess this is a "tall story."
Shh. Let's listen!

(continued on next page)

M1: In all our history, there has never been a lumberjack to equal Paul Bunyan! Why, he could cut down hundreds of trees single-handedly in just a few minutes by tying his huge ax to the end of a long rope and swinging it in circles. Now one year, here in the north, we had two winters! Yup, it snowed in winter and in summer, too. It was so cold that all the fish swam south. Milk turned to ice cream as it was being poured. And when people spoke at night, their words froze in mid-air! They had to wait until the next morning, when the sun came up, to hear the words as they defrosted!

M2: Didn't Paul have a pet ox?

M1: That's true. One day that winter, Paul was jogging through the snow to keep warm—by the way, that small lake over there is from one of his footprints—when he spotted a little ox almost hidden by the snow. The ox was blue with cold, and he stayed blue even when he warmed up. Paul named him Babe. Babe grew fast, and was soon huge and super strong.

Paul and Babe his blue ox became quite a team—no work was too hard for them. Babe could haul the logs away as fast as Paul could cut them. Sometimes, though, it was difficult to get the tall logs out of the forest on twisty logging roads. So Paul tied the ends of the roads to Babe's horns, and Babe pulled those roads straight as an arrow . . .

Video
Buying a Lie: An Internet Stock Hoax

Students watch a *20/20* news segment which investigates a man who pulled off a stock hoax costing investors millions of dollars. This video segment can be played on the Teacher's *ActiveTeach* disc and projected for classroom viewing or the disc can be played on any DVD player. Teaching notes and video scripts are also provided on the *ActiveTeach* disc.

Tests

A **Unit 3 Test** is provided in the Test Bank as a Word file on the *ActiveTeach* disc. It includes discrete sections on: Grammar, Vocabulary, Reading, and Writing. An Answer Key is also provided. If you wish, this test can be easily modified to suit the particular needs of your class.

Extra Vocabulary: Metaphors

Extra Vocabulary activities for this unit can be found in both the Student's *ActiveBook* and in the Teacher's *ActiveTeach*, along with an answer key.

UNIT 4
Moving forward

Unit Overview

Warm Up Lesson	
LESSON 1	**CAN DO** describe the chances of something happening **GRAMMAR** future probability
LESSON 2	**CAN DO** talk about plans and arrangements **GRAMMAR** future forms review **VOCABULARY** arrangements
LESSON 3	**CAN DO** follow an extended piece of discourse **GRAMMAR** subject/verb inversion **VOCABULARY** special abilities
LESSON 4	**Unit Wrap Up** **Review** reinforce lessons 1–3 **Communication** make an argument for research funding
Grammar and Vocabulary Reference Charts	

OPTIONAL LANGUAGE PORTFOLIO
(located in both the *ActiveBook* at the back of the Student Book and in the *ActiveTeach* at the back of this Teacher's Resource Book)

Have students review any materials (written or oral) that they created during this unit. Encourage them to select material to add to the *Achievement Portfolio* section of their Language Portfolios. These works will provide a physical representation of each student's progress over the course of the term. Also ask students to update any information in their *Personal Profiles*.

Teaching Resources

- **Workbook** pp. 28–35
- **Class Audio** CD1 Tracks 15–21
- ***ActiveBook*** Digital Student Book pages with complete unit audio plus Extra Listening Activity and Extra Vocabulary Study
- ***ActiveTeach*** Interactive whiteboard (IWB) software with video, Test Bank, and test audio

Warm Up p. 43

OPTIONAL WARM UP
Organize students into four groups. Each group looks at one of the photos on page 43. Give students one minute to brainstorm as much vocabulary as possible connected to their photo. Then have them share their ideas with students from the other groups. Finally, elicit responses from the class and write any interesting vocabulary on the board.

1 Direct students to discuss the questions in pairs. Then discuss ideas as a class.

2a Instruct students to read the news headlines and match them to the photos. Check answers with the class.

Answers: 1. D 2. B 3. C 4. A

b Tell students that they are going to listen to the four news stories that go with the headlines. Play audio 1.15 and allow students to check their answers. Then have them compare answers with a partner.

OPTIONAL EXTENSION
Play audio 1.15 again. After listening a second time, have students write a summary of the stories with their partners. Monitor and help where necessary. Ask different pairs to read their summaries to the rest of the class. Take note of any important errors. When they have finished reading the summaries, write any errors on the board and elicit the correct forms from the class.

3 Have students work with a partner to check the meaning of the words in bold in each sentence. If they do not know the meaning of the words, encourage them to help each other or check in their dictionaries before asking you. Then tell students to discuss the questions with their partners. Finally, compare responses as a class.

EXTEND THE WARM UP
Have students work with a partner to think of another type of progress that they would most like to see in the future and why. Ask them to justify their choices to the rest of the class.

LESSON 1 pp. 44–46

CAN DO describe the chances of something happening
GRAMMAR future probability

Summary: In this lesson, students read an article about how scientists are trying to recreate "superpowers" artificially. Through this context they look at future probability. Students finish by discussing future probabilities and by listening to an interview with Stan Lee, the creator of Spider-Man.

OPTIONAL WARM UP
If appropriate to your students, divide the class into pairs, A and B. Tell Students A to turn their chairs around so that they can't see the board. On the board write the names of the following superheroes: *Spider Man*, *Batman*, *The Incredible Hulk*, *Superman*, *The Invisible Woman*. Tell Students B to describe the superheroes to their partners, who try to guess their names from the descriptions. The winners are the pairs who describe and guess the superheroes first.

Speaking

1 Tell students to discuss the questions with their partners. Ask them to share their favorite comic book characters with the class. In a monolingual class, ask students if there are any famous comic book characters in their countries. In a multilingual class, students can tell a partner of a different nationality about the comic book characters in their country.

2a Organize students into groups to answer the questions about superheroes in four minutes. Then have them compare answers with another group and explain their answers. Elicit answers from different groups.

b Play audio 1.16 and have students check their answers. Then review answers with the class.

Answers: 1. Answers may include but are not limited to: Superman, Spider Man, Batman, The Incredible Hulk, The Fantastic Four, The Incredibles, Wonder Woman **2.** He was green. **3.** Spider Man can walk up walls using his spider-grip, he has super-strength and can lift up to ten tons, he has web shooters that he can fire to catch villains, he has spider-sense, [a kind of ESP that allows Peter Parker to sense when danger is coming], and spider-speed so he can run fast to escape danger. **4.** Planet Krypton **5.** *Spider Man* **6.** Wonder Woman

Reading

3 Have students read the article. Tell them not to worry about any words they don't know the meaning of at this stage. Discuss the article as a class and go over any unfamiliar vocabulary.

OPTIONAL VARIATION
Assign paragraphs to different students. After reading their paragraphs, have students mingle and tell each other about what they have read and whether they think the research is important or not. Students then read the rest of the article to check the information they have been told.

4 Have students discuss the questions in small groups. Encourage them to give reasons and examples to support their opinions. Compare responses as a class.

Grammar

OPTIONAL WARM UP
Write the following phrase on the board: *One of the students in this class will . . .* In another column, write: *. . . become president of the country, . . . become an international soccer player, . . . do his or her homework tonight, . . . begin studying another language in the next year, . . . buy the newspaper tomorrow.*
Have students work in small groups to discuss these prompts and decide how likely it is that students in the class will do these things. Monitor carefully for use of expressions of probability. When students have finished talking, elicit responses from the class and draw students' attention to the ways that they expressed probability.

5 Direct students to read the Active Grammar box, underline the phrases in the article on pages 44–45, and to complete the chart in the box. Then have students compare their answers with a partner. Check answers with the class.

Answers: 1. are bound to . . . (Web-shooter) **2.** There is a fairly good chance that . . . (Wall climbing); there is a distinct possibility that . . . (Super-strength); There is every likelihood that . . . (Regeneration) **3.** there is very little chance that . . . (Force field); the odds are against . . . (X-ray vision); It is doubtful that . . . (Flying) **4.** you don't stand a chance of . . . (Super-strength); stands no chance of . . . (Web-shooter)

Direct students to the Reference section on page 130.

6 Before students look at the exercise have them close their books. Write the Example sentence on the board: *There is no chance that she's borrowing my laptop.* Write *stand* below this sentence. Refer students back to the chart in the Active Grammar box and ask them to rewrite the sentence using the word *stand*. Write the answer on the board and direct students to look at the example in their books.

Ask students to rewrite the sentences. Then have them compare their sentences with a partner. Finally, check answers with the class.

Answers: 1. It is doubtful that they will make a breakthrough in the near future. 2 It's inconceivable that we'll be able to travel to Mars by 2050. **3.** They're bound to notice it's missing. **4.** There's a chance that the information is not secure. **5.** We're being met at the airport, so presumably we don't need train tickets. Or: Presumably we're being met at the airport, so we don't need train tickets. **6.** There's a distinct chance (*or* possibility) that China will win the space race. **7.** It's doubtful that the relationship will improve.

OPTIONAL PRESENTATION

If you prefer a more deductive approach, use the complete grammar charts and explanations on the Reference page to present the concepts. (page 130)

Speaking

7 Have students discuss the predictions with a partner. Monitor conversations for errors and correct use of language to express probability. Then discuss students' ideas as a class. Point out any important errors you have heard and call on students to correct them.

Listening

8 Tell the class that they are going to hear an interview with Stan Lee, the creator of Spider Man. Give students time to read the questions. Play audio 1.17 and ask students to number the questions 1–4, according to the order in which they are asked in the interview. Have students compare answers with a partner. Then check answers with the class.

Answers (order questions are answered in):
1. c **2.** b **3.** d **4.** a

OPTIONAL EXTENSION

Write the following topics on the board: *diseases, going to Mars, genetics.* Play audio 1.17 again and ask students to work in small groups to discuss whether or not they agree with what Stan Lee says about these topics. Monitor conversations for use of phrases to express probability. Then discuss as a class and draw students' attention to any interesting language they have used.

NOTES

LESSON 2 pp. 47–49

CAN DO talk about plans and arrangements
GRAMMAR future forms: review
VOCABULARY arrangements

Summary: In this lesson, students look at vocabulary used in making arrangements. They review future forms. Students listen to two telephone conversations and look at different ways of generalizing. They finish by playing *Twenty Questions*.

OPTIONAL WARM UP

Write the following questions on the board: *When was the last time you arranged to do something with a friend? Who did you arrange to meet? Where did you meet? How did you arrange to meet?* Ask students to discuss the questions with a partner or in groups. Then elicit responses from the class.

Vocabulary

1 Ask students to discuss the questions in pairs. Monitor conversations for errors. You may want to discuss the quotation as a class. To initiate the conversation, write the following headings on the board: *Communications technology has made our lives better. Communications technology has made our lives worse.* Elicit examples from the class to write under each heading and discuss.

2a Direct students to read the emails to find out what Tom is trying to do and what happens in the end. Tell them not to worry about words or expressions they don't understand at this stage. Have students compare ideas with a partner. Then check answers with the class.

Answers: Tom is trying to organize a barbecue, but since no one can come, he cancels it.

OPTIONAL VARIATION

Organize students into groups of four. Have each student in the group read one of the emails and remember the information. Students then tell the others in their group about the content of their email. Then have students read all the emails and decide what Tom is trying to do and what happens in the end.

b Before students look at the definitions, ask them to try to figure out from context what the words and phrases in bold in the emails mean. Check answers with the class.

Direct students to match the words and phrases in bold to the definitions. Then have students compare answers with their partners.

Answers: 1. be up to **2.** come up **3.** tied up **4.** lined up **5.** get out of **6.** call off **7.** swamped **8.** fall through **9.** be on **10.** be free **11.** wind down

Ask the class if there are any other words or phrases in the emails that they don't understand. Encourage students to answer each others' questions or check in a dictionary before asking you.

3 Direct students to read the sentences and complete them by adding one word to each one. Check answers with the class.

Answers: 1. The tennis match was called **off** due to rain. **2.** If you aren't **up** to anything this afternoon, why don't you come over? **3.** I'm sorry—I won't be able to make it at 5:30. Something has come **up**. **4.** I'm tied **up** all of January, but I'll have some free time in February. **5.** There's a great new band lined **up** for tonight. **6.** I need to wind **down** after this lousy week. **7.** Despite the rain, the festival is still **on**. **8.** She can't come tomorrow because she's **swamped** with work. **9.** I have to clean the house today. I can't get out **of** it. **10.** The picnic plans fell **through** when the forecast called for rain.

Grammar

OPTIONAL WARM UP

Write the following sentences on the board: *1. The class starts at 3:00. 2. I'll close the windows right away. 3. Most of the students will do their homework this evening. 4. There's going to be a party this weekend. 5. I'm meeting the rest of the class for a coffee tomorrow morning. 6. It's going to snow tomorrow. 7. I'll be traveling at this time tomorrow. 8. I'll have finished this book before the end of the month.*

Have students work with a partner to decide which future forms are used in each sentence and why they are used. For example, in sentence number 1 the simple present is used for a fixed schedule.

Next, have students write 5–7 sentences about themselves using different future forms. Some of the sentences should be true and some false. Have students read their sentences aloud to a partner. The partner guesses which sentences are true and which are false.

4 Direct students to match the beginning of each rule in the Active Grammar box with the correct ending. Encourage them to use the examples to help them. Check answers with the class.

Answers: 1. e **2.** c **3.** a **4.** g **5.** d **6.** f **7.** b

Direct students to the Reference section on page 130.

5a Have students complete the questions using the correct future form of the verb in parentheses.

b Play audio 1.18 and allow students to check their answers. Then play the audio again, this time instructing students to listen for the words that are contracted. Play the audio again and ask students to repeat the questions, paying attention to the contracted forms.

Answers: 1. 'll still be studying **2.** 'll have **3.** 'll be living **4.** will have **5.** 'll have changed **6.** 'll have **7.** 'll have **8.** 'll have seen

6 Have students interview a partner by asking the questions from Exercise 5a, paying attention to contracted forms. Encourage students to ask follow-up questions. Monitor for correct use of future forms and the use of contracted forms. Then ask students to share information about their partners with the class. Finally, write errors on the board and ask different students to correct them. Draw students' attention to their use of contracted forms and praise them for correct usage.

OPTIONAL PRESENTATION

If you prefer a more deductive approach, use the complete grammar charts and explanations on the Reference page to present the concepts. (page 130)

Listening

OPTIONAL WARM UP

Write these questions on the board: *How often do you talk on the phone? Who do you talk to? How long do you spend on the phone every day?* Have students discuss the questions with a partner. Then discuss as a class and decide who spends most time on the phone every day.

7 Tell the class that they are going to hear two telephone conversations. Play audio 1.19. Direct students to listen and decide what the relationship between the speakers is and what plans they are trying to make. Then have students compare answers with a partner. If necessary play the audio again.

Answers: Conversation 1: They are friends. They are making plans to go out on Saturday night.
Conversation 2: They are a couple. They are discussing what to make for dinner.

8 Play audio 1.19 again. Have students listen for the expressions in the How To box. Discuss the context in which the expressions are used. For example, Kevin in Conversation 1 says that he is busy pretty much all day, making his answer a little vague and imprecise.

9 Direct students to unscramble the sentences, starting each one with the underlined word and paying attention to expressions used to generalize. Then have students compare answers with a partner. Check answers with the class.

Answers: 1. We still go to that café every so often. **2.** I'm sort of busy this weekend. **3.** Her job involves solving problems and that kind of thing. **4.** I'll be working pretty much all evening. **5.** Because I'm so busy, I only see my sister once in a while. *or* Because I'm so busy, I see my sister only once in a while. **6.** By this time next year, I'll have met tons of new people. **7.** We're hoping to meet at about four-ish. **8.** I'll be arriving at ten or so.

10 Have students ask and answer the questions with a partner. They should include expressions from the How To box in their responses. Then have students switch partners and tell their new partner what they learned about their first partner.

Speaking

11 Ask the class if they know how to play *Twenty Questions*. If any students know how to play, have them explain the rules to the class. If they don't, direct students' attention to the instructions in the box. Then have students play the game in pairs. Encourage them to include vague or imprecise expressions in their answers.

When students have finished, encourage them to tell the class about which famous people they chose and which students guessed their partner's famous person. If some students finish early, they can repeat the activity with a different famous person.

NOTES

LESSON 3 pp. 50–52

CAN DO follow an extended piece of discourse
GRAMMAR subject / verb inversion
VOCABULARY special abilities

Summary: In this lesson, students read an article about gifted children. Then they look at ways of emphasizing information through subject/verb inversion. They listen to an expert on gifted children discussing a strange case, then write a summary of the expert's description.

Note: There are many characteristics of gifted children. They may learn to read early and tend to demonstrate high reasoning ability, creativity, curiosity, a large vocabulary, and an excellent memory. However, they can sometimes have problems with teachers and other authority figures, because they may frequently question authority. Gifted children often have problems in school if they are not challenged enough. Some famous gifted children include Ruth Lawrence, the youngest student to enter Oxford University at the age of 11; Steve Wozniak, who started developing complex electronics while still in school and went on to develop the world's first screen and keyboard desktop computer; the writer H.P. Lovecraft, who recited poetry at age two and was writing poetry at the age of five; and Mozart, who wrote his Symphony no. 1 at the age of eight.

OPTIONAL WARM UP
Write these prompts on the board: *school, friends, food, TV, sports, games*. Tell students to think back to when they were ten years old. Then have students tell a partner about their lives when they were ten years old, using the prompts on the board to help them. Finally, discuss as a class to see whose childhoods were the most similar and the most different.

Vocabulary

1 Ask students to work with a partner to make three lists of things that they think are normal for children to be able to do by the time they are two, five, and ten years old. Write students' ideas on the board. Then ask if anyone knows of any child prodigies. Discuss answers as a class.

2 Ask the class to cover the right-hand column (a–g). Ask students to discuss what they think the words in the left-hand column mean. Then have them uncover the right-hand column and match them with the words on the left. Check answers with the class.

Answers: 1. d **2.** a **3.** f **4.** e **5.** g **6.** b **7.** c

3 Have students look at the photos and at the words and phrases in Exercise 2. Ask students to make predictions about the topic of the article. Then have students read the article quickly to check their predictions. To ensure that students skim through the article, you may want to give them a time limit for this first reading. Then have students discuss with a partner if any of their predictions were correct.

Finally, have students read the article more carefully and answer the questions that follow. Have students compare answers with a partner and then check answers with the class.

Answers: 1. Because Son could play chess when he was three years old. **2.** It's nothing unusual. It is natural for him. **3.** They receive lots of attention, not all of it positive. "They have also been objects of suspicion and superstition. They often must deal with teasing by other children, attention from the press, and pressure and high expectations from their parents." **4.** The "big question" is whether geniuses are born or made. **5.** It is a combination of nature and nurture. ("Prodigies are half born, half made.")

4 Have students discuss the questions with a partner. Monitor conversations for errors and any interesting language. Then ask different pairs to share their ideas with the rest of the class. Write errors on the board and ask different students to correct them. Finally, read the interesting language students have used and congratulate them on its use.

Grammar

OPTIONAL WARM UP
Write two sentences on the board about things that you are able to do. For example: *I speak English. I also speak French.* Below, write the sentence prompt: *Not only . . .* Ask the class how you could make one sentence using the two original sentences and the sentence prompt. If students can't give you the sentence, write it on the board: *Not only do I speak English, but I also speak French.* Explain that this is an example of subject/ verb inversion and elicit why this structure is used. (To add variety and to emphasize certain parts of the sentence.) Focus students' attention on the change in word order (*I do* becomes *do I*) and how the order in this type of sentence is the same as in a question.

Ask students to write two sentences about things that they are able to do. Then ask them to write a third sentence combining the information in the two sentences, beginning with *Not only . . .* Monitor the class and check students' sentences as necessary. Then have students share their sentence with a partner. Finally, have students read their sentences to the rest of the class.

5 Direct students to complete the tasks in the Active Grammar box. Then have students compare answers with a partner. Check answers with the class.

Answers: 2. Only recently has science begun to investigate the cultural and biological factors . . . (paragraph 4); Nowhere is this illustrated more clearly than in the case of Indian prodigy Tathagat Avatar Tulsi. (paragraph 4)
Matching: **1.** c **2.** d **3.** b **4.** a

Direct students to the Reference section on page 130.

6 Direct students to read the six pairs of sentences and circle the correctly written sentence in each pair. Then have students compare answers with a partner. Finally, check answers with the class.

Answers: 1. b **2.** a **3.** a **4.** a **5.** b **6.** a

OPTIONAL PRESENTATION
If you prefer a more deductive approach, use the complete grammar charts and explanations on the Reference page to present the concepts. (page 130)

OPTIONAL EXTENSION
Have the class form two groups, A and B. Tell Students A that they are journalists writing a report on child prodigies. The journalists are going to interview Nguyen Ngoc Truong Son. Tell Students B to pretend that they are Son. Instruct Students A to prepare questions to ask in the interview, and Students B to prepare what they would like to say in an interview. Encourage Students B to be imaginative and invent details about Son and his life. When students have finished preparing, have each student find a partner from the other group and conduct the interview. Monitor for errors. If any pair feels confident enough, ask them to act out their interview for the rest of the class. When students have finished, write errors you have heard on the board and ask students to correct them.

Speaking

OPTIONAL WARM UP
Organize the class into two groups, A and B. Tell Students A to look at the first picture and Students B the second. Give them three minutes to discuss what they think the child in the photo is like. You may wish to put the following prompts on the board: *age, nationality, family, special talent*. When students have finished preparing, have each student find a partner from the other group and share their ideas about the children in the photos.

7a Ask students to work in pairs, A and B. Refer Students A to the paragraph on page 141 and Students B to the paragraph on page 142. Have students complete the paragraphs and then make notes relating to the categories on page 52 (name, special talent, and what others think of him or her).

Answers:
Paragraph A: **1.** did **2.** also **3.** when *or* after **4.** did **5.** does **6.** Only
Paragraph B: **1.** only **2.** also **3.** had **4.** when *or* after **5.** does **6.** No

Name:	Junichi Ono	Abigail Sin
Special talent:	Pop artist	Pianist, mathematician
What others think:	He's a little strange.	determined—never stops practicing

b Have students use their notes to tell a partner about the person they have read about.

Listening

8a Give students time to read the notes and to think briefly about what type of information they will need to fill in the blanks. Draw their attention to the usefulness of this tip in an exam situation.

b Play audio 1.20. As students listen, they should complete the notes. Then have students compare their answers with a partner. Play the audio again for students to check their answers. Last, check answers with the whole class.

Answers: 1. John and Michael **2.** small **3.** laughed **4.** the day of the week of any date **5.** numbers **6.** everything about that day **7.** visual **8.** We can see the answers

9 Have students discuss the questions in groups of three or four. Monitor the conversations closely for errors. Then discuss as a class. Write any errors you have heard on the board and ask different students to correct them.

Writing

10 Ask students to discuss with a partner what the most important parts of John and Michael's story are. Then have students work on their own to write a summary of the story. You may wish to have students read their summaries aloud for the class.

LESSON 4 pp. 53–54

Unit Wrap Up
Review reinforce lessons 1–3
Communication make an argument for research funding

Summary: In this lesson, students review the unit's language. They listen to different people talking about important discoveries and inventions. Then they read some information about new technology before presenting a case for research funding of one of these areas to the rest of the class.

Review

1

Answers: Answers may vary. Following are some possible answers:
1. There's a good chance the weather will improve in the coming months./There's a distinct possibility that the weather will improve in the coming months./The weather may well improve in the coming months.
2. There's a remote possibility that they will contact us./They probably won't contact us./The chances are slim that they will contact us.
3. There's every likelihood that we will move in the spring./There's a good chance that we will move in the spring./We're bound to move in the spring.
4. I doubt they will offer him the job./There's very little chance that they will offer him the job./There's a distinct possibility that they won't offer him the job.
5. Attendance will presumably be high this year./Attendance is bound to be high this year./There's a strong possibility that attendance will be high this year.

2

Answers: 1. will retire, 'll be looking **2.** coming **3.** 'll be **4.** be seeing **5.** 'm going to work **6.** will have gotten

3

Answers: 1. b **2.** c **3.** b **4.** c **5.** b

4

Answers: 1. in a while **2.** free **3.** up to **4.** pretty much **5.** came up **6.** every so often **7.** swamped **8.** fell through

OPTIONAL EXTRA LISTENING

These audio tracks, activities, and audioscripts are available on both the *ActiveBook* CD-ROM at the back of each Student Book and on the *ActiveTeach* DVD at the back of this Teacher's Resource Book. The audio can also be found on the Audio Program CD. The audioscripts can also be found at the back of the Workbook. These listening activities can be completed in class or done as homework.

Communication

make an argument for research funding

OPTIONAL WARM UP

Ask students to think of the three most useful inventions that affect their daily lives. Have them explain to a partner why these inventions are important to them. Encourage students to ask follow-up questions where possible. Then discuss as a class.

5 Play audio 1.21. Tell students to write down the inventions and discoveries mentioned and to take notes about them. Then have them compare what they have written with a partner.

Play the audio again and have students add more information. Then allow students to discuss questions 2 and 3 with a partner.

Answers: Speaker 1: x-rays, penicillin, and the structure of DNA **Speaker 2:** a rocket / sending man to the moon **Speaker 3:** computers and the Internet **Speaker 4:** domestic appliances, advances in travel (bicycle, car, airplane)

6 Have students think about the questions while reading the paragraphs. They will probably need time to take notes to answer the questions. Monitor and help with any unknown vocabulary. Encourage students to use an English-English dictionary or ask their partners if there are any unknown words.

7 Have the class form three groups, A, B and C. Tell Group A that they are going to present a case for research into space travel, Group B that they are going to present a case for research into how robots can help mankind, and Group C that they are going to present a case for research into genetic engineering. Students should discuss the questions in their groups and decide how they are going to present a case for their research. Give them time to prepare what they are going to say and help where necessary.

Give each group a chance to present their case to the rest of the class. Encourage the students listening to take notes and write questions to ask after the presentation. Decide as a class which group made the most convincing case.

Notes for using the CEF

The Common European Framework (CEF), a reference document for language teaching professionals, was produced by the council of Europe as a means of ensuring parity in terms of language teaching and language qualifications across Europe. It has since increasingly become an accepted standard for English learners throughout the world. It can be downloaded as a PDF file fro free from www.coe.int from the section on Language Policy. There is also a link to the site from the *English in Common* website: www.PearsonELT.com/EnglishinCommon.

The CEF recommends that language learners use a portfolio to document, reflect on, and demonstrate their progress. *English in Common* has a Language Portfolio, which can be downloaded from your *ActiveTeach* disc (at the back of this Teacher's Resource Book) or from the *ActiveBook* disc (at the back of each Student Book). Suggested tasks are provided at the beginning of every unit on the Unit Overview page.

CEF REFERENCES

Lesson 1 CAN DO: describe the chances of something happening
CEF C1 descriptor: Can qualify opinions and statements precisely in relation to degrees of, for example, certainty / uncertainty, belief / doubt, likelihood, etc. (CEF page 129)

Lesson 2 CAN DO: talk about plans and arrangements
CEF C1 descriptor: Can use language flexibly and effectively for social purposes. (CEF page 76)

Lesson 3 CAN DO: follow an extended piece of discourse
CEF C1 descriptor: Can understand enough to follow extended speech on abstract and complex topics beyond his or her own field, though he or she may need to confirm occasional details, especially if the accent is unfamiliar. (CEF page 66)

Additional Resources

Activity Worksheets and Teaching Notes—Unit 4

Photocopiable worksheets for this unit can be found on pages 120–125 and Teaching Notes can be found on pages 169–170 of this Teacher's Resource Book. They consist of games and other interactive activities for: Vocabulary, Grammar, and Speaking.

Extra Listening Activity—Unit 4

This activity is designed to provide students with additional opportunities to listen to and practice comprehension of spoken English. The audio can be accessed by clicking the Extra Listening folder in both the Student's *ActiveBook* (for independent student use) and in the Teacher's *ActiveTeach* (for classroom use). The audio is also provided at the end of the Audio Program CD. An activity worksheet can also be printed out from either the *ActiveBook* or *ActiveTeach*.

Extra Listening Unit 4—Audioscript

F1: OK, folks, lunch is cleaned up. Chances are the kids won't get back from ice skating until around 4 o'clock. What should we do until then? Go for a walk? Read by the fire? Just sit and talk?

M1: How about a game of Jeopardy? I've got the set right here.

F2: Sounds like fun, Mike. Remind me of the rules.

M1: Well, to start, I'll be the host and you three can be the contestants. Questions are worth between one hundred and 500 dollars, depending on difficulty. If you know the answer, push the buzzer. And remember, your answers have to be in question form. The categories in this round are children's books, inventions we use everyday, and the Olympics. Sally, will you keep score?

M2: She'll probably cheat! We'd better watch her!

F1: Oh shush! Stop teasing your sister, Bill! You know, I think you don't have a hope of winning with these categories unless she gives you extra points by mistake!

M1: Are you guys ready? We'll start with Children's Books for one hundred dollars. This young woman fell through a rabbit hole and met a cat with a crazy smile.

M2: Who is Alice in Wonderland?

M1: Correct! Sally, give Bill one hundred dollars.

F2: How did you get that question, Bill? You never read a book when we were little!

M2: Did too!

F2: You did not!

M1: OK, children, it's time to grow up or I'll send you to your rooms!

F2:, M2: We'll be good, promise!

(continued on next page)

M1: Next, Inventions for 300 dollars. This product was invented by Mary Anderson in 1903 to help streetcars operate safely in the rain.
F1: What is a windshield wiper?
M1: Correct, 300 dollars for Lisa. Next question is Olympics for 400 dollars. By summer 2016, this city will have hosted the 31st Olympiad.
F2: What is London?
M1: Sorry. Wrong answer.
M2: What is Rio?
M1: Correct. 400 dollars more for Bill. Looks like he's going to win.
Next, Inventions for 200 dollars.
These little brown pieces of candy weren't invented until 1930. They revolutionized cookies in America.
F1: What are chocolate chips?
M1: Correct, Lisa. I was pretty sure you'd get that one, judging by the delicious smell wafting in here. Uh oh. Look at the time! We're going to have to finish up.
F1: Sally, what's the score so far?
F2: Bill is ahead by 200 dollars. You and I are tied. The next question may well be the decider.
M1: Well, good luck everyone. And the last question is worth 500 dollars. This machine was patented in 1889 by Josephine Garis. A handle sprayed hot, soapy water into a tub. At first it was used only by some restaurants and hotels.
M2: What is a dishwasher?
M1: Correct! And the winner is Bill. Congratulations!
F1: Good job, Bill!
F2: You're smarter than I thought, kid brother! Well done!
F1: OK—who'd like some coffee and chocolate chip cookies?
All: Me, I would! Me, too . . .

Video
Born Genius: Children Who are Beyond Gifted

Students watch a *20/20* news segment about three amazing talented child prodigies. This video segment can be played on the Teacher's *ActiveTeach* disc and projected for classroom viewing or the disc can be played on any DVD player. Teaching notes and video scripts are also provided on the *ActiveTeach* disc.

Tests

A **Unit 4 Test** is provided in the Test Bank as a Word file on the *ActiveTeach* disc. It includes discrete sections on: Grammar, Vocabulary, Reading, and Writing. An Answer Key is also provided. If you wish, this test can be easily modified to suit the particular needs of your class.

Extra Vocabulary: Two-part expressions

Extra Vocabulary activities for this unit can be found in both the Student's *ActiveBook* and in the Teacher's *ActiveTeach*, along with an answer key.

UNIT 5 Making money

Unit Overview

Warm Up Lesson	
LESSON 1	**CAN DO** talk about professional relationships **GRAMMAR** emphasis
LESSON 2	**CAN DO** discuss financial decisions and regrets **GRAMMAR** conditionals: review **VOCABULARY** money, achievement, and charity
LESSON 3	**CAN DO** express priorities **GRAMMAR** sentence adverbials **VOCABULARY** expressing priorities; expressing quantity
LESSON 4	**Unit Wrap Up** **Review** reinforce lessons 1–3 **Communication** negotiate
Grammar and Vocabulary Reference Charts	

OPTIONAL LANGUAGE PORTFOLIO

(located in both the *ActiveBook* at the back of the Student Book and in the *ActiveTeach* at the back of this Teacher's Resource Book)

Have students review any materials (written or oral) that they created during this unit. Encourage them to select material to add to the *Achievement Portfolio* section of their Language Portfolios. These works will provide a physical representation of each student's progress over the course of the term. Also ask students to update any information in their *Personal Profiles*.

Teaching Resources

- **Workbook** pp. 36–43
- **Class Audio** CD1 Tracks 22–27
- ***ActiveBook*** Digital Student Book pages with complete unit audio plus Extra Listening Activity and Extra Vocabulary Study
- ***ActiveTeach*** Interactive whiteboard (IWB) software with video, Test Bank, and test audio

Warm Up p. 55

OPTIONAL WARM UP

Ask students to write the names of three famous wealthy people from their country. Discuss as a class how the people made their money.

1 Have students discuss the meaning of the words and phrases in bold with a partner. Check answers with the class.

Answers: 1. inherited a lot of money **2.** argued about the price **3.** the business of buying and selling shares **4.** an increase in wages **5.** people who earn a lot of money **6.** worth more than money can buy **7.** paid according to how much you sell **8.** couldn't pay its debts

Ask students to decide if any of the words or phrases could be used to describe the photos. Elicit answers from different students.

Answers: Answers may vary. **A.** came into a fortune, high-income **B.** stock market, paid on commission **C.** priceless **D.** haggled

2 Have students discuss the statements with a partner. Then discuss as a class.

EXTEND THE WARM UP

Write the following sentence on the board: *High-income families should pay higher taxes.* Allow the students to decide whether they agree or disagree with the statement and have them divide into two groups. Give the groups time to prepare what they are going to say. Invite one of the students from the group that agrees to start the debate by stating why they are in favor of high-income families paying higher taxes. Then allow a student from the other group to respond. Make sure that all students in both groups contribute to the debate.

LESSON 1 pp. 56–58

CAN DO talk about professional relationships
GRAMMAR emphasis

Summary: In this lesson, students read about a unique business model. Then they look at how to add emphasis to sentences. Students finish the lesson by listening to an expert discuss what makes a successful business partnership and go on to discuss what makes partnerships successful or not.

Reading

1 Ask students to discuss the questions with a partner. Then elicit responses from the class as a whole.

2 Direct students to look at the photo and ask: *What type of business do you think Zingerman's is?* Have students read the article. Then have them read it again more carefully and answer the questions that follow. Tell students to compare their answers with a partner. Then check answers with the class.

Answers: **1.** a deli / restaurant / food store **2.** It has expanded into other related businesses around Zingerman's. **3.** They didn't franchise, anyone can pitch an idea for a Zingerman's business, employee input is encouraged, they provide excellent compensation and benefits, they share their business model through a training and consulting branch of the company.
4. on great food, great service, and financial results
5. to learn how to improve their businesses

3 Have students work with a partner. Direct them back to the article on page 56 to try to figure out the meanings from the context.

Answers: Wording of answers will vary. **1.** possibility **2.** risk harming or damaging **3.** present an idea **4.** become very successful **5.** pay and other advantages that you get as part of a job, such as health insurance; programs that offer employees reasons to remain employed by a company **6.** the ideas that guide the actions and behavior of a person or organization

OPTIONAL EXTENSION

Ask students if Zingerman's sounds like a place where they would like to work. What other businesses do they know of where they might like to work? Have them discuss the questions with a partner, giving reasons for their answers. Then elicit responses from the class.

Grammar

OPTIONAL WARM UP

Ask students who the first person to arrive in class was. Write the following sentence on the board, with the student's name: _____ *arrived first today.* Below write: *It was . . .* Ask students to complete the second sentence, using the information contained in the first sentence. Write it on the board: *It was _____ who arrived first today.* Ask the class why the second sentence is written in this order and explain that this is one way to emphasize important information in a sentence (in this case, who arrived first).

4 Have students read the Active Grammar box and find the examples in the article on page 56. Then ask students to compare answers with a partner. Finally, check answers with the class.

Answers: **1.** He also preferred that they stay in their **own** neighborhood. **2.** But Weinzweig was not **the least bit** interested in expanding . . . ; It actually doesn't feel like work **at all**. **3.** It's a work environment where people **truly** thrive; It **actually** doesn't feel like work at all; But this is **by no means** a secret; . . . you can **actually** order a Reuben Sandwich Kit. **4.** Zingerman's employees really **do** love coming to work. **5. It was Saginaw** who suggested franchising nationwide; **It's a work environment** where people truly thrive. **6. What is unique** about ZCoB is that anyone can pitch . . .

Direct students to the Reference section on page 131.

5a Instruct students to rewrite the sentences, adding emphasis using the words in parentheses. Then have students compare their answers with a partner.

Answers: **1.** He can't complain. It's his own fault he didn't get a raise. **2.** We are by no means certain that it is the same man committing the crimes. **3.** What I really miss is having enough time to spend with friends. **4.** They didn't understand what we wanted at all. **5.** The employees actually love coming to work. **6.** It was always Sammy who got into trouble. **7.** Keith wasn't the least bit annoyed when we cancelled the meeting.

b Play audio 1.22 for the class to check their answers. Then play it again and have students underline the stressed words in each sentence. Have students practice saying the sentences with the same stress and intonation as the audio.

OPTIONAL PRESENTATION

If you prefer a more deductive approach, use the complete grammar charts and explanations on the Reference page to present the concepts. (page 131)

Speaking

6 Have students discuss the questions with a partner. Encourage them to use different ways of adding emphasis when talking to their partners. Monitor for correct use of emphasis. Elicit feedback from the class, then congratulate students on their correct use of emphasis.

Listening

OPTIONAL WARM UP

Write the following first halves of famous business partnerships on the board: *Saatchi, Ben, Nieman, Hewlett, Johnson, Rand, Rolls.* Ask students to work in pairs to see how many of these famous business partnerships they can complete. Elicit feedback and write the second halves on the board: *Saatchi and Saatchi* (advertising agency), *Ben and Jerry's* (ice-cream makers), *Nieman Marcus* (retail department store), *Hewlett-Packard* (computer manufacturers), *Johnson and Johnson* (manufacturer of health-care products), *Rand McNally* (map publishers), *Rolls-Royce* (luxury car manufacturers). Then have students discuss what each company does and why they think it is successful.

7 Give the class time to read the sentences. Play audio 1.23 and ask students to complete the sentences. Then ask them to compare answers with a partner. Check answers with the class.

Answers: 1. friends or family members **2.** buy them out of their share **3.** a visionary, an operations person **4.** skills **5.** hire help **6.** communication **7.** long-term

8a Focus students' attention on the notes about the five sections and give them time to read them. Tell the class that they are going to listen to the audio again, but this time there will be pauses between sections. Play audio 1.24, pausing after each section to give students time to take notes on how the phrases are used. Play the audio again if necessary. Then have students compare their ideas with a partner.

b If there are any words or phrases that students don't know the meaning of, encourage them to answer each others' questions or consult a dictionary before asking you. Then have students work with a partner to reconstruct what each speaker said, using the words and phrases from Exercise 7. Finally, ask different students to tell the rest of the class what they have written. You may wish to allow students to look at the audioscript on page 152 to check their answers.

9 Ask students to discuss the questions in groups of three or four. Monitor the conversations and take note of errors. Elicit feedback from different groups.

OPTIONAL EXTENSION

For homework, ask students to look up the Zingerman's website and take notes about the products and the business. In the following lesson, have students share information that they have found with a partner. Then have students write seven or eight questions they would like to ask Ari Weinzweig and Paul Saginaw. Ask students to "interview" a partner—one partner taking the role of an interviewer, and one the role of Weinzweig or Saginaw. If a pair feels confident, ask them to role-play the interview for the rest of the class.

NOTES

LESSON 2 pp. 59–61

CAN DO discuss financial decisions and regrets
GRAMMAR conditionals: review
VOCABULARY money, achievement, and charity

Summary: In this lesson, students read an article about someone who had a lot of money then lost it. They share this information with a partner and then go on to look at conditionals. Students finish the lesson by reading an article about some of the world's greatest philanthropists.

Note: Leon Spinks went from being heavyweight champion of the world to being homeless in little more than a decade. Spinks won the heavyweight title in February 1978 by beating Muhammad Ali. Ali subsequently regained his title by beating Spinks seven months later. Spinks continued boxing, but later had personal problems and was homeless for a while.

Andrew Carnegie was a Scottish-born businessman who founded the Carnegie Steel Company in the United States. He built up one of the most important corporations in the world. Later in life he gave away most of his riches to fund libraries, schools, and universities around the world.

John D. Rockefeller was the founder of Standard Oil. He turned this corporation into one of the largest and most profitable organizations in the world. He spent the last years of his life on philanthropic ventures and gave away most of his wealth.

Bill Gates is the founder of Microsoft. He is often credited as being the richest man in the world, as well as one of the most influential. He and his wife Melinda have donated enormous sums of money to charity.

OPTIONAL WARM UP

Write *money, love, health, family* on the board. Ask students to put these four things in order of importance to them. Then tell them to compare ideas with a partner and give reasons for their order. Then have students compare their ideas with another pair and explain their choices. Finally, discuss ideas as a class.

Reading

1 Ask students to read the quotes and decide whether they agree or disagree with them. Then have them share their ideas with a partner and explain their opinions.

2a Organize students into pairs. Refer Students A to the article about Leon Spinks on page 59. Refer Students B to the article about William Post on page 143. Have students read their articles and make notes to answer questions 1–5 as they read. Tell them not to worry about any words or phrases they don't know the meaning of at this stage, because you will be dealing with them later.

Answers:

	Leon Spinks	William Post
How did he win his money? How much was it?	boxing $3.25 million	in the US lottery $16.2 million
How did he lose his money?	Others think from partying, but he denies this. He gave power of attorney to his lawyers and lost all the money.	His girlfriend sued him for $5.3 million, he made bad investments, he promised money to family members, and he couldn't control his spending.
What does he do now?	works at a McDonalds and volunteers at an after-school program	spent the last years of his life living on a Social Security check
What kind of relationship does or did he have with his family?	He says he is close to his brother, but he wouldn't ask him for financial help.	Not good. One brother tried to have him killed.
What "philosophy" does each man express at the end of the article?	He says that you do what you can. He's not going to give up on life.	He was more content without money. He wanted peace of mind.

b Now have students tell their partners about the person from their article, using the notes they have taken.

3a Tell students to find words and phrases in the articles that match the definitions. Students can compare answers with a partner and then check answers as a class.

Answers: **1.** volunteer **2.** power of attorney **3.** never saw a penny **4.** spiraled downward **5.** sue **6.** business ventures **7.** declare bankruptcy

b Have students complete the sentences and then compare their answers with a partner. To check the answers, ask different students to read aloud what they have written.

Answers: **1.** business venture **2.** seen a penny **3.** volunteered **4.** declared bankruptcy

Finally, ask if there are any words or phrases in the readings that students don't know the meaning of. Encourage them to figure out the meaning from the context before explaining them to the group.

Grammar

OPTIONAL WARM UP

Write the following scrambled sentence on the board: *If the lawyer he hadn't given power wouldn't lost of attorney, he have all money his.* Have students unscramble the sentence with a partner. If they have trouble doing so, write the first three or four words. When the class has unscrambled the sentence, ask a student to write the answer on the board: *If he hadn't given the lawyer power of attorney, he wouldn't have lost all his money.* Ask students to identify the structures used in this type of conditional sentence: *If* + past perfect + *would have* + past participle. Elicit why we use this type of conditional sentence (to talk about a hypothetical past situation) and its name (unreal conditional). Tell the class that they are going to be looking at other conditional structures in this lesson.

4 Ask students to complete the sentences with the correct form of the verb in parentheses.

Answers: 1. see **2.** hadn't gambled **3.** hadn't come into **4.** been able **5.** are **6.** would like **7.** hadn't lost **8.** Should **9.** would stop

5 Ask students to complete the sentences in the Active Grammar box by matching the left and right columns. Then have students compare their answers with a partner. Check answers with the whole class.

Answers: 1. e **2.** c **3.** a **4.** d **5.** b **6.** f

Ask the the class the following questions and write the answers on the board:

Q: What conditional structure do we use to talk about something that is always true?

A: *If* + simple present in the *if* clause + simple present in the result clause.

Q: What conditional structure do we use to talk about a possible real situation in the future?

A: *If* +present tense in the *if* clause + *will* (*might/may/could/should*) in the result clause.

Q: What structure do we use to talk about a hypothetical or unlikely situation in the future?

A: *If* + simple past in the *if* clause + *would* (*might/may/could/should*) in the result clause.

Q: What structure do we use to talk about a hypothetical past situation?

A: *If* + past perfect in the *if* clause + *would have* (*could have/should have/might have*) in the result clause.

Q: What is a typical mixed conditional structure that expresses a hypothetical present result of a past action?

A: *If* + past perfect in the *if* clause + *would/could/may/might/should* in the result clause.

Direct students to the Reference section on page 131.

6 Direct students to rewrite the sentences using the prompts in parentheses, keeping the meaning the same. Check answers with the class.

Answers: 1. If it hadn't been for the last question (being so difficult), I might/would/could have passed the exam. **2.** I would have bought some presents if I had had my credit card with me. **3.** If only there weren't so much competition, the business might be/would be doing better. **4.** If it hadn't been for Dr. Crane, I might not have recovered quickly. **5.** If they hadn't argued about money, they might/would/could still be business partners now.

OPTIONAL PRESENTATION

If you prefer a more deductive approach, use the complete grammar charts and explanations on the Reference page to present the concepts. (page 131)

Speaking

7 Have students discuss the questions in small groups. Encourage them to use conditional structures where possible. Monitor conversations for the correct use of conditionals and any important errors. Ask different pairs to summarize their answers for you. Finally, write errors on the board and encourage students to correct them for you as a class.

Reading

OPTIONAL WARM UP

Ask the class to look at the photos of Andrew Carnegie and Bill and Melinda Gates. Ask students to discuss in small groups what they know about the people in the photos and what the reading might be about. Compare information as a class.

8 Have students read the article and circle the correct choices as they read. Tell them not to worry about any words or phrases they don't understand at this stage, because they will be dealt with later in the lesson. Then have students compare answers with a partner. Finally, check answers as a class.

Answers: 1. extravagance **2.** for **3.** welfare **4.** lavishly **5.** fortune **6.** charity **7.** charged **8.** into **9.** founded **10.** mission **11.** dedicates **12.** impact **13.** admire **14.** vision **15.** deal

Ask if there are any words or phrases from the article that students don't understand. Encourage them to answer each others' questions or look in an English-English dictionary before explaining the vocabulary to the group.

OPTIONAL VARIATION

Organize the class into groups of three: A, B, and C. Have Students A read the article for information about Andrew Carnegie, Students B read about John D. Rockefeller, and Students C read about Bill and Melinda Gates. Ask students to make notes about their philanthropist(s) and then share their information with the others in their group. Then have students read the entire article and circle the correct choices in numbers 1–15 as they read. Finally, have students compare their answers with the other group members.

9 Have students discuss the questions with a partner. Monitor the conversations closely for errors and any interesting language. Then discuss students' ideas as a class. Write any errors that you have heard on the board and encourage students to come up to the board and correct them. Finally, congratulate them on any interesting language they have used.

NOTES

LESSON 3 pp. 62–64

CAN DO express priorities
GRAMMAR sentence adverbials
VOCABULARY expressing priorities; expressing quantity

Summary: In this lesson, students read an article about companies that are good to work for. Through this context students look at sentence adverbials. Then they listen to an interview with a company CEO. They finish the lesson by looking at vocabulary expressing quantity and write a paragraph using some of this vocabulary.

Note: *Fortune* is an American business magazine. Every year it publishes rankings of the top companies in the world. See: http://money.cnn.com/magazines/fortune. Wegmans Food Markets has been included in *Fortune*'s list of the "100 Best Companies to Work For" for 14 consecutive years. In 2005 it was ranked number 1, and in 2006 it was ranked number 2. See www.wegmans.com.

OPTIONAL WARM UP

Write the following question on the board: *If you could work for any company in the world, what company would you work for?* Ask students to discuss this question in pairs. Then discuss as a class.

Speaking

1 Ask students to list the most important things for them in a job. Then have them compare their lists with a partner and reach an agreement about the five most important things. Ask them to try to complete and use some of the expressions from the How To box. Ask students to share their lists with another pair and explain their choices. Monitor the conversations for errors. Compare answers as a class.

OPTIONAL EXTENSION

Ask students to discuss with a partner which of the items in the box they think are not priorities for them. Encourage them to use the expressions in the How To box. Monitor for correct use of the expressions. Ask pairs to share their ideas with the class.

Reading

2 Have students read the article and answer the questions that follow. Then have students compare answers with a partner. Finally, check answers as a class.

Answers: 1. It uses a survey, asking employees questions about their company, for example, about pay, benefits, etc. Then it compares the results for each company.
2. All of the top companies pay well, allow workers to make decisions, and offer a comfortable workplace, but the winners tend to offer things "above and beyond the norm," which other companies don't. **3.** Employees first, customers second. They also believe in giving responsibility to employees. **4.** Because the staff, even if they are very young, can make decisions that keep the customers happy.

Grammar

OPTIONAL WARM UP

Write the following sentence ending on the board: *. . . the most important thing for the majority of employees is not money.* Tell students to scan the article on page 62 quickly to find out how this sentence begins. When the they have found the sentence, write the adverbial phrase at the beginning: *Surprisingly enough, . . .* Ask the class what this adverbial phrase says about the writer's opinion of the workers' priorities (surprising, unexpected). Elicit that sentence adverbials are often used at the beginning of a sentence to show an opinion or attitude to a subject.

3 Have students read the Active Grammar box. Ask them to circle the correct choice for items 1 and 2 and then fill in the chart with words and phrases from the article on page 62. Check answers with the whole class.

Answers:
1. beginning **2.** comma

Adverbial functions	Examples
Basic ideas	*fundamentally, essentially*
Generalizations	*by and large, broadly speaking*
How something appears	*seemingly, apparently*
Contrast	*surprisingly enough, on the other hand, believe it or not*
Reflection on the past	*looking back, in hindsight*
Partial agreement	*to a certain extent, up to a point*

Direct students to the Reference section on page 131.

4 Tell students to circle the two adverbials that can complete each sentence. Check answers by asking different pairs their choices.

Answers: 1. a, c **2.** a, c **3.** a, b **4.** a, c **5.** b, c

OPTIONAL PRESENTATION

If you prefer a more deductive approach, use the complete grammar charts and explanations on the Reference page to present the concepts. (page 131)

Speaking

5 Have students discuss the statements in small groups. Monitor the conversations for errors. Ask different students to explain their views to the rest of the class. Point out any important errors you have heard and discuss them with the class.

Listening

6a Ask students to discuss the questions with a partner. Elicit responses from different pairs and discuss their ideas with the whole class.

b Tell the class that they are going to listen to an interview with a company CEO. Play audio 1.25 while students listen and take notes if they wish. Then have students respond to the questions with a partner or as a class.

Vocabulary

7a Ask students to read phrases 1–9. You may wish to play audio 1.25 again and have students listen for the phrases. Then have students complete the phrases using the words from the box. Check answers with the whole class.

Answers: 1. many **2.** bit **3.** deal **4.** plenty **5.** much **6.** most **7.** majority **8.** few **9.** handful

b Play audio 1.26 for students to check their answers.

8 Ask students to read sentences 1–6. Then have them rewrite the sentences so that they have a similar meaning. Tell students that they should use the words in bold. Then have students compare their answers with a partner. Check answers with the class.

Answers: 1. The government spends a great deal of money on defense. **2.** For the most part, the customers appreciate our top-quality service. **3.** There's plenty of room. **4.** It isn't much of a fee if you consider the amount of work involved. **5.** Only a handful of people asked questions. **6.** The vast majority of workers joined the strike.

9a Direct students to complete the sentences using their own ideas and some of the phrases from Exercise 7a.

b Have students compare their answers with a partner and discuss whether they agree or disagree. Ask different pairs to share their opinions with the class.

Writing

10 Have students choose one of the sentences in Exercise 9a to write a paragraph about. They should provide examples to support their opinion or point. Monitor and help as necessary.

When they have finished, invite different students to present what they have written to the rest of the class. Encourage the class to ask follow-up questions.

OPTIONAL EXTENSION

When students have finished presenting their topics to the class, write the following sentence on the board for students to complete: *I'd like to get a little bit more out of this class by* ______. Have students work with a partner to make a list of other ways, apart from doing more homework, that could help them get more from the class. Then have students share their lists with other pairs. Discuss as a class and write students' ideas on the board. Discuss which of the ideas are the most practical and encourage the class to put them into practice.

NOTES

LESSON 4 pp. 65–66

Unit Wrap Up
Review reinforce lessons 1–3
Communication negotiate

Summary: In this lesson, students review the unit's language. Then they listen to people talking about what they would do if their company suddenly had a fortune to spend. Then students divide into groups and negotiate, deciding how the company should spend the fortune.

Review

1

Answers: 1. He was offered the job, but surprisingly enough, he didn't accept it. Surprisingly enough, he was offered the job, but he didn't accept it. **2.** They explained how the project would be too difficult to manage, and to a certain extent I agree. **3.** They didn't know who I was talking about. Apparently, Georgia left the company years ago. **4.** I decided to leave and change careers. In hindsight, I'm not sure that I made the right decision. **5.** By and large, the new arrangements have worked out well. The new arrangements have worked out well, by and large. **6.** The new president was faced with a seemingly impossible task.

2

Answers: 1. b **2.** a **3.** b **4.** c **5.** a

3

Answers: 1. We weren't in the least bit surprised to hear that she got the part. **2.** Actually, it is surprisingly warm here. It's actually very warm here. **3.** She makes a lot of her own clothes. **4.** It is by no means certain that the game will take place. **5.** It was Rachel who had the courage to complain about the service. **6.** They have done nothing at all to fix the problem.

4

Answers: 1. founded **2.** fortune **3.** charity **4.** venture **5.** vision **6.** impact **7.** mind **8.** wealthy **9.** lavishly **10.** volunteer

OPTIONAL EXTRA LISTENING

These audio tracks, activities, and audioscripts are available on both the *ActiveBook* CD-ROM at the back of each Student Book and on the *ActiveTeach* DVD at the back of this Teacher's Resource Book. The audio can also be found on the Audio Program CD. The audioscripts can also be found at the back of the Workbook. These listening activities can be completed in class or done as homework.

Communication

negotiate

5 Tell the class that they are going to hear two people discussing what they would do if their company suddenly had a fortune to spend. Play audio 1.27 and encourage students to take notes about the ideas they hear.

Have students compare their answers with a partner and discuss how they think the speakers' characters are different. Play audio 1.27 again for students to check their answers.

Answers: She wants to: replace the chairs in the office, renovate the office, do something practical. He wants to: go on a company vacation to the Bahamas, get a house on the beach for all employees to use.

6 Have students work in small groups to discuss what their company, university, or school would do if they had $1 million to spend. Compare ideas from different groups and decide as a class which group had the best ideas.

7 Instruct students to read the profile of Fortune Foods and answer the questions. Check that students have the correct answers.

Answers: The company's strengths: It has an excellent reputation and is growing. Its clients are high-end businesses. Main problems for employees: The employees often stay late at night preparing food and are stressed. It is difficult for employees to drive to work.

8 Organize the class into two groups, A and B. Refer Students A (employees) to page 139 and refer Students B (management) to page 141. Explain that they are going to negotiate how to spend the investment. Give them time to prepare their arguments. Monitor and help where necessary.

When the groups are ready, have them start the negotiation. Monitor the conversations for errors. When students have finished the negotiation, discuss question 3 as a class. Note any important errors on the board and ask students to correct them. Finally, congratulate students on their efforts during the negotiation.

Notes for using the CEF

The Common European Framework (CEF), a reference document for language teaching professionals, was produced by the council of Europe as a means of ensuring parity in terms of language teaching and language qualifications across Europe. It has since increasingly become an accepted standard for English learners throughout the world. It can be downloaded as a PDF file fro free from www.coe.int from the section on Language Policy. There is also a link to the site from the *English in Common* website: www.PearsonELT.com/EnglishinCommon.

The CEF recommends that language learners use a portfolio to document, reflect on, and demonstrate their progress. *English in Common* has a Language Portfolio, which can be downloaded from your *ActiveTeach* disc (at the back of this Teacher's Resource Book) or from the *ActiveBook* disc (at the back of each Student Book). Suggested tasks are provided at the beginning of every unit on the Unit Overview page.

CEF REFERENCES

Lesson 1 CAN DO: talk about professional relationships
CEF B2 descriptor: Can understand and exchange complex information and advice on the full range of matters related to his/her occupational role. (CEF page 81)

Lesson 2 CAN DO: discuss financial decisions and regrets
CEF C1 descriptor: Can easily follow and contribute to complex interactions between third parties in group discussion even on abstract, complex unfamiliar topics. (CEF page 77)

Lesson 3 CAN DO: express priorities
CEF C1 descriptor: Can select an appropriate formulation from a broad range of language to express him/herself clearly, without having to restrict what he/she has to say. (CEF page 110)

Additional Resources

Activity Worksheets and Teaching Notes—Unit 5

Photocopiable worksheets for this unit can be found on pages 126–131 and Teaching Notes can be found on pages 171–172 of this Teacher's Resource Book. They consist of games and other interactive activities for: Vocabulary, Grammar, and Speaking.

Extra Listening Activity—Unit 5

This activity is designed to provide students with additional opportunities to listen to and practice comprehension of spoken English. The audio can be accessed by clicking the Extra Listening folder in both the Student's *ActiveBook* (for independent student use) and in the Teacher's *ActiveTeach* (for classroom use). The audio is also provided at the end of the Audio Program CD. An activity worksheet can also be printed out from either the *ActiveBook* or *ActiveTeach*.

Extra Listening Unit 5—Audioscript

M1: Good morning, Listeners. Steve Ross here on *Talking Business*, Radio WAMB. Today, my guest, entrepreneur Ellen Simpson, and I are going to discuss business reactions to the uncertain economic times we're living in these days. Ellen, how are most large corporations dealing with smaller profits, or the fear that banks may fail?

F1: Unfortunately, Steve, a lot of them have stopped hiring new workers, so those that remain have to work harder. At the same time, there's less opportunity for promotion and higher salaries for the employees that they already have. This leads to more stress for these workers and less job satisfaction. And if people are afraid of losing their jobs, they begin to spend less on non-essential purchases. So profits go down even more. It's a vicious cycle. And many of our big corporate leaders and CEOs have expressed their concern about the need for more cooperation and responsibility among elected officials. They want the USA to be on a firm fiscal footing. That's important for business growth and investment.

M1: What about fringe benefits that workers have become accustomed to? A lot of my friends, especially younger women with children, say that that the gains made by their mothers—like flexible working hours and money for childcare or professional development—are disappearing. Is that true?

F1: Broadly speaking, it is true. A lot of businesses are looking to save money by cutting benefits. Pensions especially, are being attacked as too expensive to sustain.

M1: Do you think this is a long-term trend?

F1: Yes, I do. There are some companies, of course, that remain committed to sharing their success with employees through the extras we used to take for granted, like health care, 401k retirement plans, and tuition reimbursement, but the packages are less generous than they used to be. If only more business leaders would realize that benefits are correlated to job satisfaction. . . .

M1: And job satisfaction to productivity! I really believe in tuition reimbursement for young workers. It's a strong incentive for continuing to learn new skills.

F1: I agree!

M1: So, what do you predict for the future, Ellen? Is this just a small dip in our economic fortunes, or is the world headed into another bad recession?

F1: If I had a crystal ball, Steve, I might be able to answer that question! I do think we're headed in the wrong direction, though.

In hindsight, if we had spent more money on creating jobs two years ago, we might not be in this mess now.

M1: Thank you Ellen. Listeners, let's hear from you now. Have any of you . . .

Video
The Millionaire: Milton Petrie, Secret Philanthropist

Students watch a *20/20* news episode about an anonymous donor who gave away millions of dollars to help complete strangers. This video segment can be played on the Teacher's *ActiveTeach* disc and projected for classroom viewing or the disc can be played on any DVD player. Teaching notes and video scripts are also provided on the *ActiveTeach* disc.

Tests

A **Unit 5 Test** is provided in the Test Bank as a Word file on the *ActiveTeach* disc. It includes discrete sections on: Grammar, Vocabulary, Reading, and Writing. An Answer Key is also provided. If you wish, this test can be easily modified to suit the particular needs of your class.

A **Review Test** is provided in the Test Bank section of the *ActiveTeach* disc to assess students' cumulative knowledge. It includes descrete sections on: Grammar, Pronunciation, Vocabulary, Reading, Writing, and Listening. The audio for the tests is provided as MP3 files in the Test Bank section of the *ActiveTeach*. The audio is also provided at the end of the Audio Program CD. Audioscripts are available on the *ActiveTeach*. If you wish, this test can be easily modified to suit the particular needs of your class.

Extra Vocabulary: Idioms 1

Extra Vocabulary activities for this unit can be found in both the Student's *ActiveBook* and in the Teacher's *ActiveTeach*, along with an answer key.

UNIT 6
Understanding power

Unit Overview

Warm Up Lesson	
LESSON 1	**CAN DO** describe an important building or structure **GRAMMAR** articles **VOCABULARY** power
LESSON 2	**CAN DO** take notes from fluent connected speech **GRAMMAR** clauses with *whatever, whoever, whenever* **VOCABULARY** fashions and fads
LESSON 3	**CAN DO** write an autobiographical statement **GRAMMAR** logical connectors of time and contrast **VOCABULARY** personal characteristics
LESSON 4	**Unit Wrap Up** **Review** reinforce lessons 1–3 **Communication** evaluate personal characteristics
Grammar and Vocabulary Reference Charts	

OPTIONAL LANGUAGE PORTFOLIO

(located in both the *ActiveBook* at the back of the Student Book and in the *ActiveTeach* at the back of this Teacher's Resource Book)

Now that students have reached about halfway through the term, ask them to take the time to fill out the *Self-Assessment* section of the Language Portfolio. This task will help learners think about their learning objectives and their particular strengths and weakness. Such tasks can help students maintain motivation to continue their learning.

Teaching Resources

- **Workbook** pp. 44–51
- **Class Audio** CD1 Tracks 28–32
- ***ActiveBook*** Digital Student Book pages with complete unit audio plus Extra Listening Activity and Extra Vocabulary Study
- ***ActiveTeach*** Interactive whiteboard (IWB) software with video, Test Bank, and test audio

Warm Up p. 67

OPTIONAL WARM UP

Ask students to list occasions when they exercise power or someone exerts power over them in their daily lives. Tell them to think about the following areas: *school, work, family, free time, sports*. Then have them compare notes with a partner and explain their ideas.

Ask different students to share with the class what they have learned about their partners.

1 Ask students to focus on the words in the box. Have them decide which of the words collocate with *power* and which collocate with *powerful*. Check answers with the class.

Answers: power: spending, nuclear, economic, brain, world, political, people, army, consumer, wind
powerful: speech, medicine, argument, reasons, influence, people, tool, army

Have students use five of the phrases in sentences.

2 Ask students to focus on the phrases in bold in questions 1–5. Have them work with a partner to check that they know the meaning of the phrases.

Answers: 1. have power over—be in a position of control over someone/something **2. in positions of power**—jobs with powerful responsibilities—for example, politicians, heads of multinational companies, etc. **3. economic power**—power that countries have because of their economic situation **4. special powers**—powers that are not within their "normal" powers **5. comes to power**—start being in a position of power (usually after an election)

Have students discuss the questions with a partner.

EXTEND THE WARM UP

Have students work in pairs. Ask each student to list who they think are the five most powerful people in their country. Then have students share this information with their partners, explaining why these people are so powerful. Ask different groups to share their results.

LESSON 1 pp. 68–70

CAN DO describe an important building or structure
GRAMMAR articles
VOCABULARY power

Summary: In this lesson, students first look at vocabulary through the context of architecture. Then students listen to information about some of the world's most important buildings. They go on to look at the grammar of articles. Students finish the lesson by writing a description of an important building or a structure.

OPTIONAL WARM UP
Have students think of a famous building in the world. Tell them to think about what words and phrases they would need to describe this building. Students can look in a dictionary or consult you for any words they don't know. Then have students describe this building to a partner, who guesses what building is being described.

Reading

1 Have students discuss questions 1–3 in pairs. Monitor conversations for errors. Ask students to justify their answers. Write important errors you have heard on the board and ask different students to correct them.

2 Have students read the article. Ask them if there are any words or phrases from the reading that they don't understand. Encourage them to answer each other's questions or to consult an English-English dictionary before you explain the vocabulary to the class.

Vocabulary

3 Instruct students to use the words in the box to complete the definitions and related example sentences 1–4. Tell them to make sure that they use the correct verb tenses in the sentences. Check answers with the class.

Answers: 1. gain, gain **2.** win over, win over **3.** be impressed by, was impressed by **4.** play (an) important part, played (an) important part

4 Have students discuss questions 1 and 2 with a partner. Monitor conversations for errors. Elicit answers from different pairs.

Answers: 1. They provided water, roads, and bridges to establish their power and built impressive public buildings. **2.** It has been used to show wealth, status, and power. Castles, palaces, etc. all glorify a particular ideal.

Listening

OPTIONAL WARM UP
Ask students to discuss the structures in the pictures in pairs and write any information they know about them. Then have them compare their ideas with their partner. Finally, discuss as a class.

5a Focus students' attention on the photos and the information in questions 1–7. Have students match the information with the structures. Elicit answers and ask students to justify their ideas to the rest of the class.

b Play audio 1.28 for students to listen and check their answers.

Answers: 1. The CN Tower **2.** Chan Chan **3.** The Great Pyramid **4.** Sydney Harbor Bridge **5.** The Pentagon **6.** The Forbidden City **7.** The Eiffel Tower

6 Have students discuss the questions with a partner. Monitor the conversations carefully for errors and any interesting language they use. Elicit answers from different pairs and discuss the students' opinions with the class. Finally, write any errors from the discussions on the board. Look at the errors with the class and encourage different students to correct them. Draw students' attention to any interesting language that they have used and praise them on its use.

Grammar

OPTIONAL WARM UP
Write these sentences on the board: *Alan is accountant. He earns $400 dollars the week. He lives on the Smith Street. He loves the music.* Tell students that there is one error in each sentence. Have them correct the errors and compare their new sentences with a partner. Elicit answers and write the correct sentences on the board: *Alan is **an** accountant. He earns $400 dollars **a** week. He lives on **Smith Street**. He loves* **music.** Have students discuss the use or non-use of articles in these sentences. Tell them they are going to look at the use of articles in more detail in this lesson.

7 Focus students' attention on the Active Grammar box. Have students circle the correct answers to complete the rules. Check answers with the whole class.

Answers: 1. a/an **2.** the **3.** no article

Direct students to the Reference section on page 132.

8 Ask students to brainstorm in pairs what they know about the city of Barcelona. Elicit information from different pairs and tell them they are going to read a passage about the designer of the Sagrada Familia church, Antoni Gaudí. Have them read the passage and complete the spaces with *a/an/the* or leave the space blank if no article is needed. Check answers with the whole class.

Answers: 1. no article **2.** no article **3.** a **4.** The **5.** the **6.** the **7.** the **8.** no article **9.** no article **10.** the **11.** the **12.** the **13.** a **14.** a **15.** the **16.** the **17.** the

OPTIONAL PRESENTATION

If you prefer a more deductive approach, use the complete grammar charts and explanations on the Reference page to present the concepts. (page 132)

Speaking

9 Have students write notes about three important buildings or structures they know. Monitor and help where necessary. Then have students compare ideas with a partner. Instruct them to reach an agreement about which are the three most important buildings or structures from their lists and why. Then have students explain their ideas to the rest of the class.

Writing

10a Have students choose two important buildings or structures that they know about. Then have them share what they know and write notes before they go on to 10b.

Alternatively, set this as a homework task so that students have time to research the buildings or structures on the Internet. In the following lesson, have students share information they have found with a partner.

b Have students write a paragraph on each of the structures they have chosen. Encourage them to use the phrases in the How To box where possible. Monitor and help students where necessary.

c Have students read their paragraphs to three or four other students. Then have them decide which of the buildings or structures students have written about have been the most influential. Congratulate students on their efforts.

LESSON 2 pp. 71–73

CAN DO take notes from fluent connected speech
GRAMMAR clauses with *whatever, whoever, whenever*
VOCABULARY fashions and fads

Summary: In this lesson, students listen to an interview about the influence children and teenagers have over the fashion and technology industries. Then they look at vocabulary connected with fashions and fads. Students go on to listen to parents and teenagers discuss various issues. Through this context they look at the use of *whatever, whoever, whenever.*

Note: Corporations are well aware of the preferences of children and teenagers, and they take these preferences into account when designing and marketing products. Corporations such as Microsoft, Sony, and Nokia have led the way in researching what appeals to teenagers. Nokia in particular has a reputation for watching teenagers. Researchers from the communications company look at teenagers around the world, trying to spot fashions that may become the next big thing among teenagers. Sony was one of the first companies to research in detail what young people wanted. Some surveys have shown that it is thought to be one of the "coolest" brands by teenagers.

OPTIONAL WARM UP

Have students discuss with a partner how they think teenagers are different from adults. Then have them share their ideas with another pair. Elicit ideas from different pairs and write differences students tell you on the board to be discussed as a whole class.

Listening

1a Have students discuss the questions with a partner. Monitor conversations for errors and interesting language. Ask different pairs to share their ideas. Note any important errors you have heard and discuss them with the class. Finally, congratulate students on any interesting language they have used.

b Play audio 1.29 and ask students to listen to find out if their answers were correct.

2a Focus students' attention on sentences 1–5. Instruct students to try to remember the audio to complete the sentences.

b Play audio 1.29 again for students to check their answers.

Answers: 1. Kids drive technology because **they have no fear of it and automatically home in on the new. 2.** Kids want technology that can be **carried around. 3.** Text messaging caught on because **kids wanted to pass notes to each other during class. 4.** Facebook developed as **a way for college students to share information. 5.** Converse sent its market researchers to **the basketball courts of New York, and other places where you find teenagers.**

Vocabulary

3a Instruct students to refer to audioscript 1.29 to review the use of the phrases in bold in 1–6. Then have them match the phrasal verbs to the definitions. Check answers with the whole class.

Answers: 1. c **2.** b **3.** e **4.** d **5.** f **6.** a

b Have students look at the phrasal verbs in Exercise 3a again. Instruct them to identify the phrasal verbs which are exact opposites and decide if these verbs are formal or informal. Check answers with different students.

Answer: *be in/be out* are opposites (informal)

4 Have students discuss questions 1–4 with a partner. Then have them share their ideas with another pair of students. Monitor conversations for errors and correct use of phrasal verbs. Then discuss students' ideas with the class. Write any important errors on the board and invite different students to correct them. Finally, congratulate students on their correct use of phrasal verbs.

Speaking

5 Organize students into groups of three or four and have them focus on questions 1–6. Then have them discuss the items with the other students in their groups. Monitor conversations for errors, which you can keep for correction after Exercise 6a. Elicit responses from different groups.

Listening

6a Tell students they are going to hear two parents and two teenagers discussing different issues. Play audio 1.30 and have students write down which of the questions from Exercise 5 are answered in each conversation. Check answers with the class.

Answers: Conversation 1: question 4 **Conversation 2:** question 1 **Conversation 3:** question 5 **Conversation 4:** question 2

b Play audio 1.30 again and have students take notes about the opinions expressed in the conversations.

Answers: Conversation 1: It depends on the age. There are some places that are not suitable for young teenagers, like bars. **Conversation 2:** It is not good for teenagers to watch whatever they want on TV, because some things are inappropriate. It is also bad for their eyes. **Conversation 3:** They want to be able to choose who they socialize with. **Conversation 4:** She thinks it's a good idea to have a time for teenagers to go to bed. He feels that teenagers can decide for themselves when to go to bed.

Grammar

OPTIONAL WARM UP

Write the following sentences a parent might say to a teenager on the board: *Whatever you do, don't stay out too late. Come home whenever you like, but don't walk home alone.* Have students work in pairs to discuss whether their parents ever say or said things like this to them. Then have them discuss the use of *whatever* and *whenever* in these sentences with their partners. Tell them that we use these words when it doesn't make any difference *what/where/how*, etc.

7 Have students read through the information in the Active Grammar box and answer the questions. Check answers with the class.

Answers: a. Stop what you are doing now. **b.** Stop whatever you are doing now./Whatever you are doing, stop it now!

Direct students to the Reference section on page 132 and give students time to read through the notes. Ask them the following questions: **Q:** What type of words are *whenever, however, whatever*? **A:** Conjunctions. **Q:** What do they join together? **A:** Clauses. **Q:** When do we use these words? **A:** When we don't have to be specific, or we don't know the exact details of *when, what, who*, etc. Then write the following sentences on the board: *1. However hard he tries, he always fails. 2. He tries hard. However, he always fails.* Elicit from the students that the first use of *however* means that it doesn't matter how hard he tries. The second use of however is to contrast the two statements.

8 Have students complete sentences 1–5 . Check answers with the class.

Answers: 1. Whatever **2.** whenever **3.** wherever **4.** Whoever **5.** However

9a Focus students' attention on the pairs of sentences 1–5. Ask them to complete the second sentences so that they have the same meaning as the first sentences. Tell students they must include *whenever, however, whatever,* etc. in each blank.

Answers: 1. Whenever you feel **2.** Wherever we go **3.** Whenever I can **4.** Whoever we hire **5.** Whatever those children do

b Tell students that they are going to check their answers by listening to a recording. Play audio 1.31 and instruct them to check their answers.

10a Have students read through *The Teenagers' Manifesto* and complete the spaces with *whoever, whenever,* etc. Check answers with the class.

Answers: 1. whatever **2.** whatever, whenever **3.** whatever **4.** whoever **5.** whenever **6.** whatever **7.** whoever, whenever

b Tell students to discuss the manifesto with a partner and decide if they would change anything about it. Have them compare their ideas with another pair and justify their ideas. Monitor conversations for errors and write important errors on the board. Ask the class to share their responses. Draw students' attention to the errors on the board and get them to correct them for you.

OPTIONAL PRESENTATION

If you prefer a more deductive approach, use the complete grammar charts and explanations on the Reference page to present the concepts. (page 132)

NOTES

LESSON 3 pp. 74–76

CAN DO write an autobiographical statement
GRAMMAR logical connectors of time and contrast
VOCABULARY personal characteristics

Summary: In this lesson, students read an article about charisma and charismatic people. Through this context students look at connectors of time and contrast. Students then look at vocabulary used for describing personal characteristics. They finish by writing an autobiographical statement.

Note: *Charisma* refers to the "magnetic" characteristic possessed by some people which can charm or influence others. Charismatic people usually project calmness and confidence and have excellent communication skills. There are many famous people who are said to have possessed charisma. Leaders such as Martin Luther King, John F. Kennedy, and Winston Churchill are commonly thought of as having been charismatic. Bill Clinton, Muhammad Ali, and Madonna are examples of living famous people who possess charisma.

OPTIONAL WARM UP

Have students work in pairs. Tell Students A to open their books to page 74 and instruct Students B keep the book closed. Tell students they are going to play *Twenty Questions* with the famous people on page 74, with Students B asking Students A questions. Refer students to Unit 4, page 49 if they can't remember the rules.

Reading

1 Write *charisma* on the board. Ask students to think of a definition for this word with a partner. They can use the photos at the top of the page for ideas. Elicit feedback from different pairs and decide who has the best definition. Then have students read the definition. Tell students to work with their partners to write a list of famous charismatic people. Then have them compare names with another pair and explain why they think these people are charismatic. Finally, have students discuss if they think the people in the photos are charismatic and in what ways.

2 Have students read the article. Ask them if there are any words or phrases from the reading that they don't understand. Encourage them to answer each other's questions or to consult an English-English dictionary before you explain the vocabulary to the class.

3 Have students discuss questions 1–5 with a partner. Check answers with the class.

Answers: 1. No. The writer says that the formula remains elusive. **2.** Education. It was a parents' night in a school, and education was common ground for everyone present. **3.** No. He mentions that charisma is associated with politicians, businesspeople, and celebrities, but other professions have charismatic people too. **4.** Because of Feynman's love of his subject and his enthusiasm. **5.** Because charisma can to some extent be learned.

Grammar

OPTIONAL WARM UP

Write this scrambled sentence on the board: *studied Ed did not hard Although well test do the he on.* Ask students to unscramble the sentence: *Although Ed studied hard, he did not do well on the test.* Underline *Although* and ask students what function this word has in the sentence. Elicit that we use *although* as a way of contrasting parts of a sentence. Have students work in pairs to write a list of any other contrast linking words or expressions they know. Ask students to share their lists with the class and write correct expressions on the board.

4 Have students read the Active Grammar box and complete the chart. Check answers with the class.

Answers: 1. It happened soon after another thing: on finding, had no sooner begun, hardly have started **It happened at the same time as something else:** during, while, when **It comes at the end of a long, continuous sequence of action:** at which point, by which time **2. Expressions that begin a clause:** although, even though, while **Expressions that can be followed by a noun phrase or gerund:** despite, in spite of **Expressions that use adjective/adverb + *as* + subject + verb to emphasize the contrast:** Hard as we try, much as, difficult as it was

Direct students to the Reference section on page 132.

5 Tell students they are going to read about Oprah Winfrey, a charismatic woman. Have them read the article and complete it with the phrases in the boxes. Tell students that some of the phrases are not needed. Check answers with the class.

Answers: 1. Despite **2.** when **3.** even though **4.** Much **5.** No sooner

OPTIONAL PRESENTATION

If you prefer a more deductive approach, use the complete grammar charts and explanations on the Reference page to present the concepts. (page 132)

Vocabulary

6 Direct students to cover the right-hand column, a–h. Ask students to check the meaning of the adjectives in the left-hand column with a partner. Then ask them if they can think of an opposite word or expression for each of the adjectives.

Finally, ask students to match adjectives 1–8 to the phrases that have an opposite meaning. Check answers with the class.

Answers: 1. e **2.** g **3.** h **4.** c **5.** f **6.** a **7.** d **8.** b

7a Tell students they are going to hear the words and phrases from Exercise 6. Instruct them to focus on the stress and to mark it on the words and phrases. Play audio 1.32. Then play the audio again and ask students to read the audioscript on page 154 while they listen.

b Play audio 1.32 again and have students answer the questions. Ask students to practice saying the words with a partner.

Answers: *gn* in *sign* is pronounced /n/. *gn* in *dignified* is pronounced /gn/. *ch* in *much* is pronounced /tʃ/. *ch* in *charismatic* is pronounced /k/.

OPTIONAL EXTENSION

Put students in pairs, A and B. Have Students A choose an adjective from Exercise 6 without telling Students B the word. Tell Students A to tap the syllables of the word on the table with the correct rhythm. Tell Students B to guess the word. Repeat so that Students B are tapping and Students A guessing. Continue until the students have tapped all the words.

8 Focus students' attention on the photos of the different famous people. Ask them to discuss in pairs what they know about the people and why they are famous. Tell students to also decide which adjectives from Exercise 6 they could use to describe the people. Elicit responses from different pairs and write the adjectives on the board.

Then have students write a list of other famous people who could be described using the adjectives and phrases in Exercise 6. Have students compare their lists with a partner.

Writing

9a Refer students to the autobiographical statement in the Writing Bank on page 145. Give them time to do the exercises. Monitor and help as necessary. Check answers with the class.

Answers: **1.** **c.** The writer is trying to enroll in an academic program. **2.** **1.** I always enjoyed designing things → I always enjoyed designing objects (The rewrite avoids repetition of "things," which is in the previous sentence and sounds too informal). **2.** I was also really good at math → I also found that I had a particular aptitude for math (The original sentence sounds too informal, like spoken English). **3.** doing tasks like photocopying, sending faxes, mailing letters, and ordering materials → doing clerical work in the office (The rewrite removes the unnecessary details in the original sentence.) **4.** I'd had enough of Bilosh → I felt I needed a new challenge (The original sentence sounds too negative, which is not appropriate in this context). **5.** I will be able to work in graphic design → I will be able to work in this field (The rewrite avoids repetition of "graphic design," which is in the previous sentence).

b Tell students they are going to write their own autobiographical statement. Have students read the ad and follow the instructions. Encourage them to use the useful phrases from the box on page 145 while writing the statement. Monitor and help students where necessary.

When students have finished, ask them to read their statements to the rest of the class. Alternatively, collect the statements, read them to the class, and have students guess whose statement each one is.

OPTIONAL EXTENSION

Have students write a short biography of a partner. Give them time to prepare a list of questions to ask their partner which will form the basis of the biography. Monitor and help with ideas as necessary. Then have students work with a partner to ask the questions and write notes on the answers. Have students, either in class or as homework, write a short biography of their partner using the structure of the statement on page 145 as a guide. Finally, have students swap biographies and give positive feedback to each other on the content and language.

NOTES

LESSON 4 pp. 77–78

Unit Wrap Up
Review reinforce lessons 1–3
Communication evaluate personal characteristics

Summary: In this lesson, students review the unit's language. Then they role-play a situation where they argue their case to be the leader of a new community.

Review

1

Answers: This 1,614-foot (492-meter) high building consists of two elements that correspond to **the** Chinese concept of Earth as **a** square and **the** sky as **a** circle. **The** hole in **the** top also has **a** practical use—to relieve **the** pressure of wind on **the** building. **The** glassy tower is just blocks away from **the** 1,378-foot (420-meter) Jinmao Tower in **the** district of Shanghai that has been designated **the** Asian center for international banking. **The** tower's lower levels are used for offices, and its upper levels for **a** hotel, **an** art museum, and restaurants.

2

Answers: **1.** wherever **2.** whatever **3.** whenever **4.** whoever **5.** However

3

Answers: **1.** keep up with **2.** catch on **3.** is in **4.** came about **5.** home in on

4

Answers: An hour with the Body Earth Power Group was enough for me. No sooner ~~**but**~~ had Carin Brook entered than everyone became silent. Much as I tried to keep my mind open—and despite ~~**of**~~ the fact that I have been known to do a bit of tree-hugging myself—I couldn't help thinking that this was going to be a waste of time. Brook, even ~~**and**~~ though she is tiny, had a strong personality. We started stretching in order to "feel the Earth's rhythm", but it didn't last long. I'd hardly ~~**but**~~ lifted my hands up when she told us all to sit down, close our eyes and "re-visualize ourselves from above". Hard as ~~**though**~~ I tried, I just couldn't imagine what the top of my head looked like, and in ~~**the**~~ spite of her promptings to "relax," the hard floor was getting very uncomfortable. Thankfully 4.00. came, by which ~~**the**~~ time I was desperate for a nice soft chair and a good meal.

OPTIONAL EXTRA LISTENING

These audio tracks, activities, and audioscripts are available on both the *ActiveBook* CD-ROM at the back of each Student Book and on the *ActiveTeach* DVD at the back of this Teacher's Resource Book. The audio can also be found on the Audio Program CD. The audioscripts can also be found at the back of the Workbook. These listening activities can be completed in class or done as homework.

Communication

evaluate personal characteristics

OPTIONAL WARM UP

Write the word *leader* on the board. Elicit words from the students that they associate with leaders and write them on the board. Then have students write their own definition of a leader. Have them compare their definitions with a partner. Then have them share their definitions with the rest of the class. With the class, choose the best definition. Tell students that they are going to choose a leader in the lesson today.

5 Focus students' attention on the picture. Ask students to work with a partner to guess the identities of the different people and label the picture. Elicit answers from different pairs and ask them to justify their choices.

Answers: 1. a **2.** g **3.** c **4.** b **5.** i **6.** h **7.** f **8.** d **9.** e

6 Tell students to choose one of the people in the picture. Have students write a short profile of that person. Monitor and help students as necessary. Alternatively, you could secretly assign a role to each student by handing out slips of paper with their role.

7 Tell students to imagine that the plane they were traveling in has crashed on a desert island. Inform them that everyone has survived the crash and that they have decided to start a new community. Then tell them that their new characters all want to be the leader of the community. Give students time to think about how they are going to present their ideas to the rest of the class. Refer students to questions 1–3 to help. Monitor and help as necessary.

8a Organize students into groups. Have students take turns presenting their ideas to the rest of the group, arguing their case to become the leader of the new community. Take note of any important errors to address after Exercise 8b.

b Tell students to elect a leader of their group. Have students explain to other groups who they have elected leader and why. Write on the board any important errors you have heard. Discuss the errors with the class and ask different students to come up to the board and correct the errors. Congratulate them on any interesting ideas they have had and language they have used.

OPTIONAL EXTENSION

Tell students to work in groups and decide on a list of ten laws that they think would be most important when starting a new community. These could include the areas of money, sharing, and roles in the community. Then have students explain the laws they have written to other groups. Have students decide with the class on ten laws which they all agree on.

This activity could be further extended by asking the groups to draw up detailed plans for their community; for example, what they will eat, division of labor, how they will build housing, etc.

NOTES

Notes for using the CEF

The Common European Framework (CEF), a reference document for language teaching professionals, was produced by the council of Europe as a means of ensuring parity in terms of language teaching and language qualifications across Europe. It has since increasingly become an accepted standard for English learners throughout the world. It can be downloaded as a PDF file for free from www.coe.int from the section on Language Policy. There is also a link to the site from the *English in Common* website: www.PearsonELT.com/EnglishinCommon.

The CEF recommends that language learners use a portfolio to document, reflect on, and demonstrate their progress. *English in Common* has a Language Portfolio, which can be downloaded from your *ActiveTeach* disc (at the back of this Teacher's Resource Book) or from the *ActiveBook* disc (at the back of each Student Book). Suggested tasks are provided at the beginning of every unit on the Unit Overview page.

CEF REFERENCES

Lesson 1 Can do: describe an important building or structure
CEF C1 descriptor: Can give clear, detailed descriptions of complex subjects. (CEF page 59)

Lesson 2 Can do: take notes from fluent connected speech
CEF C1 descriptor: Can take detailed notes on topics in his/her field of interest, recording the information so accurately and so close to the original that the notes could also be useful to other people. (CEF page 96)

Lesson 3 Can do: write an autobiographical statement
CEF C1 descriptor: Can write clear, well-structured texts of complex subjects, underlining the relevant salient issues, expanding and supporting points of view at some length with subsidiary points, reasons and relevant examples, and rounding off with an appropriate conclusion. (CEF page 61)

Additional Resources

Activity Worksheets and Teaching Notes—Unit 6

Photocopiable worksheets for this unit can be found on pages 132–137 and Teaching Notes can be found on pages 173–174 of this Teacher's Resource Book. They consist of games and other interactive activities for: Vocabulary, Grammar, and Speaking.

Extra Listening Activity—Unit 6

This activity is designed to provide students with additional opportunities to listen to and practice comprehension of spoken English. The audio can be accessed by clicking the Extra Listening logo on the Unit Wrap Up page in both the Student's *ActiveBook* (for independent student use) and in the Teacher's *ActiveTeach* (for classroom use). The audio is also provided at the end of the Audio Program CD. An activity worksheet can also be printed out from either the *ActiveBook* or *ActiveTeach.*

Extra Listening Unit 6—Audioscript

M1: Hi Kate. Wake up! The library's closing. Time to go home.
F1: Huh? Oh, hi, Dan. Sorry! I wasn't sleeping. Just deep in thought. I'm trying to figure out a subject to research for my sociology paper.
M1: What's the topic?
F1: We have to write about an inspirational or charismatic leader, maybe someone who led his country in wartime, or through a difficult economic period.
M1: That shouldn't be difficult. Just Google "world leader"...
F1: Don't be silly! Anyway, I did that and thousands of pages came up! I want to research someone who doesn't waver in the face of problems, who is tireless in fighting for what he or she believes in, and who is also approachable.
M1: In other words, a pretty unusual person. Like Mahatma Gandhi?
F1: Uh-huh. But too many people have already chosen him. I want to be different.
M1: Probably a good idea—you don't want your professor to compare your research with others.
F1: Also, whoever I choose has to be incorruptible as well—so many political leaders look good until you dig deep, and find that, in spite of what they say, they are secretly indebted to lobbyists or special interest groups.
M1: You're right. Look at the recent scandals in the UK, for example. Didn't a politician get implicated in a media ethics scandal?
F1: In any case, the topic is just too big. I don't know where to start.
M1: How long does the paper have to be?

(continued on next page)

F1: My professor said to make it as long as necessary to do justice to the topic! However, I'd like to keep it to under twenty pages—about 5,000 words.

M1: Well, start by making a list of possible subjects, or time periods. Do you want someone who is still living, or someone who died in the last century? Or a much older historical figure?

F1: Mmm. Someone from long ago would be easier to research than a current leader. Maybe someone like Elizabeth the First of England. She always put her country first. I'm not sure how approachable she was, though.

M1: Well, she certainly knew how to make tough decisions. Didn't she have her cousin, Mary Queen of Scots beheaded?

F1: Yeah, remember that scene in the movie? I couldn't watch the execution, I was crying so hard. What a horrible decision to have to make!

M1: Yeah, but it was to save her throne! Well, whoever you choose, try to find just one or two events that show how he or she acted when under stress and analyze those.

F1: Good advice. I'll get started first thing tomorrow morning. Now, how about getting something to eat?

Tests

A **Unit 6 Test** is provided in the Test Bank as a Word file on the *ActiveTeach* disc. It includes discrete sections on: Grammar, Vocabulary, Reading, and Writing. An Answer Key is also provided. If you wish, this test can be easily modified to suit the particular needs of your class.

Extra Vocabulary: Idioms 2

Extra Vocabulary activities for this unit can be found in both the Student's *ActiveBook* and in the Teacher's *ActiveTeach*, along with an answer key.

UNIT 7 The natural world

Unit Overview

Warm Up Lesson	
LESSON 1	**CAN DO** explain procedures **GRAMMAR** adjective clauses
LESSON 2	**CAN DO** make inferences based on extended prose **GRAMMAR** verbs followed by infinitives or gerunds: meaning **VOCABULARY** descriptive language
LESSON 3	**CAN DO** write an ad for an object **GRAMMAR** *as . . . as*; describing quantity **VOCABULARY** buying and selling
LESSON 4	**Unit Wrap Up** **Review** reinforce lessons 1–3 **Communication** reach a compromise on a plan
Grammar and Vocabulary Reference Charts	

OPTIONAL LANGUAGE PORTFOLIO

(located in both the *ActiveBook* at the back of the Student Book and in the *ActiveTeach* at the back of this Teacher's Resource Book)

During this last half of the term, ask students to review the works contained in the *Achievement Portfolio* section of their Language Portfolios. Encourage them to remove older materials and to add more current representations of their abilities. Also ask them to update any information in their *Personal Profiles.*

Teaching Resources

- **Workbook** pp. 52–59
- **Class Audio** CD2 Tracks 2–7
- ***ActiveBook*** Digital Student Book pages with complete unit audio plus Extra Listening Activity and Extra Vocabulary Study
- ***ActiveTeach*** Interactive whiteboard (IWB) software with video, Test Bank, and test audio

Warm Up p. 79

OPTIONAL WARM UP

Tell students that they have to think of an animal for each letter of the alphabet. Pair students up and have them write as many names of animals as they can within a time limit of three minutes. Elicit responses from the class, giving one point for each correct animal name that another pair has and two points for each correct animal name that no other pair has. The winning pair is the one with the most points.

1 Focus students' attention on the animals in the photos. Ask students to discuss the questions in pairs. Monitor and make a note of any important errors to address after Exercise 2. Elicit responses from different pairs.

2 Have students work in pairs to discuss questions 1–3. Monitor the conversations. Elicit responses from different pairs. Write any important errors you have heard on the board and get different students to come to the board and correct them.

NOTES

LESSON 1 pp. 80–82

CAN DO explain procedures
GRAMMAR adjective clauses

Summary: In this lesson, students read about how animals can help warn us of natural disasters and how rats can be trained to help people in the event of a disaster. Through this context, students look at relative clauses. Then they listen to people explaining how to do something before looking at language used to explain procedures. They finish the lesson by writing explanatory notes.

Note: There have been many incidences of animals changing their behavior before a natural disaster strikes. Perhaps the most famous recent incident was before the 2004 tsunami when many animals reportedly escaped without injury by running to higher ground before the wave arrived. Some scientists believe that animals have an early warning sensory system which can detect disasters, such as earthquakes, before they happen. This may be due to the fact that animals have more sensitive hearing and smell than humans and that they also have sensory organs that detect small tremors and changes that occur before a natural disaster.

OPTIONAL WARM UP

Write *animal instinct* and *natural disaster* on the board. Organize students into two groups, A and B. Students A brainstorm words they associate with animal instinct and Students B words they associate with natural disaster. Have students share the words they thought of with a student from the other group. Elicit responses and write words students have thought of on the board in two lists.

Reading

1 Tell students to focus on the titles in the reading. Ask them to guess what they think the article will be about. Elicit responses from the class. Then have students read the article to check their predictions.

2 Have students read the passage again more carefully and answer questions 1–4. Check answers as a class.

Answers: 1. The elephants suddenly became nervous and left their habitat. The flamingos suddenly flew to higher ground even though it was the breeding season. Sharks left their natural habitat and stayed in deeper waters for two weeks. **2.** The sharks were electronically "tagged," so they could be observed. **3.** Their senses are sharper and they can feel changes in the environment. **4.** The rat's brain gives off a signal which is transmitted via a radio on the rat's back

3 Have students discuss questions 1–3 in pairs. Then check answers as a class.

Answers: 1. Unlike human beings, wild animals perceive a great deal of information about the world around them. Their senses are sharper than ours. **2.** Answers will vary. **3.** Answers will vary.

Grammar

OPTIONAL WARM UP

Write the following sentences on the board: *1. The cat <u>that had a white ear</u> caught a mouse. The cat <u>that had a striped tail</u> did not catch a mouse. 2. The cat, <u>which was sitting in the sun all morning</u>, caught a mouse.* Ask students how we know which cat caught a mouse in item 1. (Because of the underlined information.) Tell students that this information is vital to the meaning of the sentences and that this clause is a restrictive adjective clause. Elicit that in item 2 the underlined information is not vital to the meaning of the sentence and is a non-restrictive adjective clause.

4 Have students read the Active Grammar box and answer the questions. Check answers with the class.

Answers: 1. restrictive **2.** non-restrictive

Direct students to the Reference section on page 133.

5 Ask students to answer questions 1–4. Check answers with the class.

Answers: 1. restrictive **2.** before and after the non-restrictive adjective clause **3.** that we rely on; that robots are not as good at; at the beginning of the clause **4.** Of course, there are already robots that can do this job, one of which looks and moves like a snake . . .

6 Ask students to discuss the pairs of sentences with a partner and decide if they have the same meaning or if they are different and, if so, how they are different. Also instruct students to spot the sentences that are incorrect.

Answers: 1. different: The first sentence means ONLY those monkeys whose DNA is similar to humans are used in research (i.e., other monkeys are not used because their DNA is not similar to humans'). The second sentence means that ALL monkeys may be used because all monkeys have similar DNA to humans. **2.** The second sentence is wrong because it needs to be a restrictive adjective clause, therefore without the comma. **3.** The second sentence is wrong. You can't use *that* to begin a non-restrictive adjective clause. **4.** Both are correct, but the first sentence is more informal because of the use of the "dangled" preposition at the end of the sentence.

7a Tell students to rewrite the questions using the phrases in the box. Check answers with the class.

Answers: 1. Should hunting that is done only for sport and not for food be allowed? **2.** Should zoos that take animals from their natural habitat be banned? **3.** Should the Amazon Rainforest, which is being destroyed, be protected? If so, how? **4.** Should the use of fur for clothing, about which there has been much debate in the fashion industry, be banned?

b Have students discuss the questions with a partner, thinking of arguments for and against each issue. Elicit responses from different pairs.

OPTIONAL PRESENTATION

If you prefer a more deductive approach, use the complete grammar charts and explanations on the Reference page to present the concepts. (page 133)

OPTIONAL EXTENSION

After the discussion, have students choose one of the questions from Exercise 7a as the topic for a discursive essay. Ask students to write 150–200 words on the chosen topic for homework. In the following lesson, either collect the essays or have students swap their essays with a partner and comment on the content and language.

Listening

OPTIONAL WARM UP

Organize students into two groups, one in favor of rabbits as pets, the other in favor of dogs. Instruct each group to come up with reasons why their animal makes the better pet. Then pair students with a partner from the other group. Tell students to try and convince their partners that their animals are better to have as pets. Then ask pairs to share the results of their discussions with the class.

8 Tell students they are going to listen to two people explain how to do something. Play audio 2.02 and ask students to mark sentences 1–8 with a *T* if they are true, *F* if they are false, and with a *?* if the sentence is not mentioned.

Answers: 1. T **2.** F (they're picky eaters) **3.** F (you need to get rabbits vaccinated) **4.** ? **5.** T **6.** ? **7.** T **8.** ?

Pronunciation

9a Ask different students to read phrases 1–4 aloud with a partner. Tell them to pay attention to how *to* is pronounced.

b Play audio 2.03 for students to check their answers.

c Tell students to underline the unstressed prepositions in each sentence. Play audio 2.04 for students to check their answers. Give students time to practice saying the sentneces with a partner. Monitor and note any difficulties students are having with producing the weak forms. Highlight these on the board for students to correct in pairs. Give praise to the students for their efforts.

Answers: 1. of **2.** to **3.** of **4.** of

10 Have students work with a partner to complete the task. Then ask different students to read their steps to the class.

Writing

OPTIONAL WARM UP

Write the phrase *house sitter* on the board. Ask students, in pairs, to think of tasks that a house sitter does. Elicit responses from the class and write their ideas on the board.

11 Tell students that a friend is going to stay at their house while they are on vacation. Have students write three notes to leave around the house explaining how to use the washing machine, feed your pet, water your plants, etc. If students don't know anything about washing machines, pets, or plants, tell them they can write instructions for something else. Ask different students to read their notes to the class.

LESSON 2 pp. 83–85

CAN DO make inferences based on extended prose
GRAMMAR verbs followed by infinitives or gerunds: meaning
VOCABULARY descriptive language

Summary: In this lesson, students speak about places they have been to. Then they go on to listen to the story of a trip to the hottest place on Earth. In this context, students look at descriptive language. Students finish the lesson by looking at verbs that can be followed by infinitives and gerunds.

Note: Here are some of the hottest places in the world: El Azizia in Libya, the place where the highest ever temperature was recorded as 136.4° F (58° C). Marble Bar in Australia once recorded a period of 160 days from October 31, 1923 to April 7, 1924, where the maximum temperature reached or exceeded 100°F (37.8°C) every day. In terms of annual average temperature, the warmest place in the United States is Death Valley, California. The record temperature there was 134°F (56.7°C) in 1913. The hottest town in the world is Dallol, Ethiopia, with an average temperature of 94°F (34.4°C).

OPTIONAL WARM UP
In a monolingual class, have students discuss with their partners what the hottest and coldest places in their countries are. In a multilingual class, have students tell a partner of a different nationality about the hottest and coldest places in their countries. Elicit responses from various pairs.

Speaking

1 Ask students to discuss the questions with a partner. Then discuss students' ideas with the whole class.

Listening

2a Tell students that they are going to listen to the first part of a story about a trip to the hottest place in the world. Instruct them to read questions 1–3. Play audio 2.05 and ask students to answer the questions. Give them time to compare their answers with a partner. Check answers with the whole class.

Answers: 1. A visa **2.** He thinks that David's trip is a very strange one. He says that the Danakil Depression is not a tourist site. **3.** He shows his sense of humor when he says, "Typical American. Obsessed by the weather."

b Have students discuss the questions with a partner. Then have them compare their answers with another pair. Elicit answers from different pairs.

c Play audio 2.06 for students to check their predictions. Have students discuss if their predictions were correct. Check answers with the class.

3 Ask students to discuss questions 1–5 in small groups. Monitor and take note of any important errors you hear, as well as examples of interesting language students use. Then open the discussion to the whole class. Write the errors on the board and invite different students to come up to the board and correct them for you. Finally, draw students' attention to any interesting language used and congratulate them on its use.

Vocabulary

4a Ask students to focus on the words in both columns. Play audios 2.05 and 2.06 again. Tell students to match the words in the left column with the words in the right column that form common collocations. Check answers with the whole class.

Answers: 1. d **2.** c **3.** f **4.** a **5.** e **6.** b

b Focus students' attention on the photos. Ask students to discuss the places in the photos in pairs and decide where they might be. Then have students decide which of the collocations from Exercise 4a could be used to describe the photos. Elicit responses from the class. Then have students talk to a partner and decide which of the places in the photos they would like to visit most and why. Have students share their ideas with another pair and then with the whole class.

OPTIONAL EXTENSION
Have students choose one of the photos and write a description of it using collocations from Exercise 4a. Encourage students to be imaginative and invent details of the place if necessary. Monitor as students are writing, helping as necessary. Then have students read their descriptions to the rest of the class. Instruct students to listen and compare their descriptions of the same photo.

5 Focus students' attention on sentences 1–6. Tell students complete the sentences with collocations from Exercise 4a. Check answers with the class.

Answers: 1. tourist site **2.** active volcano **3.** permanent settlement **4.** below sea level **5.** ghost town **6.** spectacular landscapes

6a Refer students to the audioscript on page 155. Have them decide what things the words in the box describe. Check answers with the class.

Answers: Verbs: drone: describes the sound of the fan; zig-zag: describes how the flies in the office fly; loom: *salt statues loomed out*; trespass: *trespassing on a place nature had intended only for itself.*
Adjectives: warped: the air; vibrant: colors of the salt statues; hunched: volcano; drenched: his shirt; parched: his mouth

b Have students work with a partner to think of other things that they can use the words in the box to describe. You may wish to have them write down their descriptions.

OPTIONAL VARIATION
Have students think of other things they could describe using the adjectives, but tell them to write down only the noun and not the adjective. Students A read aloud the nouns they have written to their partners, who guess the adjectives. For example: A: "Barcelona." B: "Do you think Barcelona is a vibrant city?" Continue until Students A have read out all of their nouns, and then have Students B read out their nouns for Students A to guess.

Grammar

OPTIONAL WARM UP
Organize students into two groups, A and B. Tell Students A to write a list of things that they have to remember to do every day in their daily lives. Tell Students B to write a list of things they remember doing as children. Elicit responses from the two groups and write them on the board under two headings: *I must remember to . . .* and *I remember + -ing*. Ask students what the difference in meaning is between the two columns. Elicit that *remember* + infinitive is something that you need to do and that *remember + ing* is something you remember doing in the past.

7 Focus students' attention on the Active Grammar box. Have them read through the notes and answer the questions. Check answers with the whole class.

Answers: 1.(a) meant to write (b) means walking **2.**(a) remember to drink (b) remembers experiencing **3.** (a) regret going (b) regret to inform you **4.** (a) stopped to visit (b) stopped looking **5.** (a) tried drinking (b) tried to build **6.** (a) went on riding (b) went on to write

Direct students to the Reference section on page 133.

8 Have students add two words to sentences 1–6 to complete them. Tell students to follow the patterns from the Active Grammar box. Then check answers by asking different students to read out their sentences.

Answers: 1. After six hours of driving, we **stopped to** take a break . . . . **2.** We **tried to** visit the cathedral . . . **3.** . . . she went **on speaking/talking** loudly. **4.** She regrets **getting/waking up** so early . . . **5.** I remembered **to bring/ buy** traveler's checks . . . **6.** . . . she **went on** to become a famous lawyer.

OPTIONAL PRESENTATION
If you prefer a more deductive approach, use the complete grammar charts and explanations on the Reference page to present the concepts. (page 133)

Speaking

9a Tell students to circle the correct answers in sentences 1–4. Check answers with the class.

Answers: 1. lying **2.** to spend **3.** traveling **4.** going

b Have students read through the sentences again and mark them *T* if they are true for them and *F* if they are false. Then have them compare their answers with a partner and explain their views. Discuss as a class.

NOTES

LESSON 3 pp. 86–88

CAN DO write an ad for an object
GRAMMAR *as . . . as*; describing quantity
VOCABULARY buying and selling

Summary: In this lesson, students listen to someone talking about her job dealing with animals. They also read an article about the illegal online animal trade. In this context students look at the grammar of *as . . . as* and describing quantity. Then they look at vocabulary connected with buying and selling, and finish the lesson by writing an ad for an object they would like to sell.

Note: It is possible to buy endangered or potentially dangerous animals online. The International Fund for Animal Welfare, an organization dedicated to the protection of animals and the environment, is trying to stop online trade in wildlife. Their website is: www.ifaw.org.

OPTIONAL WARM UP

Write the following jumbled names of animals (taken from the article on page 86) on the board: *rilolga, gtier, cmpzanhiee, rafgife, okenmy.* Ask students to unscramble the words and tell you the names of the animals. Then write them on the board: *gorilla, tiger, chimpanzee, giraffe, monkey.* Ask students to work in pairs to rank these animals in order of how dangerous they are, 1 being the most dangerous, and 5 the least dangerous. Then have them justify their order to another pair. Finally, discuss as a class.

Listening

1a Have students work in pairs to think of jobs that involve animals and the skills involved in these jobs. Instruct students to share their ideas with another group. Then discuss as a class and write the jobs on the board.

b Tell students they are going to listen to a woman who works with animals discussing her job. Have students discuss the questions with a partner. Monitor conversations for errors. Then ask students to share their answers with the class.

Reading

2 Ask students to look at the heading and predict what they think the article could be about. Elicit responses from different students. Then have students read the article quickly to check their predictions.

Focus students' attention on sentences 1–3. Have them read the article again more carefully and select the best option in the sentences. Check answers with the class.

Answers: 1. toys **2.** at the size of the illegal market for wild animals **3.** illegal hunting

3 Have students discuss the questions in pairs. Monitor and take note of interesting ideas or language used. Elicit responses from different pairs. Congratulate students on any interesting ideas or language heard during their discussions.

Grammar

OPTIONAL WARM UP

Write the following sentence beginning on the board: *Virtually all of the students in the class . . .* Ask students to complete the sentence with their own idea (as long as it is true). Elicit responses and discuss the use of *virtually all* as a way of describing quantity. Then ask students to write down other ways of describing quantity. Elicit responses and write correct expressions on the board.

4 Focus students' attention on the Active Grammar box. Have students read through the notes and answer the questions. Monitor and help students where necessary. Check answers with the whole class.

Answers: 1. Examples: *bought and sold for as little as a few hundred dollars; there are as few as 150,000 left; buying wildlife online is as damaging as killing it yourself* The first two examples show surprise about a statement. The third example means the two things are equal **2.** as much as: as little as; well under: well over; a tiny minority of: a large majority of; virtually all: virtually none; precisely: approximately; as many as: as few as; a minimum of: a maximum of **a.** as much as, as little as, well under, well over, precisely, approximately, as many as, as few as, a minimum of, a maximum of **b.** as much as, as little as

Direct students to the Reference section on page 133.

OPTIONAL PRESENTATION

If you prefer a more deductive approach, use the complete grammar charts and explanations on the Reference page to present the concepts. (page 133)

Pronunciation

5a Play audio 2.08. Tell students to listen to how *as* is pronounced in *as much as, as big as*, etc. (*as* is pronounced /əz/). Refer students to the audioscript on page 155 and ask different students to read the sentences aloud using similar pronunciation.

b Have students work with a partner to create sentences with some of the phrases from the Active Grammar Box. Ask different students to read their sentences to the rest of the class.

6 Have students put the words in sentences 1–5 in the correct order. Tell students to start and finish with the underlined words. Check answers with the whole class.

Answers: 1. Hamsters can give birth to as many as eight offspring at a time. **2.** The vast majority of domestic parrots are able to repeat human speech. **3.** The life of a housefly is as short as 17 days. **4.** Koalas spend virtually all of their lives asleep: 22 hours per day. **5.** Tortoises can live well over 100 years, a great deal longer than humans.

Speaking

7 Focus students' attention on questions 1–2. Have them discuss the questions with a partner. Monitor conversations for important errors.

Ask students to report back to the class. Encourage students to use some of the phrases from the Active Grammar box while doing so. Write any important errors you have heard on the board. Ask students to discuss the errors with their partners. Ask different students to come to the board and write the correct forms.

Vocabulary

8a Have students match each phrase on the left with a similar meaning on the right. Check answers with the class.

Answers: 1. h **2.** j **3.** b **4.** c **5.** f **6.** g **7.** i **8.** d **9.** a **10.** e

b In pairs, have students look at the expressions again. First, have Students A close the book. Students B say one of the phrases, and Students A respond with a phrase with a similar meaning. After Students B have said a few phrases, change roles and have Students B close their books and Students A read out phrases.

Speaking

9 Focus students' attention on the photos. Ask students to discuss in pairs what phrases from Exercise 8a they could use to describe the things in the photos and what animals were used to make them.

Writing

10a Focus students' attention on the ads on Sellit.com. Tell them there are five spelling mistakes and five preposition mistakes. Then have students read through the excerpts and find the mistakes. Check answers with the class.

Answers: Spelling mistakes: slitely = slightly; feeturing = featuring; chose = choose; availlable = available; tare = tear

Preposition mistakes: on excellent condition = in excellent condition; choose for = choose between/from; one in a kind = one of a kind; State in the art = State of the art; as good of new = as good as new.

b Have students choose a possession they would like to sell. Tell them they can choose things like furniture, books, toys, clothes, etc. Then have students write an ad of about 30–40 words for Sellit.com describing the object, price, condition, etc. Monitor and check what the students are writing.

c Organize students into groups. Have students show their ads to the others in their groups. Encourage them to ask each other questions about the item and to choose one of the items they would like to buy.

d Have students tell the rest of the class about the item they decided to buy and why they chose to buy it.

OPTIONAL EXTENSION

Organize students into two groups, A and B. Students A are journalists who need to prepare questions for an interview with a representative of IFAW. Ask them to include questions about quantities in their interviews. Students B are representatives of IFAW who will be interviewed by the journalists. The journalists will ask them, among other things, about the quantity of animals bought and sold online. Students B look back through the article on page 86 to prepare for the interview. When students are ready, pair Students A with Students B and get them to conduct the interview. Monitor for use of *as . . . as* and ways of describing quantity. Last, highlight any important errors on the board for students to correct in pairs. Give praise to students for correct use of phrases to describe quantity.

NOTES

LESSON **4** pp. 89–90

Unit Wrap Up
Review reinforce lessons 1–3
Communication reach a compromise on a plan

Summary: In this lesson, students review the unit's language. They read notes about an island and discuss with a partner what they could do with the land. Then they listen to two people discussing what they could do with the land and finish with a role-play.

Review

1

Answers: One problem that faces prison inmates, **who spend** most of their time locked up, is how to develop self-esteem and do something useful. One idea **that has** been piloted at a prison in Washington is to get the inmates to train dogs **that will** eventually help disabled people. The project has been a great success. The relationship between the inmates and the guards **who work** at the prison has improved considerably. Many of the inmates, **when they** leave the prison, go on to work with animals.
In another scheme, Pilot Dogs, a company **that trains** dogs for the blind in Ohio, put five dogs in the hands of prison inmates, **who trained** the dogs successfully.

2

Answers: **1.** I got a new dog at the animal shelter that rescues homeless animals. **2.** Rats, which can smell more efficiently than robots, are sent into damaged buildings. **3.** The explorer, who had hiked for hours up the mountain, was amazed by the view. **4.** The volcano, which hadn't been active for years, erupted last night. **5.** Many animals that are sold on the Internet are sold illegally. **6.** Zoos can help save endangered species that might otherwise become extinct.

3

Answers: **1.** to say **2.** to think **3.** to lock **4.** to tell **5.** talking **6.** drinking **7.** to become

4

Answers: **1.** as **2.** vast **3.** approximately **4.** virtually **5.** maximum **6.** well **7.** much **8.** none

OPTIONAL EXTRA LISTENING
These audio tracks, activities, and audioscripts are available on both the *ActiveBook* CD-ROM at the back of each Student Book and on the *ActiveTeach* DVD at the back of this Teacher's Resource Book. The audio can also be found on the Audio Program CD. The audioscripts can also be found at the back of the Workbook. These listening activities can be completed in class or done as homework.

Communication

reach a compromise on a plan

OPTIONAL WARM UP
Write the following prompts on the board: *situation, weather, people, vegetation, buildings*. Ask students to look at the picture of the island and discuss in pairs what they think life on the island is like, using the prompts to help.

5 Focus students' attention on the photo of the island and the notes. Have students read the notes.

6 Have students work in pairs. Tell them to make a list of all the things they could do with the island. Then have them compare their ideas with other students. Elicit responses from different students.

7 Tell students they are going to listen to two people discussing what they could do with the land. Play audio 2.09 while students listen and make notes about what the people say. Ask them to compare their ideas with the ideas of the people on the audio.

8 Organize students into groups of three, Students A, B, and C. Refer Students A to page 138, Students B to page 141, and Students C to page 142. Give them time to read and memorize their roles.

Have students discuss what to do with the land, trying to convince the others of their point of view. Tell them that they must agree on something, and this might mean a combination of their ideas. Monitor conversations for errors and interesting language that students use.

9 Ask the different groups to report their decisions back to the rest of the class. Decide with the class whose solution is the best one for the island.

Notes for using the CEF

The Common European Framework (CEF), a reference document for language teaching professionals, was produced by the council of Europe as a means of ensuring parity in terms of language teaching and language qualifications across Europe. It has since increasingly become an accepted standard for English learners throughout the world. It can be downloaded as a PDF file for free from www.coe.int from the section on Language Policy. There is also a link to the site from the *English in Common* website: www.PearsonELT.com/EnglishinCommon.

The CEF recommends that language learners use a portfolio to document, reflect on, and demonstrate their progress. *English in Common* has a Language Portfolio, which can be downloaded from your *ActiveTeach* disc (at the back of this Teacher's Resource Book) or from the *ActiveBook* disc (at the back of each Student Book). Suggested tasks are provided at the beginning of every unit on the Unit Overview page.

CEF REFERENCES

Lesson 1 Can do: explain procedures
CEF B2 descriptor: Can give a clear, detailed description of how to carry out a procedure. (CEF page 81)

Lesson 2 Can do: make inferences based on extended prose
CEF C1 descriptor: Is skilled at using contextual, grammatical, and lexical cues to infer attitude, mood, and intentions and anticipate what will come next. (CEF page 72)

Lesson 3 Can do: write an ad for an object
CEF C1 descriptor: Can write clear, detailed, well-structured and developed descriptions, and imaginative texts in an assured, personal, natural style appropriate to the reader in mind. (CEF page 62)

Additional Resources

Activity Worksheets and Teaching Notes—Unit 7

Photocopiable worksheets for this unit can be found on pages 138–143 and Teaching Notes can be found on pages 177–178 of this Teacher's Resource Book. They consist of games and other interactive activities for: Vocabulary, Grammar, and Speaking.

Extra Listening Activity—Unit 7

This activity is designed to provide students with additional opportunities to listen to and practice comprehension of spoken English. The audio can be accessed by clicking the Extra Listening logo on the Unit Wrap Up page in both the Student's *ActiveBook* (for independent student use) and in the Teacher's *ActiveTeach* (for classroom use). The audio is also provided at the end of the Audio Program CD. An activity worksheet can also be printed out from either the *ActiveBook* or *ActiveTeach*.

Extra Listening Unit 7—Audioscript

F1: Good morning, everyone. Welcome to the West coast job fair for applicants who are interested in working on "The Ice"—that is in Antarctica—at one of our permanent stations, in a field camp, or on a research ship. As you probably already know, conditions there are challenging. You'll be on duty 6 or even 7 days a week, working in unpredictable weather, with average temperatures around zero degrees centigrade, or 32 degrees Fahrenheit, even in the summer. Any questions so far? No?

OK. As our recruitment materials make clear, most of our scientists are military, or university professors on research grants. Civilians, like you here today, are mainly hired for support services. I want to stress that everyone on the team is important! Without people who can cook, clean, and fix broken machinery and computers, our astrophysicists and astronomers could not succeed in their important work. I see a hand up in the back. What's your question, sir?

M1: Actually, I'm here with my daughter, as a concerned Dad. I'd like to know why you, a young woman, went to Antarctica? Weren't you very lonely?

F1: Good question! I went mostly for personal adventure! But I was pleasantly surprised to learn that nearly half of the staff at McMurdo station, where I was based, are female, including our base commander, and some of the leaders of scientific teams. Your daughter will be fine.

M1: Thank you!

F1: Yes? The woman in front . . .

F2: What do the staff do during the dark months?

(continued on next page)

F1: I myself overwintered there for six months last year, so I can fill you in on what the "Big Dark" was like. Of course, we continued focusing on research projects, but it was quieter, with only about 50 people instead of around 200. There was more time for reading, relaxation—we have a library and 3 TV channels—and exercise. I remember my first time skiing over miles of completely clean snow that sparkled like diamonds in the moonlight. Next question . . . Yes? The gentleman in the third row?

M2: I have two questions. First, what happens if you get sick?

F1: Well sickness, of course, can be a problem. We do have a physician who remains with us during the winter and stays in contact with other doctors through the internet for advice. And we stock an excellent pharmacy for routine illnesses. It's almost impossible to get supplies dropped in, although in 1999, the station's overwintering doctor, Jerri Nielsen, discovered that she had breast cancer. There was a daring July drop of chemotherapy supplies for her.

M2: And food? What do you eat when you can't bring in fresh supplies?

F1: The station has a small greenhouse. We grow a variety of vegetables and herbs, hydroponically, without soil, using only water and nutrients. Most fruits have to come frozen or in cans, of course. Some of you here might be assigned as gardeners!

Any more questions? No? Then let me conclude by saying . . .

Video
Pick your Poison: Exotic Pets

Students watch a *Nightline* news episode about the rise in popularity of exotic, and sometimes dangerous, pets. This video segment can be played on the Teacher's *ActiveTeach* disc and projected for classroom viewing or the disc can be played on any DVD player. Teaching notes and video scripts are also provided on the *ActiveTeach* disc.

Tests

A **Unit 7 Test** is provided in the Test Bank as a Word file on the *ActiveTeach* disc. It includes discrete sections on: Grammar, Vocabulary, Reading, and Writing. An Answer Key is also provided. If you wish, this test can be easily modified to suit the particular needs of your class.

Extra Vocabulary: Suffixes

Extra Vocabulary activities for this unit can be found in both the Student's *ActiveBook* and in the Teacher's *ActiveTeach*, along with an answer key.

UNIT 8
Problems and issues

Unit Overview

Warm Up Lesson	
LESSON 1	**CAN DO** stall for time when asked a difficult question **GRAMMAR** reporting verbs
LESSON 2	**CAN DO** discuss lifestyle **GRAMMAR** continuous forms **VOCABULARY** lifestyles
LESSON 3	**CAN DO** explain everyday problems **GRAMMAR** fronting **VOCABULARY** cause and effect
LESSON 4	**Unit Wrap Up** **Review** reinforce lessons 1–3 **Communication** summarize opinions on issues
Grammar and Vocabulary Reference Charts	

OPTIONAL LANGUAGE PORTFOLIO

(located in both the *ActiveBook* at the back of the Student Book and in the *ActiveTeach* at the back of this Teacher's Resource Book)

During this last half of the term, ask students to review the works contained in the *Achievement Portfolio* section of their Language Portfolios. Encourage them to remove older materials and to add more current representations of their abilities. Also ask them to update any information in their *Personal Profiles*.

Teaching Resources

- **Workbook** pp. 60–67
- **Class Audio** CD2 Tracks 10–12
- ***ActiveBook*** Digital Student Book pages with complete unit audio plus Extra Listening Activity and Extra Vocabulary Study
- ***ActiveTeach*** Interactive whiteboard (IWB) software with video, Test Bank, and test audio

Warm Up p. 91

OPTIONAL WARM UP

Ask students to research an important issue that has been in the news in the previous week. This can be a news issue from their own country or an international news issue. Tell students they can do research on the Internet or through newspapers. Encourage them to bring in newspaper clippings or printouts from the Internet if possible. Have students present the news issue to the rest of the class. Encourage them to listen and ask follow-up questions.

1 Ask students to discuss in pairs what is happening in the photos, what issues the photos represent, and if these issues are important or not. Take note of important errors for correction after Exercise 3. Elicit responses from the class.

2 Have students choose the words in the box that can be associated with each of the photos. Check answers with the class.

Answers: Answers may vary **A.** global warming **B.** pollution **C.** energy, oil, spill **D.** identity theft

3 Ask students to discuss questions 1–2 in groups of three or four. Monitor conversations for errors or any interesting language students use. Get answers from the class and discuss the students' ideas. Finally, read aloud any important errors students have made while doing Exercise 1 and Exercise 3 and discuss them with the class.

EXTEND THE WARM UP

Ask students to work in pairs to write a short news report about one of the news issues they talked about in Exercise 3. When they have finished, have students swap their reports with another pair. Then have students read each others' reports and write comments on the content of the news report. Have them return the reports to the students who wrote them so they can read the comments.

LESSON 1 pp. 92–94

CAN DO stall for time when asked a difficult question
GRAMMAR reporting verbs

Summary: In this lesson, students discuss different issues of global importance. Then they read an article about possible future inventions and in this context look at reporting verbs. Students go on to listen to people talking about inventions they would like to see and to discuss these inventions.

Note: There has always been speculation about what the inventions of the future will be and how they will help the world. Necessity has always been the mother of invention, and this will be true of inventions of the future, which will have to tackle problems such as the depletion of the world's oil, processing of the world's waste, and identifying future illnesses. In the United States, there is an organization called the Da Vinci Institute which is dedicated to finding important future inventions and which has designed a museum dedicated to them. (See: http://www.davinciinstitute.com)

OPTIONAL WARM UP

Organize students into groups of three or four. Have them make a list of what they think are the top three inventions the world has ever seen. Then have them share their lists with another group, justifying their choices and explaining why these inventions have been so important for the world. Elicit responses from each group and then try to reach agreement with the class about the most important inventions in history.

Speaking

1a Ask students to match each sentence to a photo. Check answers with the class.

Answers: 1. C **2.** B **3.** A **4.** D **5.** B **6.** D **7.** C **8.** A

b Organize students into pairs, A and B. Have Students A give an opinion on one of the issues from Exercise 1a and have Students B respond with an alternative opinion. Monitor the conversations for use of expressions for giving opinions and expressing contrasting opinions. Continue until students have discussed all the issues. Write good examples of these expressions being used by the students on the board. Congratulate students on accurate usage of the expressions.

Reading

2 Have students discuss the questions in pairs. Monitor conversations for errors. Ask students to justify their answers. Write important errors you have heard on the board and ask different students to correct them.

3 Have students read the article. Ask them if there are any words or phrases from the reading that they don't understand. Encourage them to answer each other's questions or to consult an English-English dictionary before you explain the vocabulary to the class.

4 Focus students' attention on questions 1–4. Tell them to read the article more slowly and circle the correct option in each sentence. Check answers with the class.

Answers: 1. b **2.** a **3.** b **4.** a

Grammar

OPTIONAL WARM UP

While students are discussing the article in the Reading exercises, take note of an exact sentence that one of the students says. Write this sentence on the board with quotation marks around it to show that it is direct speech. Ask the class if they remember who said this sentence and write the student's name beside it. Now ask students to report what the student said. Write the reported sentence on the board and discuss the differences between the original sentence and the reported version.

5 Have students go back to the article on page 92 to answer the questions. Check answers with the class.

Answers: Paragraph 1: He said that whatever hadn't happened would happen, and no one would be safe from it. **Paragraph 2:** A teenager . . . wrote that it would take over a hundred years to produce fresh oil./. . . scientist Hilary Craft said we had already found the answer: solar power. **Paragraph 3:** Another inventor, Clara Petrovic, said she was working on a prototype that would convert waste into bricks and other building material. **Paragraph 4:** Criminal investigator Alexis Smithson said that in the past, thieves had always taken objects. **Paragraph 5:** Glen Hiemstra of Futurist.com recently claimed that somewhere on planet Earth there is a young child who will be the first person to live forever. When we report speech, verb tenses usually shift back to the past. However, in paragraph 5 the reported speech does not revert to the past; it stays in the present.

6 Have students read through the Active Grammar box and complete the exercise. Then have students compare their answers with a partner. Check the answers with the whole class.

Answers: 1. d **2.** e **3.** f **4.** c **5.** b **6.** g **7.** a

Direct students to the Reference section on page 134.

7 Focus students' attention on sentences 1–5. Have them complete the exercise. Tell them to refer to the Active Grammar box for help if necessary. Check answers with the class.

Answers: **1.** threatened **2.** implied discussing **3.** informed **4.** told **5.** suggest

8 Organize students into pairs. Have students report the conversation using the correct words from the box. Tell them that in one sentence they need to change a positive adjective to a negative one. Check answers with the class.

Answers: (Verb tenses may vary, as tenses do not always need to shift back.) Sarah warned that if they/we didn't start recycling, the consequences would be serious for the planet. David suggested starting a recycling group in the community. Sarah remembered that there already was one. Mike confessed that there had been one. He had started it, but then it became too much work, so they stopped.

OPTIONAL PRESENTATION

If you prefer a more deductive approach, use the complete grammar charts and explanations on the Reference page to present the concepts. (page 134)

Listening

9 Focus students' attention on the pictures. Ask them to guess what each of the inventions do. Elicit answers from the class.

10 Tell students they are going to listen to seven people talking about the invention they would most like to see. Play audio 2.10 and ask them to write the number of the speaker next to the pictures. Check answers with the class.

11a Have students discuss questions 1–5 with a partner. Encourage them to use the expressions in the How To box while doing so. Monitor the conversations for students' use of the expressions and make a note of any important errors. Discuss correct usage of the expressions that you heard and note any errors on the board for the students to correct.

b Ask pairs to change partners so that they are working with a different student. Have them report to their new partner what their original partner said. Monitor for students' use of the reported speech features from page 93. Write any important errors on the board and elicit corrections from the students.

LESSON 2 pp. 95–97

CAN DO discuss lifestyle
GRAMMAR continuous forms
VOCABULARY lifestyles

Summary: In this lesson, students listen to two people talking about their work/life habits. Then they look at vocabulary connected with lifestyles before studying continuous forms. Students finish the lesson by interviewing their partners.

Note: Modern life is increasingly stressful and there are many people who become disenchanted with the way they live and the jobs they do. This can result in depression and other health problems. Some people have found an answer to the problems of their stressful lives in "downshifting," a term that refers to people giving up their jobs and leading a different life, often in the country. This change normally results in a reduction in earnings but can bring about an improvement in the quality of life.

OPTIONAL WARM UP

Give students time to think about any areas of their life they would like to change. Tell them to take notes about how they would like to change these areas. Then have students share this information with a partner. Tell them to discuss what they would have to do to make these changes and if it would be easy to make these changes to their lives or not. Then discuss as a class.

Listening

1 Ask students to work in pairs to discuss the people in the photos by answering the question. Monitor conversations and take note of important errors. Elicit answers from different pairs. Write any important errors you have heard on the board and get different students to correct them.

2 Tell students that they are going to hear the people in the photos talking about their work/life habits. Play audio 2.11 and ask students to take note of how the two lifestyles differ. Check answers with the class.

Answers: Thomas leads a relaxed lifestyle, living near the beach. He believes that money isn't everything and that there is no point in hurrying. Elise has a hectic city lifestyle. She believes that she wouldn't like living in the country and that she would miss the noise of the city.

3a Focus students' attention on questions 1–5. Ask students to read the questions and possible answers and choose the best answer for each question.

b Play audio 2.11 again for students to check their answers.

Answers: **1.** b **2.** c **3.** a **4.** c **5.** c

Vocabulary

4 Refer students to the audioscript on page 156. Play audio 2.11 again and ask them to read along with the audioscript.

Focus students' attention on the idiomatic expressions a–e. Have students try to work out the meaning of the expressions from the context of the audioscript. Elicit responses from different students. Then have them complete the exercise. Check answers with the class.

Answers: **1.** e **2.** d **3.** c **4.** b **5.** a

5 Ask students to discuss questions 1–2 in pairs. Elicit responses from different students. In a monolingual class, ask students to tell you whether they think people in their country are stressed out compared to other countries. In a multilingual class, tell students to tell a partner of a different nationality about whether people are generally stressed out in their country. Then have students tell the rest of the class what they have learned about their partner's country.

OPTIONAL EXTENSION

Ask students to work in pairs or small groups. Have them prepare and write a survey addressing work/life habits to ask the other students in the class. Then have them ask their questions and make notes on the answers. The results can be presented in the form of charts or tables and displayed around the classroom.

Grammar

OPTIONAL WARM UP

Prepare a short paragraph about yourself that includes an example of the following structures: present continuous, past continuous, present perfect continuous, past perfect continuous, and future continuous. Tell students you are going to read the paragraph once at normal speed and that they should try to write down as much as they can. If they can't write everything, they should leave a space and continue. Read the paragraph. Have students compare what they have written with a partner. Write on the board any parts of sentences students can give you. Have students try to fill in the spaces to reconstruct the article. Help them until the full article is on the board. Underline all of the continuous forms on the board. Ask students to decide what they have in common. Finally, have students discuss the use of the continuous forms with a partner.

6 Tell students to look at the sentences from the listening and have them match each sentences to the correct continuous form. Check answers with the class.

Answers: **1.** d **2.** b **3.** e **4.** c **5.** a

7 Focus students' attention on the Active Grammar box. Ask students to do the tasks in the box. Check answers with the whole class.

Answers: **1.** (a) (sentences 1 and 2) (b) (sentence 4) (c) (sentence 3) (d) (sentence 5) **2.** Another example would be: I was hoping . . . **3.** Verbs of personal feeling; for example, *like, love, hate, want, prefer, dislike, wish* Verbs of thought; for example: *know, believe, imagine, mean, realize, understand, doubt, feel (have an opinion)* Verbs of the senses; for example: *appear, hear, sound, taste, see, smell, resemble, seem*

Direct students to the Reference section on page 134.

8a Focus students' attention on sentences 1–7. Have students change the verb forms into the continuous. Check answers with the whole class and discuss how the meaning of the sentences can change with the use of the continuous forms.

Answers: **1.** I've been reading that book. Simple = she's finished the book. Continuous = she hasn't finished it **2.** I'll be working until about 8:00 tonight. Simple and continuous = basically the same meaning here. **3.** She was hitting me. Simple = she did it once. Continuous = she did it repeatedly. **4.** The first chapter is being written. Simple = it is finished. Continuous = it isn't finished. **5.** What music are you listening to? Simple = generally. Continuous = at this particular moment it's happening. **6.** He had been losing his hair. Simple = the hair was all gone. Continuous = the hair was in the process of going. He still had some left. **7.** We're going to work at 8:00. Simple and continuous = basically the same meaning here, BUT Simple = for a formally organized timetable. Continuous = may be a decision made by an individual.

b Have students write potential responses to the sentences in Exercise 8a. Check answers with the class.

9 Focus students' attention on the words in the box. Discuss the definitions of the words. Tell students to look up any new words in a dictionary if necessary. Ask different students to give explanations of the words to the class.

Have students complete the paragraphs with the words from the box. Tell students they may need to change the verb form to fit the context. If both the simple and continuous forms are possible, tell students to use the continuous form. Check answers with the whole class.

Answers: 1. were going back 2. were beginning 3. are questioning/have been questioning 4. seem 5. is growing/has been growing 6. are urging 7. have been advocating 8. quotes 9. was driving

OPTIONAL PRESENTATION

If you prefer a more deductive approach, use the complete grammar charts and explanations on the Reference page to present the concepts. (page 134)

Speaking

OPTIONAL WARM UP

Write the following words on the board: *store clerk, anthropology student, work in a bar, jogging, studying for a test, learning German, master's degree, play tennis, go dancing*. Ask students to discuss in pairs if they have ever done or been any of these things. Ask different students to share their experiences with the class. Then ask students to cover the profile of Dana Kolansky, look at her photo, and predict which of these things she does. (She does all of these things). Tell them to read the profile and check if their predictions were correct.

10 Have students read the profile and decide if Dana leads a busy life. Elicit opinions from different students and ask them to explain why they think this.

11a Focus students' attention on the profile outline. Tell students to think of the questions they would need to ask to complete the profile with information about someone else. Elicit responses from different students and write the correct questions they give you on the board.

b Organize students into pairs. Have them interview their partners using the questions they have written. Monitor the interviews for errors. Elicit responses from different pairs and ask students to tell the rest of the class one or two pieces of information about their partner. Write any important errors you have heard on the board. Invite different students to come to the board and write the correct forms. Congratulate students on any interesting language they have used while doing the interviews.

LESSON 3 pp. 98–100

CAN DO explain everyday problems
GRAMMAR fronting
VOCABULARY cause and effect

Summary: In this lesson, students read problems and advice on an advice website. They study fronting. They also listen to people complaining about problems they have had with machines. Then students look at the vocabulary connected to cause and effect. Students finish the lesson by writing an essay about a problem or issue.

Note: Advice columns have always been a traditional part of magazines. People can write to the magazine with a problem and an expert (or other readers) writes back in an open letter, giving advice about what to do in this situation. The advent of the Internet has meant that it is possible to ask for advice on the Internet in the same way.

OPTIONAL WARM UP

Have students make a list of machines they come into contact with in their daily life. Then have them share their lists with a partner. Elicit responses from the class and write the list of machines on the board. Discuss with the class which of these machines they would most miss if they stopped working.

Reading

1 Have students discuss with a partner what is happening in the photo. Then have them tell their partners if they have ever been in a situation like the one shown. Instruct students to describe to their partner what happened and how they resolved the problem. Write any errors you hear on the board. Ask students to tell you what they have learned about their partners.

2a Have students read Problem A and Problem B and identify the problem each person has. Tell them not to worry about difficult vocabulary at this stage, as you will be dealing with it later. Have students discuss the problems with a partner and decide which of the problems is more serious and why. Then have them think of advice that they would give to Silvia and Jake. Elicit responses from the class and agree who has thought of the best advice.

b Have students read the advice in comments 1–4. Then have them compare this advice with the advice they came up with and decide if they agree with the suggestions given. Discuss as a class. Ask students if there are any words or phrases in the bulletins they don't understand. Encourage them to answer each others' questions before explaining the vocabulary to the class.

OPTIONAL EXTENSION

Assign students an area of life (for example: love, family, friends, money) that they need to write about. Give students time to prepare and write about their problem. Then have them swap with a partner and write a letter of advice to him or her. Have students return the letters of advice to their partners. Discuss as a class to see who gave the best advice.

Grammar

OPTIONAL WARM UP

Write the following sentence beginning on the board: *I get really irritated . . .* Have students finish the sentence with their own ideas. Then discuss students' ideas with the class. Now write: *What . . .* on the board. Ask students to complete this sentence so that it has the same meaning as the first sentence they completed. Elicit the following beginning of the sentence: *What I get really irritated by is . . .* Discuss what effect this structure has on the sentence. Explain that we use this type of order to emphasize the subject of the sentence or to provide a clear link with a previous sentence.

3 Focus students' attention on the Active Grammar box. Ask them to complete the tasks. Check answers with the whole class.

Answers: 1. What you need to do is to put yourself in your friend's shoes. (comment 1) What might also work is having some games available for them. (comment 1) There's not much you can do. (comment 2) What they really care about is your ability to do the job. (comment 4) **2.** Other examples of "fronting phrases" in comments 1–4: The fact remains that you . . . (comment 1) The point is, . . . (comment 2) The truth is, . . . (comment 3) The fact of the matter is . . . (comment 4)

Direct students to the Reference section on page 134.

4 Focus students' attention on sentences 1–5. Have them change the sentences so that the meaning stays the same. Tell students to start the sentences with the underlined word.

Check answers with the class and write the sentences on the board.

Answers: 1. What bothers me is their bad behavior. **2.** How long he hoped to get away with the lie I'm not sure. **3.** How she manages with those kids I don't know. **4.** The problem was that she didn't discipline them. **5.** What worries me is (the fact) that my colleague lost his job.

5 Organize students into groups of three, A, B, and C. Refer Students A to page 139, Students B to page 141 and Students C to page 142. Give them time to read through the problems. Monitor to make sure that students understand their problems. If students prefer, they can make up their own problem. If so, monitor to check what problems the students come up with.

Then have students tell the other two students in their group about their problem. Tell the students listening to offer advice and to use fronting expressions where possible. Monitor the conversations, taking note of errors and correct use of fronting expressions. Elicit responses from different groups and decide with the class if the advice given by students was good advice or not. Write any errors you have heard on the board and ask different students to come to the board and write the correct forms. Finally, congratulate students on their use of fronting expressions.

OPTIONAL PRESENTATION

If you prefer a more deductive approach, use the complete grammar charts and explanations on the Reference page to present the concepts. (page 134)

Listening

6a Refer students back to the list of machines they came up with in the Warm Up at the start of the lesson. Ask them to discuss with a partner what can go wrong with each machine and if they have any experiences of these or any other machines going wrong. Elicit responses from different pairs.

b Tell students they are going to hear three people complaining about problems they have had with machines. Play audio 2.12 and ask them to take notes about which machines the people are talking about and what the problem is in each case. Check answers with the whole class.

Answers: 1. photocopier—keeps getting jammed **2.** computer—won't shut down **3.** air conditioner—can't turn it on

7 Organize students into pairs. Tell students to imagine that there is a problem with an item of technology in their home. Have them make notes about the problem. Then have them describe the problem to their partners without mentioning the name of the item. Encourage students to use phrases from the How To box. Tell students who are listening to guess what the item is and come up with a solution if possible. Monitor conversations for errors and discuss the solutions to the problems students have offered. Write any errors you have heard on the board and ask different students to correct them.

OPTIONAL EXTENSION

On the board write the following prompts: *where?*, *when?*, *how much?*, *problems*, *expected action*. Have students write a letter of complaint to the store where they bought the machine they have described in Exercise 7. Instruct students to include the prompts on the board in their letters.

Vocabulary

8 Focus students' attention on sentences 1–4 and a–d. Have them put a word in each space to complete the sentences. Check answers with the class.

Answers: **1.** influence **2.** resulted **3.** consequence **4.** from **a.** gives **b.** origins **c.** source **d.** bring

Tell students to match the problems with each piece of advice. Check answers with the class.

Answers: **1.** d **2.** a **3.** c **4.** b

9 Organize students into groups of three or four. Have students finish sentences 1–5 so they are true for them. Then have them compare their answers with other students in their group. Encourage students to ask each other follow-up questions where possible. Monitor the conversations for errors. Finally, read aloud any important errors you have heard and get different students to correct them for you.

Writing

10a Refer students to the Cause and Effect essay section in the Writing Bank on page 146. Ask students to work through the exercises with their partners. Monitor and help where necessary before checking answers with the whole class.

Answers: Exercise 1: a Insomnia—Causes and Effects
Exercise 2: **1.** c **2.** a **3.** c **4.** b **5.** b

b Focus students' attention on the problems and issues suggested. Have them choose one of the problems or issues and make notes about its causes, the effect it has had on them or others, and possible solutions to this problem. Monitor and help students as necessary. Discuss as a class.

c Have students write an essay of 200–250 words about the problem or issue. You may want to show students this paragraph plan: paragraph 1: introduction; paragraph 2: causes of the problem; paragraph 3: the effect on them and on others; paragraph 4: possible solutions. It may be a good idea for students to write the essay for homework. Then have them read each others' essays and comment on the problems and possible solutions given.

OPTIONAL VARIATION

You may wish to have students look at the Extra Vocabulary for this unit (Academic English) before writing this essay. The Extra Vocabulary can be found on both the Student's *ActiveBook* and the the Teacher's *ActiveTeach*. Students would then be able to include the language in their essays. Encourage students to also include expressions from the useful phrases box on page 146.

NOTES

LESSON 4 pp. 101–102

Unit Wrap Up
Review reinforce lessons 1–3
Communication summarize opinions on issues

Summary: In this lesson, students give and exchange opinions about five different topics they have chosen.

Review

1

Answers: "We propose **adopting** . . . explained **to** us . . . people **to** think . . . for **destroying** the local . . . deliberately **harming** the . . . We **suggest adopting** this . . . to **consider** spiritual . . . guaranteed to **open** our . . ."

2

Answers: **1.** Were you planning **2.** Why are you wearing **3.** Where were you going **4.** How long have you been playing **5.** Had he been living **6.** Do you see

3

Answers: (paragraph 1) My family . . . The **problem** is . . . but the fact of the **matter** is that . . . (paragraph 2) What **surprises** me . . . thing **is**, she has . . . (paragraph 3) **Why** you're complaining . . . idea **would** be to . . .

4

Answers: **1.** influence **2.** resulted **3.** consequences **4.** gives, for **5.** bring, consequences **6.** sources **8.** origins

OPTIONAL EXTRA LISTENING

These audio tracks, activities, and audioscripts are available on both the *ActiveBook* CD-ROM at the back of each Student Book and on the *ActiveTeach* DVD at the back of this Teacher's Resource Book. The audio can also be found on the Audio Program CD. The audioscripts can also be found at the back of the Workbook. These listening activities can be completed in class or done as homework.

Communication

summarize opinions on issues

OPTIONAL WARM UP

Write the following expressions on the board: *I agree, I'm not sure about that, I don't think so, I agree with you up to a point, but . . . , I disagree, I suppose you're right, You could have a point there.* Have students divide the expressions into two groups with a partner; agreeing and disagreeing. Then have students decide if any of these expressions are particularly formal or informal. (*I suppose you're right* sounds more informal than the others.)

5a Ask students if they have ever been in situations or places like the ones shown in the photos, and in which situation or place they would most like to be now.

Have students read statements a–k and decide if any can be used to describe the photos.

b Have students give the statements a number from 1 to 5, with 1 being something they completely disagree with, and 5 being something they completely agree with.

6a Organize students into small groups. Tell students to decide which five of the topics their group is going to discuss. Then have them discuss the topics and exchange opinions.

b Ask each group to report to the class about what they talked about and what the group's views and opinions were. Monitor students and note any important errors. Write errors you have heard on the board and ask students to correct them. Finally, congratulate students on their use of interesting language during the lesson.

NOTES

Notes for using the CEF

The Common European Framework (CEF), a reference document for language teaching professionals, was produced by the council of Europe as a means of ensuring parity in terms of language teaching and language qualifications across Europe. It has since increasingly become an accepted standard for English learners throughout the world. It can be downloaded as a PDF file for free from www.coe.int from the section on Language Policy. There is also a link to the site from the *English in Common* website: www.PearsonELT.com/EnglishinCommon.

The CEF recommends that language learners use a portfolio to document, reflect on, and demonstrate their progress. *English in Common* has a Language Portfolio, which can be downloaded from your *ActiveTeach* disc (at the back of this Teacher's Resource Book) or from the *ActiveBook* disc (at the back of each Student Book). Suggested tasks are provided at the beginning of every unit on the Unit Overview page.

CEF REFERENCES

Lesson 1 Can do: stall for time when asked a difficult question
CEF C1 descriptor: Can select a suitable phrase from a readily available range of discourse functions to preface his/her remarks appropriately in order to get the floor, or to gain time and keep the floor while thinking.
(CEF page 124)

Lesson 2 Can do: discuss lifestyle.
CEF B2 descriptor: Can express his/her ideas and opinions with precision, and present and respond to complex lines of argument convincingly. (CEF page 77)

Lesson 3 Can do: explain everyday problems
CEF B2 descriptor: Can outline an issue or a problem clearly, speculating about causes or consequences, and weighing advantages and disadvantages of different approaches. (CEF page 79)

Additional Resources

Activity Worksheets and Teaching Notes—Unit 8

Photocopiable worksheets for this unit can be found on pages 144–149 and Teaching Notes can be found on pages 177–178 of this Teacher's Resource Book. They consist of games and other interactive activities for: Vocabulary, Grammar, and Speaking.

Extra Listening Activity—Unit 8

This activity is designed to provide students with additional opportunities to listen to and practice comprehension of spoken English. The audio can be accessed by clicking the Extra Listening logo on the Unit Wrap Up page in both the Student's *ActiveBook* (for independent student use) and in the Teacher's *ActiveTeach* (for classroom use). The audio is also provided at the end of the Audio Program CD. An activity worksheet can also be printed out from either the *ActiveBook* or *ActiveTeach*.

Extra Listening Unit 8—Audioscript

F1: Good afternoon, listeners. I'm Alison Berlin, and this is *Issues in the News*. Today my two guests are on opposing sides of proposals to allow deep-sea drilling off the northern coast of Alaska. Stuart Ross, your firm represents some of the big oil companies that are pushing for increased exploitation of Alaskan oil. Is that environmentally safe?

M1: Yes, indeed, Alison. In the last few years, we've developed several innovative technologies that will allow us to drill with much less damage to the ocean.

F1: For example?

M1: Well, one is called "through-tube" drilling. A new well is drilled through the production tubing of an older well. Not needing to redrill, or pull out the old tubes, can potentially save about 1 million dollars in labor costs. Let me stress that the benefits of achieving energy independence through increased production of domestic oil are worth the risks.

F1: Bryan Adams, what do you think?

M2: Alison, the fact of the matter is that the environment can't tolerate deep sea drilling. Let's remember that the BP blowout in the Gulf of Mexico took five months to get under control. One hundred seventy million gallons of crude oil poured into the gulf, and it will take years to clean up the mess. The shrimp industry was almost destroyed, not to mention the thousands of birds and fish that died. And we still don't know what the long-term effects on the environment will be.

F1: Are you saying that it's irresponsible to drill in the Beaufort Sea, off the North Slope of Alaska?

(continued on next page)

M2: Yes, I am. We're just not technologically ready to risk Arctic waters and the pristine ecosystem that exists there. The oil companies have admitted that they don't know how to cope with leaks that occur miles under the ocean floor. We're talking about a location that's blocked in by ice for 8 months every year, and one thousand miles away from Coast Guard help.

F1: Stuart Ross, would you like to comment on these points?

M1: Yes, thank you. I understand the issues that my fellow guest has brought up. The fact remains, however, that our country and the world are dependent on oil today and will remain so for the foreseeable future. We need additional sources of energy! And, of course, development of new oil fields means more jobs and tax revenue, both of which we sorely need.

F1: Can you expand on that?

M1: Studies have shown that allowing drilling in Alaska could generate 1.4 million new jobs by 2030, along with 800 billion dollars in additional revenue for the government. By the way, our own domestic consumption will probably remain about the same in the next twenty years, so we'll see a big drop in the amount of oil we need to import.

M2: I'd much rather we spent our time and money on developing alternative, clean energy sources, like wind and solar power! Those could create jobs as well!

F1: I'm afraid that time is up. Thank you gentlemen for your insightful analysis of a controversial issue.

M1: Thank you.

M2: Thank you . . .

Video
Living the Real Simple Life

Students watch a *Nightline* news episode about a suburban family that grows all of their own food. This video segment can be played on the Teacher's *ActiveTeach* disc and projected for classroom viewing or the disc can be played on any DVD player. Teaching notes and video scripts are also provided on the *ActiveTeach* disc.

Tests

A **Unit 8 Test** is provided in the Test Bank as a Word file on the *ActiveTeach* disc. It includes discrete sections on: Grammar, Vocabulary, Reading, and Writing. An Answer Key is also provided. If you wish, this test can be easily modified to suit the particular needs of your class.

Extra Vocabulary: Academic English

Extra Vocabulary activities for this unit can be found in both the Student's *ActiveBook* and in the Teacher's *ActiveTeach*, along with an answer key.

UNIT 9
People with vision

Unit Overview

Warm Up Lesson	
LESSON 1	**CAN DO** express a degree of certainty **GRAMMAR** collocations with prepositions
LESSON 2	**CAN DO** using colloquial expressions to explain your tastes **GRAMMAR** discourse markers **VOCABULARY** describing art
LESSON 3	**CAN DO** respond to hypothetical questions **GRAMMAR** unreal past
LESSON 4	**Unit Wrap Up** **Review** reinforce lessons 1–3 **Communication** collaborate on a proposal
Grammar and Vocabulary Reference Charts	

OPTIONAL LANGUAGE PORTFOLIO

(located in both the *ActiveBook* at the back of the Student Book and in the *ActiveTeach* at the back of this Teacher's Resource Book)

During this last half of the term, ask students to review the works contained in the *Achievement Portfolio* section of their Language Portfolios. Encourage them to remove older materials and to add more current representations of their abilities. Also ask them to update any information in their *Personal Profiles*.

Teaching Resources

- **Workbook** pp. 68–75
- **Class Audio** CD2 Tracks 13–16
- ***ActiveBook*** Digital Student Book pages with complete unit audio plus Extra Listening Activity and Extra Vocabulary Study
- ***ActiveTeach*** Interactive whiteboard (IWB) software with video, Test Bank, and test audio

Warm Up p. 103

OPTIONAL WARM UP

Have students talk to a partner about famous painters from their country. Then ask different students to tell you about the different painters.

1 Focus students' attention on the photos. Ask them to discuss which art forms they can see represented in the photos. Then have them think of other forms of visual arts and discuss with a partner which they prefer and why. Monitor and take note of errors which you can correct after Exercise 3. Elicit responses from different pairs.

Answers: A. fine art/painting **B.** theater **C.** architecture **D.** movies

2 Ask students to discuss in pairs the words and phrases in bold in sentences 1–7 and decide if they refer to books, movies, theater, art, or architecture (there may be more than one answer). Draw five columns on the board and write *books*, *movie*, *theater*, *art*, and *architecture* at the top of the columns. Elicit responses from different pairs, write the words and phrases in the correct columns, and discuss which might go in more than one column.

Answers: 1. movie and theater **2.** book, movie, and theater **3.** movie and theater **4.** book **5.** architecture and art **6.** movie **7.** art

3 Organize students into small groups. Have them talk about their favorite paintings, buildings, movies, and novels. Encourage them to use the vocabulary from Exercise 2 while doing so. Elicit responses from different groups. Write important errors you have heard on the board and encourage students to self-correct.

EXTEND THE WARM UP

In a monolingual class, have students think of five cultural or artistic places that a tourist to their city or town should visit. Have them compare their places with a partner and justify their choices. Then ask students what they have learned about their partner's city or town.

LESSON **1** pp. 104–106

CAN DO express a degree of certainty
GRAMMAR collocations with prepositions

Summary: In this lesson, students read biographies about three important visionaries. They look at collocations with prepositions. Then they listen to an interview about the relationship between creativity and genius and go on to look at ways of expressing certainty and uncertainty.

Note: Leonardo da Vinci: Italian architect, sculptor, scientist, anatomist, engineer, mathematician, and painter. He is considered to be one of the greatest painters and thinkers of all time. The Yellow Emperor: Chinese emperor thought to have lived in the 27th century B.C. Much of Chinese culture is attributed to his systems and inventions. Sir Isaac Newton: English physicist, mathematician, astronomer, and alchemist. He is commonly thought to be one of the most important figures in the history of science. Wolfgang Amadeus Mozart: one of the most important and influential classical composers. Albert Einstein: one of the greatest physicists of all time. He formulated the theory of relativity. Vincent Van Gogh: a Dutch painter whose paintings have reached record prices. He committed suicide in 1890, reputedly because of a lack of recognition for his paintings.

Reading

1 Ask students to discuss in pairs what the three people in the pictures have in common. Also have them talk about what they know about the three people and their achievements. Elicit responses from different pairs.

2 Tell students to read the biographies quickly to compare their ideas from Exercise 1 with the information in the reading and to find out more information. You may want to set a time limit for this initial reading to encourage students to skim the biographies. Tell them not to worry about any words or phrases they don't understand at this stage. Then discuss as a class.

OPTIONAL VARIATION

Organize students into groups of three, A, B, and C. Having discussed what they know about the people in the pictures (Exercise 1), tell Students A to read the biography of Leonardo da Vinci, Students B to read about The Yellow Emperor, and Students C to read about Sir Isaac Newton. Then have students tell the rest of their group what they have learned about the person they have read about.

3 Have students read the biographies again more carefully and discuss the questions with a partner. Ask students if there are any words or phrases in the biographies they don't understand. Encourage them to work out the meanings from the context or use a dictionary before you explain the vocabulary to the class.

Grammar

OPTIONAL WARM UP

Write the following sentences on the board: *Sir Isaac Newton was famous of his mathematical theories. Leonardo da Vinci immersed himself on painting for a time.* Ask students to spot the mistakes and elicit the correct sentences: *Sir Isaac Newton was famous* ***for*** *his mathematical theories. Leonardo da Vinci immersed himself* ***in*** *painting for a time.* Ask them why the prepositions *for* and *in* are correct here. (These prepositions collocate with these adjectives and are "dependent" on them.) Tell students that there is no rule for which prepositions go with which adjectives, verbs, and nouns. Also tell them to note collocations with prepositions they see when they are reading, and that it would be a good idea to have a separate section in their notebooks for examples of collocations.

4 Focus students' attention on the Active Grammar box and give them time to read through the notes and do the tasks. Check answers with the whole class.

Answers:
1. a. verb + preposition: range **from** . . . (to . . .); work **on**. . . ; attribute **to** . . .
b. verb + object + preposition: draw inspiration **from** . . . ; made contributions **to** . . .
c. noun + preposition: in the fields **of** . . . ; ideas **for/of** . . . ; the development **of** . . .
d. adjective + preposition: (be) famous **for** . . . ; (be) immersed **in** . . .
e. prepositional phrases (beginning with a preposition): **in** a time of . . . ; **on** one occasion . . .
2. succeed in: a; improve on: a; of all time: e; in later life: e; make observations about: b; hope for: a; specialize in: a; a solution to: c; the quality of: c; admiration for: c; in recognition of: e; devote your life to: b; (be) obsessed with: d

Direct students to the Reference section on page 135.

5 Focus students' attention on a–f. Have them refer to the chart in the Active Grammar box and list the correct expressions. Check answers with the class.

Answers: a. devote your life to **b.** attributed to **c.** (be) obsessed with **d.** (be) immersed in **e.** improve on **f.** admiration for

6 Instruct students to choose the correct options. Check answers with the class.

Answers: **1.** of **2.** to **3.** to **4.** of **5.** in **6.** to **7.** on **8.** on **9.** for **10.** In (The scientist described is Albert Einstein.)

7 Have students work in pairs. Tell them to think of other famous "visionaries" or inspirational people. Have them ask and answer questions about them using the phrases in the Active Grammar box.

OPTIONAL VARIATION

Tell students to check the rules for *Twenty Questions* on page 49 again. Have them work in pairs. Have Students A think of a famous visionary and Students B ask questions to find out the identity of the visionary. When asking questions, they should try to use expressions from the Active Grammar box. When students have guessed the identity of the visionary, students change so that Students A are asking Students B questions.

OPTIONAL PRESENTATION

If you prefer a more deductive approach, use the complete grammar charts and explanations on the Reference page to present the concepts. (page 135)

Listening

8 Tell students they are going to listen to a radio interview with someone who is talking about people who have invented or discovered something. Play audio 2.13. Ask students to make notes under the three headings.

Answers:

1. Discoveries made outside the laboratory:
- Physicist Richard Feynman saw a plate flying through the air and was inspired to calculate electron orbits.
- Alexander Fleming was making mold for his hobby when he accidentally discovered penicillin.

2. The psychology of high achievers:
- A study of high achievers (Nobel Prize winners vs. other scientists) found that more than 50% were also artistic, and nearly all had a long-lasting hobby.
- 25% Nobel Prize winners played a musical instrument, 18 % drew or painted.
- Less than 1% of non-Nobel winners had a hobby.

3. Can only creative people be geniuses?
- No, but creative thinking can help solve problems.
- Often the solution to a problem will come when you are not thinking about it.
- The brain has the ability to make connections from one part of your life to another.
- People who have creative hobbies and interests often excel in their fields.

9 Have students discuss questions 1–4 with a partner. Monitor the conversations for errors to correct after Exercise 11. Then ask students to share their ideas with the rest of the class.

10 Focus students' attention on the How To box. Tell them to read the words and phrases in the box and then complete the exercise by circling the correct answers. Check answers with the class.

Answers: **1.** debatable **2.** not 100 percent certain **3.** unquestionably **4.** not clear-cut **5.** irrefutably **6.** questionable **7.** indisputably

Speaking

11 Ask students to discuss statements 1–4 in groups, saying whether they agree or disagree with them. Encourage students to use phrases from the How To box while doing so. Monitor for errors and correct use of the expressions from the How To box. Have students share ideas with another group. Read aloud any errors you have heard in Exercise 9 and Exercise 11 and discuss them with the class.

NOTES

LESSON 2 pp. 107–109

CAN DO using colloquial expressions to explain your tastes
GRAMMAR discourse markers
VOCABULARY describing art

Summary: In this lesson students look at language to express likes and dislikes. They listen to people talking about different pictures. Then they look at discourse markers. Students go on to discuss their favorite artists. They finish the lesson by reading an article about art thieves.

Note: The National Portrait Gallery in London holds the most extensive collection of portraits in the world. Every year the Gallery holds a competition for the best portrait. For more information about the gallery, go to http://www.npg.org.uk/.

OPTIONAL WARM UP

Organize students into pairs, A and B. Ask students to think of a famous painting. Have Students A describe their paintings to Students B. Then have Students B try to guess what the famous painting is. Students B can draw what their partners are describing if it will help them. When Students A have finished describing the painting, have students swap so that Students B describe their paintings to Students A.

Vocabulary

1 Ask students to discuss in pairs the type of art that they like and don't like. Monitor conversations and take note of errors for later correction.Have students share their ideas with another pair. Elicit responses from different pairs.

2 Focus students' attention on sentences 1–4 and a–d. Check that they understand the meanings of the phrases in bold. Then have students match sentences 1–4 with their opposites in a–d. Also instruct them to decide which of the words in bold are used to show personal opinions and which are used to describe facts. Check answers with the whole class.

Answers: 1. d **2.** c **3.** a **4.** b **personal opinions:** striking, tranquil, disturbing, dull, striking **facts:** abstract, avant-garde, figurative

3 Focus students' attention on the phrases in the box. In pairs, have students talk about a painting or photograph they like or don't like. Instruct them to use phrases from the How To box.

Listening

4a Tell students they are going to hear people talking about three paintings. Have them read the questions and answer choices, and then play audio 2.14. Have students circle the correct answers. Check answers with the class. Then have students discuss with their partners which words or phrases helped them decide on the answers.

Answers: Conversation 1: c **Conversation 2:** b **Conversation 3:** a

b Play audio 2.15 and have students listen for which picture actually won and what the speaker thinks of the winner. Then have students compare answers with a partner. Check answers with the class.

Answers: a. It's good, but it's not his favorite.

Grammar

OPTIONAL WARM UP

Prepare an anecdote about something interesting that has happened to you recently and in it include discourse markers from the Active Grammar box. Tell the anecdote to the class. Ask students to listen and take notes. When you have finished telling the anecdote, have students compare notes with a partner and retell the story. Elicit from them the discourse markers you have used and write them on the board. Ask students what function these expressions have. Elicit that we use these expressions to help organize what we are saying and that they can also show our attitude to a subject. Refer students to the Active Grammar box.

5 Have students complete the tasks in the Active Grammar box. Check answers with the class.

NOTES

Answers:

Focusing on the main topic	Returning to the main point	Returning to a previous line of discussion
regarding as for as far as ___ is concerned	at any rate	as I was saying anyway, what I was going to say was . . . anyway
Introducing a strong opinion or criticism	**Softening an opinion or criticism**	**Making additional (often contrasting) points**
to be honest to tell you the truth frankly	kind of sort of more or less	mind you in fact as a matter of fact

Direct students to the Reference section on page 135.

6 Ask students to circle the best choices in conversations 1–5. Check answers.

Answers: 1A: To be honest, **B:** At any rate **2A:** kind of, **B:** Mind you **3A:** As a matter of fact, **B:** Frankly **4A:** As for, **B:** more or less **5A:** Regarding, **B:** To tell you the truth

OPTIONAL PRESENTATION

If you prefer a more deductive approach, use the complete grammar charts and explanations on the Reference page to present the concepts. (page 135)

Speaking

7 Have students discuss the questions with a partner. Encourage students to use discourse markers to help organize their speech and show their attitude toward the subject. Monitor conversations for errors and use of discourse markers. Elicit responses from the class. Then discuss any errors you have heard with the class. Ask students which of the discourse markers they have used in their conversations and congratulate them on their use.

Reading

8a Have students discuss in pairs what is happening in the cartoon and what the famous painting is (it's Munch's *The Scream*).

b Have students read the article and answer questions 1–4. Check answers with the class.

Answers: 1. Officials thought the painting was so famous that it wouldn't be stolen. **2.** Paintings by famous artists Vermeer and Gainsborough. The paintings were stolen and treated badly by the thieves. **3.** He posed as a buyer for the J. Paul Getty Museum. He also had to learn everything about the paintings. He even memorized the patterns of wax droplets left on one version of the painting. **4.** An art thief. He stole paintings for the love of art, not money.

9 Have students discuss questions 1–4 with a partner. Monitor conversations. Ask different groups to share their ideas with the class. Write errors on the board and ask students to correct them.

10a Have students answer questions 1 and 2 about the word *thug*. Check answers.

Answers: 1. *thug*: a violent person who may attack people **2.** They're called art thieves, and the negative connotation of the word *thieves* helps one to guess that *thug* is a negative word.

b With their dictionaries students answer the same questions about the words and phrases. Then drill the words with the class.

Answers: mastermind: to organize a complicated plan aesthetes: people who know about and appreciate beautiful art objects, like paintings, sculpture, etc. hideout: a place where you can hide track down: find, after searching for a long time stuffed: pushed roughly into a small space crack a case: solve a case (informal) haul: amount of things that have been stolen

OPTIONAL EXTENSION

Give students the website address for the National Portrait Gallery in London (http://www.npg.org.uk/) or for the Smithsonian's National Portrait Gallery in Washington, D.C. (http://www.npg.si.edu/). For homework ask students to look at one of the websites and find three portraits that they like. In the following lesson, students mingle and tell other students about the three portraits they have chosen and why they would recommend the other students see them.

LESSON 3 pp. 110–112

CAN DO respond to hypothetical questions
GRAMMAR unreal past

Summary: In this lesson, students write a short paragraph about a photograph. Then they talk about cameras and photography. Students go on to read different articles and share information about these articles with a partner. Through the context of what they have read, students look at the unreal past. Then they look at expressions used for responding to hypothetical questions. Students finish the lesson by writing a story.

OPTIONAL WARM UP

In the previous lesson, ask students to bring a photo that is important to them to the next class. Write these questions on the board: *Who took the photo? Where were you? Who were you with? What time of day was it? What were you doing? How old were you? Why is this photo important to you?* Have students tell a partner about the photo, using the questions on the board. Ask different students to explain to the class why the photo is so important to their partners.

Writing

1a Focus students' attention on the three photos. Tell students to imagine they are in one of the photos. Have them write a short paragraph about what they are feeling and doing in the situation shown in the photo. Monitor and check what students are writing.

b Have students read their paragraphs to the rest of the class. Then have them compare their impressions of the situations shown in the photos with what other students have written.

Speaking

OPTIONAL WARM UP

Ask students to brainstorm with a partner words and expressions they know that are related to either cameras or photography. Write correct words and expressions on the board.

2 In pairs, students discuss questions 1–2. Monitor conversations for interesting language the students use and errors which you can correct after Exercise 3.

Reading

3a Organize students into two groups, A and B. Refer Students A to the article on page 138 and Students B to the article on page 140. Have students read the articles and take notes. When they have finished reading, have students check their answers with the other students in their groups.

b Pair students so that Students A are working with Students B. Have students tell their partners about the main ideas in the article and their answers to areas 1–4 in Exercise 3a. Check the answers with the whole class.

Answers:
Article 1
1. The best time to do it: early morning or late afternoon **2. Stories:** N/A
3. The local culture: ask before photographing, take time to get to know the local culture, learn a few words of the language **4. Learning from the professionals:** spend time looking through big coffee table books and magazines; watch for different uses of light, perspective, and color
Article 2
1. The best time to do it: it doesn't matter what time of day you write as long as you do it every day **2. Stories:** look for stories, find something unusual that has happened, look for a beginning, a middle and an ending; or find an original angle **3. The local culture:** interact with the local culture; talk to people, try the food, haggle in the markets **4. Learning from the professionals:** travel writers don't just see the normal things; they spot things most tourists don't see

OPTIONAL EXTENSION

Organize students into two groups, photographers and travel writers. In their groups, have students imagine a typical day in the life of this person and make notes about it. Then have them pair off with someone from the other group and describe their days to the other student. Then decide with the class whose typical day is more interesting.

4 Pair students so that Students A work with Students B. Give them time to discuss the questions. Then ask different pairs to share their opinions with the class.

Grammar

> **OPTIONAL WARM UP**
> Tell students that you had a problem today and they are going to guess the problem. Read aloud the following sentences to the class one by one: *If only I had woken up earlier. I wish I'd set the alarm clock. If only I'd got to the bus stop sooner. I wish I'd left the house sooner.* Have students try to guess the problem you had: *I missed the bus and was late for work.* Write the sentences on the board and focus students on the verb tense used (past perfect). Tell students that when we are talking about imaginary situations in the present we use the simple past and that when we are talking about imaginary situations in the past we use the past perfect.

5 Focus students' attention on the Active Grammar box. Have students read through the notes and complete the tasks. Check answers with the class.

Answers:
1. Examples from article 1: If only I'd taken a better picture, I wish I had a decent camera; from article 2: Ah, if only I were a travel writer, I wish I could live like that
2. (a) the present = *wish/if only* + simple past (b) the past = *wish/if only* + past perfect
3. Examples in article 1 introduction: it's high time you learned a few basics. article 2 section 1: it's about time you started—no excuses.
4. (a)
5. *It's high time / It's about time* + simple past
6. Example in article 1: In many cultures, people would rather you asked before photographing them Example in article 2: Travel writers would rather go to the jungle
7. *would rather* + (a) base form (b) simple past
8. Examples in article 1: Suppose you see a beautiful landscape article 2: . . . what if you could interview someone who lived in it . . .
9. *what if/suppose* + (a) simple past (b) past perfect (c) simple past

Direct students to the Reference section on page 135.

6 Have students complete the second sentences in 1–7 so that they convey a similar idea to the first sentences. Tell students to include the verbs in parentheses, but that they will need to change the tense. Check answers with the class.

Answers: 1. time we began **2.** offered you **3.** you didn't take **4.** I had entered **5.** I were **6.** choose *or* we chose **7.** time you finished (writing)

7 Have students complete the sentences so they are true for them. Monitor and check the sentences students are writing and help as necessary. Then have them share their sentences with their partners. Ask different pairs to share their sentences with the class.

> **OPTIONAL PRESENTATION**
> If you prefer a more deductive approach, use the complete grammar charts and explanations on the Reference page to present the concepts. (page 135)

Speaking

8a Have students discuss situations 1–6 in pairs. Encourage them to extend the conversations for as long as possible by asking each other follow-up questions. Monitor the conversations for errors and correct use of the phrases from the How To box.

b Have students think of two more hypothetical questions. Then have them ask a partner the questions, starting with *What if . . .* or *Suppose . . .* ? Read aloud important errors you have heard and elicit the corrections from the class. Congratulate students on their use of the phrases from the How To box.

> **OPTIONAL VARIATION**
> Have students write their two or more hypothetical questions on slips of paper and then collect them. Then have students choose a question and tell their answer to the class. The rest of the class then has to guess the question that they answered. Continue so that all students have a taken a question and told their answer to the class.

Writing

9 Focus students' attention on the words in the How To box and discuss with the class when people might use them. Have students choose one of the situations shown in the pictures in Exercise 8. Instruct them to write the story of what happened in about 150 words. Tell them to use at least four of the words/phrases from the How To box in their story. Monitor and check what the students are writing; correcting and helping where necessary. Ask different students to read their stories to the rest of the class.

LESSON 4 pp. 113–114

Unit Wrap Up
Review reinforce lessons 1–3
Communication collaborate on a proposal

Summary: In this lesson, students listen to how two popular products were developed. Students then present a proposal about a new product to the rest of the class.

Review

1

Answers: 1. a **2.** g **3.** b **4.** c **5.** e **6.** f **7.** d

2

Answers: 1. be honest **2.** kind **3.** As far as my work is concerned **4.** Regarding **5.** more or less **6.** In fact

3

Answers: 1. left **2.** know **3.** could **4.** went **5.** had gotten up **6.** run **7.** learned **8.** hadn't brought

4

Answers: 1. disappointing **2.** over the top **3.** heavy **4.** contemporary **5.** finest piece **6.** incredible

OPTIONAL EXTRA LISTENING

These audio tracks, activities, and audioscripts are available on both the *ActiveBook* CD-ROM at the back of each Student Book and on the *ActiveTeach* DVD at the back of this Teacher's Resource Book. The audio can also be found on the Audio Program CD. The audioscripts can also be found at the back of the Workbook. These listening activities can be completed in class or done as homework.

Communication

collaborate on a proposal

5a Ask students to discuss the photos and what they know or can guess about the products shown. Then have them read statements 1–6. Play audio 2.16 and ask students to listen and mark the statements *T* if they are true and *F* if they are false.

b Play audio 2.16 again for students to check their answers.

Answers: 1. F (He saw native people in the Arctic using the method.) **2.** T **3.** F (He sold the patent for $22 million.) **4.** F (It involved making multiple copies of patent documents by hand.) **5.** T **6.** T

6 Have students discuss questions 1 and 2. Monitor conversations and take note of errors for correction after Exercise 7b.

7a Organize students into pairs. Have students choose one of the business ventures or come up with an idea of their own. Then tell students to plan how they would "sell" the venture to the rest of the class.

b Have students write a short summary of the main ideas behind the business venture with their partners. Monitor and help them as necessary. Then have students take turns to present their proposals to the rest of the class. Encourage students listening to ask follow-up questions. Decide with the class which of the proposals are most interesting and which they would invest in if they could. Write any errors you have heard on the board. Have students discuss the errors with their partners and correct them. Finally, praise the students for any interesting language they have used.

OPTIONAL EXTENSION

For homework, have students write an advertisement for the product, service, or movie. Check the advertisements in the following lesson. Have students perform the advertisement for the rest of the class. If possible, record the advertisements on audio, video, or DVD so that students can see and judge their own performance.

NOTES

Notes for using the CEF

The Common European Framework (CEF), a reference document for language teaching professionals, was produced by the council of Europe as a means of ensuring parity in terms of language teaching and language qualifications across Europe. It has since increasingly become an accepted standard for English learners throughout the world. It can be downloaded as a PDF file for free from www.coe.int from the section on Language Policy. There is also a link to the site from the *English in Common* website: www.PearsonELT.com/EnglishinCommon.

The CEF recommends that language learners use a portfolio to document, reflect on, and demonstrate their progress. *English in Common* has a Language Portfolio, which can be downloaded from your *ActiveTeach* disc (at the back of this Teacher's Resource Book) or from the *ActiveBook* disc (at the back of each Student Book). Suggested tasks are provided at the beginning of every unit on the Unit Overview page.

CEF REFERENCES

Lesson 1 Can do: express a degree of certainty
CEF C1 descriptor: Can qualify opinions and statements precisely in relation to degrees of, for example, certainty/uncertainty belief/doubt, likelihood, etc. (CEF page 129)

Lesson 2 Can do: use colloquial expressions to explain your tastes
CEF B2 descriptor: Can adjust what he/she says and the means of expressing it to the situation and the recipient and adopt a level of formality appropriate to the circumstances. (CEF page 124)

Lesson 3 Can do: respond to hypothetical questions
CEF B2 descriptor: Can take an active part in informal discussion in familiar contexts, commenting, putting point of view clearly, evaluating alternative proposals and making and responding to hypotheses. (CEF page 77)

Additional Resources

Activity Worksheets and Teaching Notes—Unit 9

Photocopiable worksheets for this unit can be found on pages 150–155 and Teaching Notes can be found on pages 181–182 of this Teacher's Resource Book. They consist of games and other interactive activities for: Vocabulary, Grammar, and Speaking.

Extra Listening Activity—Unit 9

This activity is designed to provide students with additional opportunities to listen to and practice comprehension of spoken English. The audio can be accessed by clicking the Extra Listening logo on the Unit Wrap Up page in both the Student's *ActiveBook* (for independent student use) and in the Teacher's *ActiveTeach* (for classroom use). The audio is also provided at the end of the Audio Program CD. An activity worksheet can also be printed out from either the *ActiveBook* or *ActiveTeach*.

Extra Listening Unit 9—Audioscript

M1: Good afternoon. Today's art history lecture will focus on a controversial topic, "graffiti art." I am aware that many people, and most police and public officials, consider graffiti to be a form of vandalism, a crime that should be punished. Frankly, if someone's name in black spray paint appeared on my freshly painted garage door, I would probably agree and be very annoyed. However, as an art historian, I have a broader view of the subject. I think that it's high time for us to start appreciating that art is found all around us, and not only in museums.

Graffiti is not, in fact, new. It has existed for at least 2,500 years, with examples commonly found on ancient Egyptian temples and on the walls of buildings in Pompeii and Rome, including Latin curses and political slogans. At any rate, modern graffiti art began in the United States in the late 1960's, with the invention of permanent markers and spray paint. Some people believe that it started as a way to express political and social anger, a part of hip hop culture, and is closely related to rap music.

Although it may have started as a form of rebellion, graffiti has crossed over into the mainstream art world. Exclusive galleries in Europe have shown works on canvas by graffitists. Artists you may have heard of include Keith Haring, whose designs on t-shirts and bags had first been seen spray-painted on city walls, and the French crew 123Klan, a group of artists that has produced logos, illustrations, and designs for Nike, Coca Cola, and Sony among other corporations. I think you'll agree that that is definitely mainstream!

(continued on next page)

I see that some of you are shaking your heads. Let me backtrack for a minute. Not all graffiti is art, of course. In the early days, teens simply sprayed their initials and part of their street address, all over subway cars, kind of a competition to say "I was here; notice me." We call this "tagging." At first the tags were monochromatic, in only one color. Later they became more elaborate and creative. But was this art? I would say, "Not yet."

In my opinion, graffiti became art when it became less spontaneous. Today's artists often start out with a sketch, decide on colors, and plot out the size of their design. They want to communicate feelings and ideas to as many viewers as possible, and so choose a public location, like the side of a building or highway wall. Of course, when a graffitist paints without permission, his or her work can be legally removed, sometimes by the next day. Still, just because the work is not hanging on a museum wall, doesn't mean it is not art.

To sum up, all new forms of art shock! Think of how your grandparents reacted to Picasso's cubist portraits. Or how their grandparents felt when looking at an impressionist landscape by Monet. That's how New Yorkers must have felt when they stepped inside of rainbow-colored subway cars back in the 1970s. . . I wish I had been there . . .

Tests

A **Unit 9 Test** is provided in the Test Bank as a Word file on the *ActiveTeach* disc. It includes discrete sections on: Grammar, Vocabulary, Reading, and Writing. An Answer Key is also provided. If you wish, this test can be easily modified to suit the particular needs of your class.

Extra Vocabulary: Confusing words

Extra Vocabulary activities for this unit can be found in both the Student's *ActiveBook* and in the Teacher's *ActiveTeach*, along with an answer key.

UNIT 10
Expressing feelings

Unit Overview

Warm Up Lesson	
LESSON 1	**CAN DO** discuss how feelings affect you **GRAMMAR** modals (and verbs with similar meanings) **VOCABULARY** outlook and attitude
LESSON 2	**CAN DO** make guesses about imaginary situations **GRAMMAR** modals of deduction (past and present) **VOCABULARY** strong feelings
LESSON 3	**CAN DO** describe a childhood memory **GRAMMAR** uses of *would*
LESSON 4	**Unit Wrap Up** **Review** reinforce lessons 1–3 **Communication** express strong feelings about an issue
Grammar and Vocabulary Reference Charts	

OPTIONAL LANGUAGE PORTFOLIO

(located in both the *ActiveBook* at the back of the Student Book and in the *ActiveTeach* at the back of this Teacher's Resource Book)

The Language Portfolio can be updated with new information as the student continues with his or her English studies and moves from one level of *English in Common* to another. Encourage students to review each section of their Language Portfolios and update information to reflect their progress as they continue to study and use English.

Teaching Resources

- **Workbook** pp. 76–83
- **Class Audio** CD2 Tracks 17–20
- ***ActiveBook*** Digital Student Book pages with complete unit audio plus Extra Listening Activity and Extra Vocabulary Study
- ***ActiveTeach*** Interactive whiteboard (IWB) software with video, Test Bank, and test audio

Warm Up p. 115

OPTIONAL WARM UP

Have students work with a partner. Ask them to discuss the last time they felt extreme emotions, such as anxiety, excitement, sadness, anger, etc. Encourage students to ask follow-up questions to find out more information when appropriate. Ask different students to explain to the rest of the class what they have learned about their partners.

1 Ask students to discuss in pairs how they think the people in the photos are feeling and why. Take note of any important errors the students make. Elicit responses from the class.

2 Focus students' attention on sentences 1–6. Have students check that they understand the meaning of the idioms in bold and then have them decide which idioms apply to the people in the photos. Tell students to use a dictionary to look up unfamiliar words if necessary. Then discuss with the class.

Answers: Photo A: He's "pleased with himself," probably because he just scored a point or won the match.
Photo B: They're at their wits end, possibly with worry about bills
Photo C: She's wound up because she's stuck in traffic. She should "chill out."
Photo D: He's "down in the dumps." Maybe he's having a rough day at work.

Ask students to match sentences 1–6 with sentences a–f. Check answers with the class.

Answers: 1. e **2.** c **3.** d **4.** a **5.** f **6.** b

EXTEND THE WARM UP

Ask students to work in pairs to think of famous people whose current feelings might be described by the idioms. You could collect pictures of famous people from magazines to help students think of examples. Have students write a list of the names of the famous people and show them to another pair who guess which idiom can be matched with the feelings of each famous person; for example, "You wrote *Derek Jeter* because he's over the moon about a home run he hit."

LESSON 1 pp. 116–118

CAN DO discuss how feelings affect you
GRAMMAR modals (and verbs with similar meanings)
VOCABULARY outlook and attitude

Summary: In this lesson, students listen to an interview about optimism and pessimism. Then they look at modals and verbs with similar meanings. Students go on to read about overcoming obstacles to achieve dreams and goals. They finish the lesson by talking about a dream or a goal they would like to realize.

OPTIONAL WARM UP
Have students discuss with a partner whether they think they are optimistic or pessimistic. Tell them to give examples. Then discuss as a class.

Listening

1 Ask students to discuss the questions in pairs. Then discuss the questions with the class.

2 Tell students they are going to listen to an interview with someone talking about optimistic and pessimistic people. Have students read sentences 1–5. Play audio 2.17 and instruct students to choose the correct phrases to complete the sentences. Check answers with the class.

Answers: 1. b **2.** a **3.** b **4.** b **5.** a

3 Have students discuss questions 1–4 in pairs. Ask different pairs to share their views with the rest of the class.

Grammar

OPTIONAL WARM UP
Write the following prompts on the board: *punctuality, language spoken, homework, study of English outside class*. Tell students that you want to make a list of rules for the class. Have them work in pairs to write a list of rules, using the prompts. Monitor for students' use of modals. Then have students compare their list of rules with another pair. Elicit responses from each pair and write examples of modals used by the students on the board. Discuss with the class how modal verbs such as *must* and *can't* are used to express obligation.

4 Have students discuss with a partner the use of the words in bold in sentences 1–12. Then discuss students' ideas as a class. Next, have them match the words in bold to their correct usage in the Active Grammar box. Check answers with the class.

Answers: 1. h **2.** b **3.** f **4.** a **5.** k **6.** j **7.** d **8.** e **9.** l **10.** c **11.** g **12.** i

Direct students to the Reference section on page 136.

5 Have students work in pairs to discuss questions 1–4. Monitor the conversations. Then open the discussion to the whole class. Write any errors you have heard in the board and encourage students to self-correct.

OPTIONAL PRESENTATION
If you prefer a more deductive approach, use the complete grammar charts and explanations on the Reference page to present the concepts. (page 136)

Vocabulary

6a Check with students that they understand the meaning of the phrases in bold in the questionnaire.

Answers: going through = experiencing **look on the bright side** = be optimistic **dwell** = to focus one's attention on **chances are** = it is likely **tend to** = have a tendency to **work out in the long run** = it will work out in the long term

Then have students complete the questionnaire by writing numbers from 1 to 5 in the boxes depending on how strongly they agree or disagree with the statements.

b Have them read the results of the questionnaire on page 143. Then have them compare their results with other students in the class. Tell them to discuss whether they agree with the rating they received or not.

Reading

7 Have students work with a partner to discuss whether or not they agree with the statement. Monitor and help students as necessary.

8 Have students read the article. Go over vocabulary students are having trouble with.

9 Have students work in groups to discuss the meaning of statements 1 and 2. Elicit responses from the class.

Speaking

10a Organize students into small groups. Have them think of a dream they would like to realize or a goal they would like to achieve. Have them make notes about the areas given. Monitor and help students as necessary.

b Have students tell their partners about their dream or goal and try to offer advice on how to fulfill or achieve it. Ask different students to tell the rest of the class about their partner's dream or goal.

NOTES

LESSON 2 pp. 119–121

CAN DO make guesses about imaginary situations
GRAMMAR modals of deduction (past and present)
VOCABULARY strong feelings

Summary: In this lesson, students listen to three people talking about the first people to see or experience something amazing and how they might have felt at the time. Then they study modals of deduction. Students go on to read a book review before looking at adjectives used to describe strong feelings.

Note: Macchu Picchu is a well-preserved ruin of an Inca city in Peru. Yuri Gagarin was the first human in space and the first to orbit the earth. Orville and Wilbur Wright were the first people to make a controlled flight in 1903.

OPTIONAL WARM UP

Ask students to work in groups to put the three photos on page 119 in order of excitement, with 1 being the most exciting thing to do and 3 the least exciting. Have students share their ideas with another group and justify their order.

Listening

1 Have students discuss in pairs what is happening in the photos. Tell them to talk about what it would be like to be in each situation and what problems there might be. Elicit responses from different pairs.

2 Tell students they are going to listen to three people discussing similar situations to the ones shown in the photos. Play audio 2.18 and ask students to answer questions 1–4. If necessary, play audio 2.18 again for students to check their answers. Then check answers with the class.

Answers: 1. Aircraft were not sophisticated—difficult to fly, physically and mentally—lots of calculations to do, how to control the landing. **2.** Would the landing be more like a crash? **3.** It was covered in vegetation and hidden. Now you can see it as soon as you arrive. **4.** Positive: thrill/excitement, awe of what he's experiencing, seeing Earth from space for the first time, the vastness of space; Negative: didn't know if he would get back home, alone and probably scared.

Grammar

OPTIONAL WARM UP
Bring a photograph to class. It can be any type of photo, the bigger, the better, so students can see it. Put a piece of paper in front of the photo and hold it up for the class. Ask students to speculate what is in the photo. Move the paper so that students can only see a small part of the photo. Have students discuss with a partner what they think they can see. Ask pairs what they think the photo shows. If students don't use a modal verb of deduction in their predictions, elicit *might* and encourage students to use it. Ask them if there are any verbs similar to *might* in order to elicit *may* and *could*. Continue slowly revealing the photo and have students continue making deductions until the whole photo is uncovered.

4 Have students answer the questions in the Active Grammar box. Check answers with the class.

Answers: 1. might, may, could **2.** can't, couldn't **3.** must **4.** *Must be* is about the present and *must have been* is about the past.

Direct students to the Reference section on page 136.

5 Ask students to note the difference in meaning (if any) between the two options in sentences 1–4. Check answers with the class.

Answers: 1. different: *can't* is a deduction about how he feels, *shouldn't* is a statement about how he should feel *normally does* is a statement about how he usually performs, *could've done* means it was possible for him to have done better **2.** same meaning **3.** different: *might be* is about the present, *could have been* is about the past **4.** same meaning

OPTIONAL PRESENTATION
If you prefer a more deductive approach, use the complete grammar charts and explanations on the Reference page to present the concepts. (page 136)

Speaking

6a Organize students into groups of three or four. Have students discuss with the other group members what they think is happening in each of the photos on page 142 and why. Encourage them to use their imaginations when looking at the photos. Ask different groups to share their ideas with the rest of the class. Decide with the class which group has come up with the best story.

b Refer students to the stories behind the photos on page 139. Have them read the stories and check if any of their speculations about the photos were correct.

Reading

OPTIONAL WARM UP
Write the following questions on the board: *Where would you normally see a book review? Do you often read book reviews? Why or Why not? How do you choose a book to read? Would you buy a book because you saw a good review?* Have students discuss these questions in groups of three or four. Monitor their discussions for any interesting language they use. Elicit responses from different groups. Draw students' attention to interesting words or phrases you heard while monitoring and discuss their meaning.

7 Organize students into groups. Have students read the introduction to a book review and discuss with their group what they think "some of the biggest highs" and "some of the biggest lows" might be. Ask different groups to share their ideas with the class.

8 Have students read the rest of the review and decide with a partner if statements 1–5 are true or false, and why. Have students compare answers with another pair. Check answers with the class.

Answers: 1. True **2.** False (it also covers stories of normal, unexceptional people who find themselves in exceptional circumstances) **3.** False (he says how responsible he felt "If we made a mistake, we would regret it for quite a while.") **4.** True **5.** False (it has a humorous tone)

OPTIONAL EXTENSION
Organize students into pairs. Tell Students A they are reporters from *Esquire* magazine. Have Students B choose one of the people mentioned in the article (Buzz Aldrin, Max Dearing, Craig Strobeck, or Geoffrey Petkovich). Give them five minutes to prepare the interview between the reporters and the interviewees. Monitor and help students where necessary. When students are ready, have them conduct the interview.

Vocabulary

OPTIONAL WARM UP
Before the lesson, look through some magazines and newspapers to find photos of faces showing strong feelings. Bring these to class to show the students and elicit any adjectives to describe feelings that they already know.

9 Focus students' attention on sentences 1–15. Have students put the adjectives in bold in the correct box in the chart. If students are not sure of the meaning of any of the adjectives, tell them to check them in a dictionary. Check answers with the whole class.

Answers:

1. happy	**2. unhappy**	**3. neither happy nor unhappy**
thrilled ecstatic delighted	miserable upset	indifferent uninterested
4. scared	**5. surprised**	**6. angry**
terrified petrified	taken aback flabbergasted dumbstruck	furious outraged livid

10 Focus students' attention on sentences 1–7. Have students discuss in pairs how they would feel in these situations and why. Encourage students to use the adjectives from Exercise 9 in their discussions. Monitor conversations for use of the adjectives and for errors. Then discuss as a class.

OPTIONAL VARIATION

Have students look at the different situations and write an adjective to describe how they would feel in each one. Tell them to write the adjectives in a different order from the order of the questions. Then have them swap their list of adjectives with a partner. Have students guess which adjective their partner has written to go with each situation; for example: "Would you feel dumbstruck if you were offered a job as a model for a clothing company in Milan?"

NOTES

LESSON 3 pp. 122–124

CAN DO describe a childhood memory
GRAMMAR uses of *would*

Summary: In this lesson, students listen to people describing childhood memories. They read an excerpt from *The House on Mango Street.* Through this context students look at the different uses of *would.* Then students read excerpts of stories about childhood memories and look at different expressions to describe a childhood memory. Students go on to talk about a childhood memory of their own. They finish the class by writing a paragraph about a childhood memory.

Note: Sandra Cisneros was born in Chicago in 1954 and started writing poetry while in high school. Her best-known novel is *The House on Mango Street,* which was published in 1984. She has also published short stories and poetry and has won literary awards for her writing.

OPTIONAL WARM UP

Write the following ages on the board: 4, 8, 12, and 14 years old. Have students discuss with a partner what they can remember about being each of these ages. Ask different students to share their memories with the rest of the class.

Listening

1 Focus students' attention on the situations in the box. Have students discuss with a partner how each of the situations made them feel. Monitor conversations for errors. Ask different students to tell the rest of the class what they have learned about their partners. Read aloud any important errors and discuss them with the class.

2 Tell students they are going to listen to different people talking about childhood memories. Play audio 2.19 while students listen and mark the topics from Exercise 1 that each speaker mentions. Check answers with the class.

Answers: Speaker 1 mentions moving, changing schools, making friends Speaker 2 mentions playing sports Speaker 3 mentions summer vacation, making friends Speaker 4 mentions summer vacation, playing games

OPTIONAL VARIATION

Organize students into groups of three. Have each student choose four of the topics in the box to listen for. Play audio 2.19 and have the students listen and mark which of their four topics are mentioned. Then have them share their answers with the other students in the group. Check answers with the class.

3 Focus students' attention on questions 1–6. Play audio 2.19 again and ask them to answer the questions. If necessary, play audio 2.19 again for students to check their answers. Then check answers with the whole class.

Answers: 1. She found it difficult to get along with other children because they knew each other and had already formed small groups of friends, and she felt "out of it." **2.** She learned to become very outgoing, energetic, and entertaining in order to make new friends. **3.** Having to run in wind, rain, and traffic. **4.** She talks about the hot temperatures when they got off the plane (the "wall of heat"), the smell of the air (a "wonderful smell"), and the color of the pool ("I remember the pool, and how blue it was"). **5.** The breakfasts took a long time ("breakfasts that went on forever") **6.** It made him feel happy, and free. He says "It was such a great feeling of freedom—something every kid should have."

Reading

4a Focus students' attention on the picture. Have students answer the questions. Then discuss as a class.

b Have students read the story quickly to check if their predictions from Exercise 4a were correct or not. Elicit responses from different students.

5 Have students discuss in pairs how the story made them feel and what they think life will be like the house on Mango Street. Check the meaning of words that students had trouble with. Encourage them to help each other with the vocabulary before they ask you.

OPTIONAL EXTENSION

Have students write a paragraph describing the place they lived as a child. Encourage them to use imaginative vocabulary and *would* where possible. Have them read their paragraphs to the class.

Grammar

OPTIONAL WARM UP

Write the following sentences on the board: *1. If I had more time, I **would** take up a hobby. 2. **Would** you please help me with my homework?* Have students discuss in pairs the different uses of *would* in the sentences. (sentence 1: imagined situation, sentence 2: polite request)

6 Focus students' attention on the Active Grammar box. Have students match example sentences 1–7 to the different uses of *would* in a–g. Check answers.

Answers: 1. b **2.** g **3.** f **4.** c **5.** d **6.** a **7.** e

Direct students to the Reference section on page 136.

7 Tell students to add *would* or *wouldn't* to sentences 1–6 to make them correct. Check answers with the class.

Answers: 1. If you **would** like to follow me, I'll show you to your rooms. **2.** I **would** have more time for work if you took care of the kids more often. **3.** When we were alone at home, we **would** always cook for ourselves. **4.** He **would** never help me with my homework. **5.** If only he **would** answer the phone, I could explain what happened. **6.** We hid the package in the cupboard so that she **wouldn't** notice it.

8 Have students complete the sentences in a way that is true for them. Then have them share what they have written with a partner. Encourage them to ask each other follow-up questions. Monitor conversations for the correct use of *would*. Write errors on the board and ask different students to correct them. Draw students' attention to examples of their correct use of *would* and congratulate them for using it.

OPTIONAL PRESENTATION

If you prefer a more deductive approach, use the complete grammar charts and explanations on the Reference page to present the concepts. (page 136)

Reading

9 Ask students to read the stories and decide on a title for each one. Have students share their ideas with the class and decide which are the best titles. Check the meaning of any words and phrases that students have not seen before. Encourage them to use a dictionary for vocabulary they don't know before explaining it yourself.

Possible Answers: 1. Childhood Sweethearts **2.** The Black Sheep **3.** Walking Tall **4.** Brotherly Love **5.** Hard Rain

OPTIONAL VARIATION

Put students in groups of five. Have them read one of the stories and think of a title for it. Then have them tell the others in their groups what they have read about and the title they have chosen. Have students read all the stories and decide if the titles chosen by the other group members were good ones. Discuss as a class.

10 Have students cover the stories and think of different ways of completing the phrases in the How To box. Elicit responses from different students. Then have them uncover the stories and compare their own expressions to the original ones in the stories.

Speaking

11a Have students think of two or three childhood memories that they can remember clearly. Have them write notes about their memories. Monitor and encourage students to use the expressions in the How To box.

b Organize students into groups of three or four. Have students share their stories with other students in their group. Monitor for correct use of the expressions from the How To box. Ask different groups to tell the rest of the class about the most interesting childhood memory they have heard in their group. Write errors on the board for students to correct and give praise for correct use of phrases from the How To box.

Writing

12 Have students write a paragraph about an early childhood memory. Instruct them to use phrases from the How To box while doing so. Then have them read their paragraphs to the class. Encourage students listening to ask follow-up questions. Ask them to think of titles for the stories they have heard. Then have students choose the title they like best. Write errors on the board and ask different students to correct them.

NOTES

LESSON 4 pp. 125–126

Unit Wrap Up
Review reinforce lessons 1–3
Communication express strong feelings about an issue

Summary: In this lesson, students review the unit's language. Then they listen to three people who are complaining, raving, or taking a stand on something. Students then complain about, rave about, or take a stand on an issue they feel strongly about.

Review

1

Answers: 1. The manager is likely to be angry about the situation. **2.** They're bound to call us this morning. **3.** I'm supposed to be there at 10:30. **4.** This can't be the only way out of the building. **5.** We might have time to chat before the meeting. **6.** They won't pay the bill until the dispute has been resolved. **7.** Should we wait for you outside the conference hall? **8.** He ought to bring his own laptop.

2

Answers: 1. can't have/must not have **2.** couldn't have **3.** might have been/could have been **4.** must have been **5.** must have/should have **6.** must have been **7.** must have been

3

Answers: 1. If **I'd** known, I'd have called you earlier. **2.** I wish she **wouldn't** always tell me what to do. **3.** Correct **4.** We left the keys in the office so you **would** see them when you got there. **5.** Correct **6.** Correct **7.** I told Marcella that we**'d** meet her outside the theater. **8.** My parents wouldn't **ever** have dreamed/**would** never have dreamed of sending me to private school.

4

Answers: 1. pleased **2.** aback **3.** delighted/thrilled **4.** minds **5.** tends **6.** upset **7.** end **8.** calm **9.** terrified **10.** worked **11.** thrilled/delighted

OPTIONAL EXTRA LISTENING

These audio tracks, activities, and audioscripts are available on both the *ActiveBook* CD-ROM at the back of each Student Book and on the *ActiveTeach* DVD at the back of this Teacher's Resource Book. The audio can also be found on the Audio Program CD. The audioscripts can also be found at the back of the Workbook. These listening activities can be completed in class or done as homework.

Communication:

express strong feelings about an issue

OPTIONAL WARM UP

Tell the class about something that you complain about. In pairs, have students share their "top five" complaints. Try to come to an agreement about the top five complaints of the whole class.

5 Check that students understand what the three verbs mean by reading the definitions. Ask students to talk about the last time they complained about something, raved about something, or took a stand on an issue.

6 Play audio 2.20 and have students decide whether these people are complaining, raving, or taking a stand on something. Have them take note of what the people are talking about and what their opinions are on the subjects. Check answers.

Answers: Speaker 1: raving about a great restaurant
Speaker 2: complaining about public transportation
Speaker 3: taking a stand about smoking in public

7 Tell students that they are going to complain, rave about, or take a stand on something. If students can't think of an issue, tell them to look at the pictures to help them. Give them time to make notes. Help students as necessary.

8 Organize students into groups. Have students take turns to talk about the issue they have prepared. Have students listening take note of the topic that students are talking about and a question they would like to ask. When students have finished talking, the other students in the group should ask them questions. Monitor carefully for errors and any interesting language the students use. Write errors on the board and encourage students to correct them. Finally, congratulate students on their efforts in this lesson and in the course as a whole.

Notes for using the CEF

The Common European Framework (CEF), a reference document for language teaching professionals, was produced by the council of Europe as a means of ensuring parity in terms of language teaching and language qualifications across Europe. It has since increasingly become an accepted standard for English learners throughout the world. It can be downloaded as a PDF file for free from www.coe.int from the section on Language Policy. There is also a link to the site from the *English in Common* website: www.PearsonELT.com/EnglishinCommon.

The CEF recommends that language learners use a portfolio to document, reflect on, and demonstrate their progress. *English in Common* has a Language Portfolio, which can be downloaded from your *ActiveTeach* disc (at the back of this Teacher's Resource Book) or from the *ActiveBook* disc (at the back of each Student Book). Suggested tasks are provided at the beginning of every unit on the Unit Overview page.

CEF REFERENCES

Lesson 1 Can do: discuss how feelings affect you
CEF B2 descriptor: Can convey degrees of emotion and highlight the personal significance of events and experiences. (CEF page 76)

Lesson 2 Can do: make guesses about imaginary situations
CEF C1 descriptor: Can qualify opinions and statements precisely in relation to degrees of, for example, certainty/uncertainty belief/doubt, likelihood etc. (CEF page 129)

Lesson 3 Can do: describe a childhood memory
CEF B2 descriptor: Can highlight the personal significance of events and experiences, account for and sustain views clearly by providing relevant explanations and arguments. (CEF page 74)

Additional Resources

Activity Worksheets and Teaching Notes—Unit 10

Photocopiable worksheets for this unit can be found on pages 156-161 and Teaching Notes can be found on pages 181-182 of this Teacher's Resource Book. They consist of games and other interactive activities for: Vocabulary, Grammar, and Speaking.

Extra Listening Activity—Unit 10

This activity is designed to provide students with additional opportunities to listen to and practice comprehension of spoken English. The audio can be accessed by clicking the Extra Listening logo on the Unit Wrap Up page in both the Student's *ActiveBook* (for independent student use) and in the Teacher's *ActiveTeach* (for classroom use). The audio is also provided at the end of the Audio Program CD. An activity worksheet can also be printed out from either the *ActiveBook* or *ActiveTeach*.

Extra Listening Unit 10—Audioscript

F1: Hi, I'm Carol, a roving reporter for our local newspaper, *The Sun*. My topic for today is "Happiness." Would you be willing to share your thoughts and a memory or two with me?

M1: Sure. I'll be happy to.

F1: I've heard that one before!

M1: Sorry. Well, I think happiness is determined by your outlook on life.

F1: How so?

M1: Well, I tend to look on the bright side of things. For example, I don't particularly like my long commute to work, and I wish I had a higher salary, but I'm really happy to have a job! It took me a year to find one in my field after I graduated from college.

F1: Were you miserable while you were job hunting?

M1: Not really. I'm pretty much an optimist. I was sure that I'd find something sooner or later, and I did. Luckily, I was able to live at home with my folks while I job-hunted. And I'll be even happier when I've saved enough to move out!

F1: What is your earliest happy memory?

M1: Uh, I guess I was around four years old. We always went to my grandparents' house on a lake for a week or two in the summer. My father was trying to teach me to swim, in very shallow water, but I was terrified of getting my face wet.

F1: Mmm, I can relate to that. I'm still not a good swimmer.

M1: You should take lessons! Anyway, my father was at his wits end, trying to make me relax. Then he saw a school of small golden fish swimming by, and pointed them out to me. I wanted to see them more clearly, took a breath, and put my face in the water. I can still remember how pleased I was with myself when I realized I could do something that had frightened me. It was a good life lesson.

F1: And another memory, as you got older?

M1: Mmm. I have to think . . . Oh, OK. Of course! It was in college. Looking back, it's hard to believe that I had the nerve to try out for the basketball team. As you can see, I'm only 5'9"—not nearly as tall as most of the players. But I loved the game. Luckily, not too many people wanted to play that year.

F1: And?

M1: Well, the coach was impressed with my shooting ability. Actually, he was flabbergasted that I could make a basket from halfway across the court. It was the happiest day of my life when he put me on the team.

F1: Did you play a lot?

M1: Actually, no . . . I sat on the sidelines most of the time. But I learned a lot from him about coaching, and now I volunteer at a local school with special-needs kids. I have a great time with them.

F1: It sounds like you're a really positive person. Thanks for letting me interview you.

M1: You're welcome. Um . . .

F1: Yes?

M1: It would make me very happy if you'd have a cup of coffee with me . . .

Tests

A **Unit 10 Test** is provided in the Test Bank as a Word file on the *ActiveTeach* disc. It includes discrete sections on: Grammar, Vocabulary, Reading, and Writing. An Answer Key is also provided. If you wish, this test can be easily modified to suit the particular needs of your class.

A **Review Test** is provided in the Test Bank section of the *ActiveTeach* disc to assess students' cumulative knowledge. It includes descrete sections on: Grammar, Pronunciation, Vocabulary, Reading, Writing, and Listening. The audio for the tests is provided as MP3 files in the Test Bank section of the ActiveTeach. The audio is also provided at the end of the Audio Program CD. Audioscripts are available on the *ActiveTeach*. If you wish, this test can be easily modified to suit the particular needs of your class.

Extra Vocabulary: Phrasal verbs and particles

Extra Vocabulary activities for this unit can be found in both the Student's *ActiveBook* and in the Teacher's *ActiveTeach*, along with an answer key.

Activity Worksheets

Photocopiable Masters

Contents

Preposition pairs

opt	distinguish	from	with
short	stem	to	about
lacking	rely	from	in
bother	benefit	for	on
nervous	appeal	from	in
succeed	riddled	about	of

1. Where to send your children to school is a difficult decision, but in the end we ______________ _________ private schools for both our kids.
2. The library has been ______________ _________ up-to-date resources ever since the college ran into financial problems.
3. To be honest, this book is ______________ _________ clear explanations and useful exercises.
4. I've never really ______________ _________ organizing my notebook, but I can definitely see the benefits.
5. At first I was ______________ _________ making mistakes when I was talking to a native speaker, but now I don't really think about it.
6. I find it almost impossible to ______________ American accents ______________ Canadian accents, though some people say the difference is obvious.
7. Juan's problems ______________ _________ his inability to listen carefully to what he's being asked, as well as the fact that he's kind of lazy.
8. I think I ______________ _________ my dictionary far less these days than when I first started learning English here.
9. Self-study doesn't really ______________ _________ me. I want to be in a class with other students and a teacher who can answer all my questions.
10. I tell students to proofread their work before handing it in, but I still get essays ______________ _________ errors.
11. He believes he would ______________ _________ studying more grammar, but in actual fact it's his vocabulary that's really weak.
12. Because of the fact she works with native speakers, she's ______________ _________ getting promoted in just six months.

Where's Jonny Star?

Reporter A

Where's Jonny Star?

People believe Jonny has checked into an exclusive clinic. (believe)

He is said to be suffering from chronic depression.

People think that he has checked into the Pine Hill Clinic. (think)

It is said that treatment there costs $4,000 a day.

People think the record company will cancel the upcoming tour. (seem)

It is thought that canceling the tour will cost the record company over $3 million.

It looks like his girlfriend, Suzy Lee, is back with her ex-boyfriend, actor Eddie X. (appear)

They seem to have gone on vacation together.

People claim the reason she's gone back to Eddie is that she hates Jonny's mood swings. (claim)

There appears to be a lot of tension between Jonny and Eddie.

People believe that X broke Star's nose in a fight recently. (believe)

It is claimed the reason for this is that Star said X's films are awful.

It looks likely that his relationship with Suzy is over. (seem)

It appears that this isn't the last we'll hear about the notorious Jonny Star.

Reporter B

Where's Jonny Star?

It is believed that Jonny has checked into an exclusive clinic.

People say he's suffering from chronic depression. (say)

He is thought to have checked into the Pine Hill Clinic.

People say that treatment there costs $4,000 a day. (say)

It seems as if/though the record company will cancel the upcoming tour.

People think that canceling the tour will cost the record company over three million dollars. (think)

It appears that his girlfriend, Suzy Lee, is back with her ex-boyfriend, actor Eddie X.

It's likely they have gone on vacation together. (seem)

It is claimed the reason she's gone back to Eddie is that she hates Jonny's mood swings.

It seems there is a lot of tension between Jonny and Eddie. (appear)

X is believed to have broken Star's nose in a fight recently.

People think the reason for this is that Star said X's films are awful. (claim)

It seems as if/though his relationship with Suzy is over.

It looks as if this isn't the last we'll hear about the notorious Jonny Star. (appear)

Perfect sports stars

Student A

Adam Samson—Soccer Player (age 33)
interviews Tanya Smith—Ice-skater

Questions

1. You've had a fantastic career. How did you feel about winning an Olympic Gold at just 18?
2. Was this the highlight of your career?
3. You've never won a World Championship Gold. Is this a major disappointment?
4. Why did you pull out of the National Championships last month?
5. Is it better now?
6. You said you might retire next year. Is this true?
7. How did you meet Tony Scott, your present coach?
8. Well, thanks for talking to me.

Answers

a. None really. I've scored more goals than any other midfielder in the league.
b. Well, I started young. I'll have been playing for 15 years next season.
c. To be honest, I'm not getting any younger, and I hadn't been getting along with the coach.
d. It's definitely something I've been thinking about.
e. Apart from the fact that I haven't been team captain at a World Cup, yes.
f. Basically, because he'd left me out of the last few games, and I'd been playing really well.
g. I've been surrounded by so many great players, and I've been able to learn so much from them.
h. It's funny, because I'd never won anything like that before, so it was a bit of a shock.

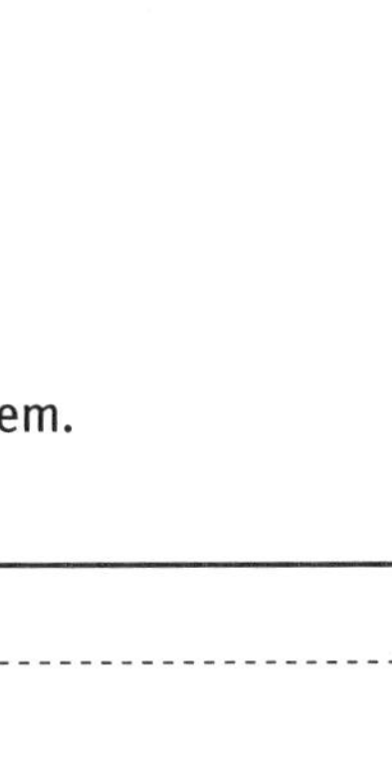

Student B

Tanya Smith—Ice-skater (age 26)
interviews Adam Samson—Soccer Player

Questions

1. Why did you quit the national team?
2. So, no regrets about retiring then?
3. There are reports that you got into a fight with the coach. Why?
4. So how long have you been playing professionally?
5. What's been especially important to your career?
6. Will you retire having fulfilled all your ambitions?
7. So how did you feel winning World Player of the Year Award two years ago?
8. Are you going to go into coaching?

Answers

a. Well, I've been going to a specialist, so it should be fine soon.
b. I'd only been skating professionally for three years, so it was kind of shocking!
c. Actually, I'd been spotted by a former skater of his, and later he offered to coach me.
d. No problem. It's been fun!
e. Well, I'll have been skating for almost 20 years next month, so maybe it's time for a change.
f. Kind of. I'll have been to six by next year, so hopefully I can win gold then!
g. Well, I've never done any better, so I guess it was.
h. Because I'd injured my ankle in training.

Collocation maze

START

set	achieveable goals	deal with	the top	a learning	experience	exceed
rivals	burning	problems	exceed	the potential	face	expectations
risk	challenges	face	an achievement	have	daunting	pursue
an ambition	make	potential	an element	of risk	difference	a dream
take on	a difference	rise to	forward	set	an opponent	take on
the right attitude	have	head	look	the right attitude	believe in	pursue
paid	for the top	ultimate	ambition	barriers	yourself	attitude
off	rise	to the challenge	face	a risk	head for	the top

FINISH

40 things to do

1. Throw a huge party and invite every one of your friends
2. Swim with dolphins
3. Skydive or a parachute jump
4. Be an extra in a film
5. Buy an around-the-world airline ticket and a backpack and run away
6. Grow a beard, shave your head, or grow your hair long
7. Give your mother a dozen red roses and tell her you love her
8. Send a message in a bottle
9. Ride a camel into the desert
10. Plant a tree
11. Learn to ballroom dance properly
12. Fall deeply in love—helplessly and unconditionally
13. Get a tattoo or get something pierced
14. Shower in a waterfall
15. Spend a night in a haunted house by yourself
16. Experience weightlessness
17. Drive across the US from coast to coast
18. Sleep under the stars
19. Learn to juggle with three balls
20. Run a marathon or do a triathlon
21. ....
22. ....
23. ....
24. ....
25. ....
26. ....
27. ....
28. ....
29. ....
30. ....

31. ....
32. ....
33. ....
34. ....
35. ....
36. ....
37. ....
38. ....
39. ....
40. ....

and **never ever**..

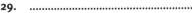

English in Common 6, Teacher's Resource Book

Prefix dominoes

"That's ***irrelevant***."	"I had no idea he was seeing Josie!"	"Yeah, I was totally ***unaware*** of it too."	"Why were you arguing with her?"	"Don't worry, it was just a little ***misunder-standing***."	"I'm not sure I want to continue."
"Why, do you feel ***unmotivated***?"	"I don't know what to do."	"Don't be so ***indecisive***."	"I can't think of one good reason to go."	"Yes, the disadvantages seem to ***outnumber*** the advantages."	"She's looking a little heavy these days."
"Yeah, she is a little ***overweight***."	"I've painted my living room white."	"Isn't that a little ***unimaginative***?"	"I think she'll do much better than me."	"Don't ***overestimate*** her."	"Do you think we'll finish before Friday?"
"Yes, but it'll require a ***superhuman*** effort."	"How was the meeting with the boss?"	"Terrible! He claims my work is ***substandard***."	"Do you think they deserved to lose?"	"Absolutely. They were totally ***outplayed***."	"He never ever says *Thank you*."
"I know. He's so ***impolite***."	"You look fed up."	"I'm overworked and ***underpaid***."	"Who do you want to win the election?"	"I don't care. I'm completely ***apolitical***."	"Is there anything he's not good at?"
"Not really. You could say he's ***multitalented***."	"I didn't think it was a particularly good performance."	"I agree. The beginning was particularly ***unimpressive***."	"He's a typical teenager."	"What, moody and ***monosyllabic***?"	"It seems too risky. I think I'll wait."
"Don't be so ***overcautious***. Just go for it!"	"What's he famous for?"	"He sailed around the world ***single-handedly***."	"He gets out of breath just walking upstairs."	"Yes, he's totally **unfit** to be a firefighter."	"But he was fired because he wore sneakers to work."

Life changing verbs

Student A

You left city life in the United States for a small Mediterranean fishing village, but after five years you have decided to return home. You had wanted to set up a business, but bureaucratic and legal problems made it impossible, and you are now broke.

feel like / don't mind / advise / warn / succeed in / dislike / can't stand / persuade / afford

I'm really excited about moving home.
You're looking forward to moving home.

I used to really hate spending so much time stuck in traffic.
You used to detest spending so much time stuck in traffic.

I absolutely loved living near the beach.
You adored living near the beach.

My parents persuaded me and supported my decision to come home.
Your parents encouraged you to come home.

I didn't get permission to open a café in the village.
You weren't allowed to open a café in the village.

The court said I had to pay the legal costs of the case.
You were ordered to pay the legal costs of the case.

In the end, I had to leave because of financial problems.
You were forced to leave because of financial problems.

I would advise you to rent a house rather than buy one.
You'd recommend renting a house rather than buying one.

I really think you should consider a big step like this carefully.
You're urging me to consider a big step like this carefully.

Student B

You and your spouse have recently moved from the United States to a cottage in rural Italy. It's in an isolated location, and it needs a lot of renovation work—it doesn't even have water or electricity!

force / urge / order / allow / recommend / encourage / detest / adore / look forward to

We still haven't managed to sell our house in the United States.
You still haven't succeeded in selling your house in the United States.

We didn't have enough money to move to somewhere like Tuscany.
You couldn't afford to move to somewhere like Tuscany.

We have never enjoyed having to spend winters in the United States.
You've always disliked having to spend winters in the United States.

People said we shouldn't move until we spoke the language better.
People advised you not to move until you spoke the language better.

It was my brother who gave us lots of good reasons to go.
It was your brother who persuaded you to go.

A friend said we shouldn't leave the property empty for a long time.
Your friend warned you not to leave the property empty for a long time.

It's not a problem not having running water right now.
You don't mind not having running water right now.

I hate people worrying about us unnecessarily.
You can't stand people worrying about you unnecessarily.

Would you like to visit us next summer?
Do I feel like visiting you next summer?

Compare it!

START	men women	cats dogs	football basketball	guns knives
summer winter	email letters	old age youth	shopping working	GO BACK FIVE
oranges lemons	book magazine	the beach mountains	bread cakes	airplanes ships
lions wolves	GO BACK SIX	fall spring	Russia China	golf tennis
bananas grapes	houses apartments	chocolate fruit	rock jazz	bicycles motorcycles
Brazil Venezuela	opera musicals	GO BACK FOUR	trains buses	snakes crocodiles
Picasso Dali	friends family	United States Mexico	movies plays	Jeter Ramirez
FINISH	GO BACK FOUR	tea coffee	The Beatles The Rolling Stones	republics monarchies

ONE
- slightly + *-er*
- almost the same as

TWO
- much/far/miles + *-er*
- considerably + *-er*

THREE
- not as ___ as
- not nearly as ___ as

FOUR
- not nearly as ___
- nowhere near as ___

FIVE
- I'd rather . . .
- I'd prefer . . .

SIX
- the + *-er* . . . , the more/less . . .
- the more . . . , the more . . .

Try not to say it!

Student A

cost of living • price • life • expensive	**magnificent** • terrific • wonderful • outstanding	**overrated** • opinion • think • better
crime rate • level • law • wrong	**climate** • weather • temperature • situation	**freedom** • liberty • choice • independence
nightlife • clubs • music • dancing	**off the beaten track** • tourist • place • go	**bustling** • busy • move • people
unspoiled • natural • change • beautiful	**tranquil** • peaceful • calm • relax	**health** • fitness • well-being • strength

Student B

a must-see • important • place • go	**stunning** • beautiful • gorgeous • fantastic	**pollution** • litter • waste • water
overpriced • expensive • costly • cheat	**standard of living** • life • level • quality	**vast** • big • huge • large
run-down • condition • poor • look after	**diverse** • different • variety • various	**packed** • crowded • full • tight
cultural • traditions • society • background	**employment** • jobs • position • boss	**watch out** • careful • problem • danger

Vacation nightmares

Put the following in order of how bad they are. Give the worst experience "1" and the least bad "15."	You	Partner	Group
1. You book a one-week vacation at a "romantic hideaway" in the countryside, but the cottage is 10 miles from the nearest village. To say it's primitive is an understatement; there is no running water, only a well.			
2. You arrive at your beachside hotel only to find that it is not fully completed. Although your room is very pleasant, you are basically staying in a building site with a lot of noise, dust, and rubble, and the pool is not yet finished.			
3. You realize after checking in that a large group of soccer fans are also staying at the hotel. They are very loud and rude. In fact, they keep you awake all night shouting and playing loud music.			
4. You are going on vacation for a week, but because of delays caused by an air traffic controllers' strike, you lose three days of your vacation. The three days are spent in airports.			
5. You are on a luxury vacation on another continent for two weeks. After two days, a neighbor emails you to say your house has been broken into and many things have been stolen. She reassures you that she is taking care of the situation.			
6. You've booked a beach vacation on an island that is usually hot and sunny at that time of year, but the weather is terrible. It's raining and windy, and, because there's not much to do other than go to the beach, you're getting bored.			
7. The city you are staying in has a dangerous reputation, and you are robbed at gunpoint on the first day. The thief took only a little cash, and the rest of the vacation is fine.			
8. You're staying at a tropical resort where there are swarms of mosquitoes, and you get badly bitten. There are also cockroaches everywhere.			
9. You love the beach but get a terrible sunburn on the first day. It's so bad that you can barely sleep at night, and you have to stay out of the sun for the rest of the vacation.			
10. You booked a long weekend in Paris, the "City of Love," but you have a big argument with your spouse on the first day about a very trivial matter. He or she refuses to speak to you until you get home.			
11. You go on vacation with a group of five friends for a week, but you cannot agree on which beach, restaurant, or places of interest to visit. You end up not doing anything you really wanted to do.			
12. You are staying in the jungle for a week, and while you are exploring a lake, a huge snake wraps itself around your leg and tries to pull you into the water. Luckily, your friends help you, and it finally releases you.			
13. You are stopped by the police for a minor traffic violation, but they think you are a dangerous criminal that they have been looking for. You spend 48 hours in police custody before being released.			
14. Your hotel catches fire one night, and although everyone escapes unharmed, the hotel is destroyed, and you lose all of your possessions. You are given alternative accommodations and are later fully compensated.			
15. While exploring the rocky coast of a resort, you don't notice the tide coming in. You become stranded on a sand bar. As the sea is rising, you're screaming for help, believing you're going to drown. Luckily, you're seen and rescued.			

Phrasal verb eliminator

Student A

		come		
come	up	catch	back	down to
get	pay	with	up	come
hold	across	on	by	up
		fix		

He arrived late again.
He turned up late again.

I don't feel socially comfortable here.
I don't fit in here.

You need to complete the form immediately.
You need to fill out the form immediately.

He was only ensuring that everyone knew the rules.
He was only making sure that everyone knew the rules.

I liked John from the moment I met him.
I took to John from the moment I met him.

I never thought I'd successfully complete the class.
I never thought I'd get through the class.

I know about the latest trends in the fashion world.
I keep up with the latest trends in the fashion world.

I need some time off work for a while.
I need to get away from work for a while.

Student B

		fill		
up	turn	in	take	away from
to	make	get	keep	out
fit	sure	up	through	get
		with		

It'll never become popular.
It'll never catch on

It's difficult to survive financially here.
It's difficult to get by here.

We're going to redecorate the house this summer.
We're going to fix up the house this summer.

I found an old diary by chance.
I came across an old diary.

She returned the money that she borrowed.
She paid back the money that she borrowed.

Who thought of this absolutely ridiculous idea?
Who came up with this absolutely ridiculous idea?

I tell you, it's essentially all about commitment.
I tell you, it all comes down to commitment.

I'm sorry I was delayed.
I'm sorry I was held up.

Two great hoaxes

Student A

The Surgeon's Photo

	a	was suspected of being fake by some, this had never been proven.
	b	made a rather simple 8-inch neck and head which they had stuck to a toy
	c	supposedly taken by a highly respectable British surgeon, Colonel Robert
	d	respectable surgeon as a front for the plot. The picture, while never being
	e	taken the grainy black-and-white picture one morning in April 1934 from
	f	maker grandfather, Duke Wetherell, were behind the hoax. The pair had
	g	authenticated, was never exposed as being a fraud; thus the pair had
1	h	In 1994, the defining image of the Loch Ness monster, which was
	i	been humiliated by a national newspaper in the past. Already known to the press,
	j	the shores of the loch as the creature was surfacing. Although the image
	k	pulled off one of the most successful hoaxes of the 20th century.
	l	submarine. Their motive was simply revenge, since Wetherall felt he had
	m	Wilson, was finally revealed to be a fake. The Colonel claimed he had
	n	and with a dubious reputation, Wetherell had had to use the
	o	Then, shortly before his death, a man named Christian Spurling confessed that he and his film-

Answers: 1. h 2. c 3. m 4. e 5. j 6. a 7. o 8. f 9. b 10. l 11. i 12. n 13. d 14. g 15. k

Student B

The Hitler Diaries

	a	Gerd Heidemann, who discovered them, claimed the diaries had been
	b	diaries were little more than poor quality and obvious fakes. Not
	c	speeches. There were even historical errors. Within two weeks of
1	d	In 1983, the German magazine *Stern* published extracts from what they
	e	to be genuine in April, 1985. However, it soon became apparent that the
	f	rescued from an air crash in 1945, kept safe for many years until recently being
	g	Konrad Kujai, a notorious forger responsible for creating them, and
	h	only were they written on post-war whitened paper, but some of the
	i	claimed were the diaries of Adolf Hitler. The magazine had paid $4 million
	j	entries had simply been plagiarized from a well-known book on Hitler's
	k	smuggled out of East Germany. While Heidemann was trying to find a
	l	Heidemann went on trial and were each sentenced to 42 months in prison.
	m	for sixty small books covering a period from 1932 to 1945. The journalist
	n	publication, *Stern* reluctantly admitted they had been duped and both
	o	buyer, he had them verified by leading historians, and they were declared

Answers: 1. d 2. i 3. m 4. a 5. f 6. k 7. o 8. e 9. b 10. h 11. j 12. c 13. n 14. g 15. l

Who sits where?

1 2 3 4 5 6 7 8 9

Compound Character Adjectives
- hard-working
- fun-loving
- single-minded
- self-sufficient
- thick-skinned
- stand-offish
- career-oriented
- level-headed
- absent-minded

Office Workers
- Claire
- Maria
- Joe
- Ann
- Mark
- Sara
- Martin
- Paulina
- Teresa

Student A

- The person who can take criticism is next to the door. ***(Start with this one)***
- Teresa sits next to a window.
- Sara is **level-headed**.
- The **hard-working** person has a desk closer to the window than Martin.
- The **absent-minded** person is next to the person who thinks their job and work are the most important things.
- The central desk belongs to the person who likes to have a good time.
- The person who is generally determined and focused person is in a corner.
- The **career-oriented** person is between the forgetful person and Mark.
- Paulina and Maria are next to each other.
- The person next to the water-cooler isn't very friendly.

Student B

- The person who doesn't panic has a desk nearer the window than Joe.
- Paulina is forgetful.
- The **single-minded** person is next to the **self-sufficient** person.
- The person who works 12 hours a day has a desk behind Sara.
- Martin is further from the window than Teresa.
- Maria is across from the elevator.
- The **thick-skinned** person is Mark.
- Claire is in front of Ann.
- The **fun-loving** person is behind Joe.
- The **stand-offish** person is Ann.

Sentence conversions

Student A

I felt tired, so I went to bed. *Feeling tired, I went to bed.*	**It's impossible to get him to listen to you.** *Getting him to listen to you is impossible.*	**She picked up the book and started to flick through it.** *Picking up the book, she started to flick through it.*
He was really intelligent, but it made no difference. *Being intelligent made no difference.*	**If you mix it with fruit juice, it tastes even better.** *Mixed with fruit juice, it tastes even better.*	**Since he had forgotten his ID, he wasn't allowed to enter.** *Having forgotten his ID, he wasn't allowed to enter.*
James, who was caught by the police, eventually confessed. *Caught by the police, James eventually confessed.*	**As they brought no food, they drew attention to themselves.** *Having brought no food, they drew attention to themselves.*	**The boy remembered the time and started to run.** *Remembering the time, the boy started to run.*

Student B

I saw the spider, so I screamed. *Seeing the spider, I screamed.*	**He hadn't studied, so he couldn't do any of the test.** *Not having studied, he couldn't do any of the test.*	**These machines, which are made in Germany, are very reliable.** *Made in Germany, these machines are very reliable.*
If you look after them well, they'll last you a lifetime. *Looked after well, they'll last you a lifetime.*	**They were dishonest. It was second nature to them.** *Being dishonest was second nature to them.*	**Michelle lost her balance. She fell over.** *Losing her balance, Michelle fell over.*
He got out of bed. He put on his robe. *Getting out of bed, he put on his robe.*	**The most difficult thing to do is to apologize.** *Apologizing is the most difficult thing to do.*	**Gary had spent all his money, so he had to go home early.** *Having spent all his money, Gary had to go home early.*

Literary critics

Critic A	Critic B
a. Yes, you're right, but did you know it depicted a fictional **character**?	**1.** Yes, I know, I was almost crying; and the plot is fascinating.
b. No? What's the problem with it?	**2.** FINISH Who are you calling **bookworm**?
c. That's the new one by A.J. Wolf, isn't it? You're not **hooked** on it then?	**3.** Absolutely, **I couldn't put it down!** And it really comes alive toward the end.
d. START I'm reading *Waiting for Decades* by C.S. Murphy at the moment. It's very **readable**, don't you think?	**4.** For starters, some of the characters are a bit **one-dimensional** and unrealistic. I don't consider Wolf a very good author.
e. You have to be in this job! So, see you later, **bookworm**.	**5.** Yes, but this one was a bit of a **farce**.
f. That's strange. He's written some critically acclaimed **bestsellers**.	**6.** Let's hope so, I've got three books to finish this week. Luckily, I'm an **avid reader**.
g. That's true. Anyway, what's next on your list? Something more **gripping** maybe?	**7.** Not at all. It's not what I'd call **a page-turner**.
h. Oh no! Don't tell me what happens at the end! It's such an incredibly **moving** story, isn't it?	**8.** Really? I thought it was **based on a true story**. At any rate, it's much better than *The Trial in Surburbia*.

Discuss the following questions in small groups.

- Are you an avid reader? How many books do you read a year?
- What was the last book you couldn't put down?
- Do you know any bookworms?
- Do you prefer books that depict real events or fictional ones?
- What's the worst book you've ever read? Why was it so bad?

I'd never do that!

You back into your neighbor's car by accident one night and damage it slightly, although your car is OK. You don't particularly like him. Would you tell him it was you?	Your friend is a vegetarian, and you've invited him to dinner, but the dish you want to make contains animal fat. Would you still make the dish knowing that it wasn't suitable for a vegetarian?	Your partner has gone to work, and you find his or her diary, which is full of intimate secrets and thoughts. Would you read it?
A friend of a friend sells computers. You desperately need a new computer, and she says she can get you a really cheap one. You know it's kind of "stolen" from the company. Would you still buy it?	Your bald male friend has started to wear a wig, and it looks ridiculous. People are laughing at him. Would you tell him not to wear it?	You ran into your best friend's daughter on the street smoking with her friends. She's only 12, but you get along well with the girl. Would you tell your best friend?
You're selling your house, but before you move out, the roof starts to leak. It's not raining much at the moment. Would you have it fixed or say nothing to the buyers?	Your fiancé or fiancée gives you a new video camera as a gift. However, you drift apart, and you both decide to break off the engagement. You're asked to return the camera. Would you?	You email your picture to a gorgeous person you met on the Internet. Would you mention you had gained 15 lbs. since the photo was taken?
You're a soccer player in a "must win" game. The coach tells you to target a rival player's recent knee injury. Would you do it?	You are late for an important interview. Running down the street, you see an old lady fall down. She seems OK, and there are other people around, but she may need an ambulance. Would you stop to help and be late for the interview?	You make an expensive mistake at work, but no one knows it was you. Your co-worker is blamed for it, and unless you say it was your fault, she will get fired. However, if you do, you might lose your job. Would you admit your mistake?

It's true.	**I'm lying!**	**It's true.**
It's true.	**I'm lying!**	**It's true.**

Metaphor snap

I'm going to become a doctor like my dad.	I don't know which direction to turn.	Next year I'll be earning twice as much and have lots more responsibility.
I want to get a job with some opportunities for promotion.	He didn't make me feel welcome.	I haven't been feeling very well recently.
He's so friendly and kind.	He knows exactly what he wants. In this case, it's a new job.	Our relationship goes from one extreme to the other. We're often arguing.

Dice of prediction

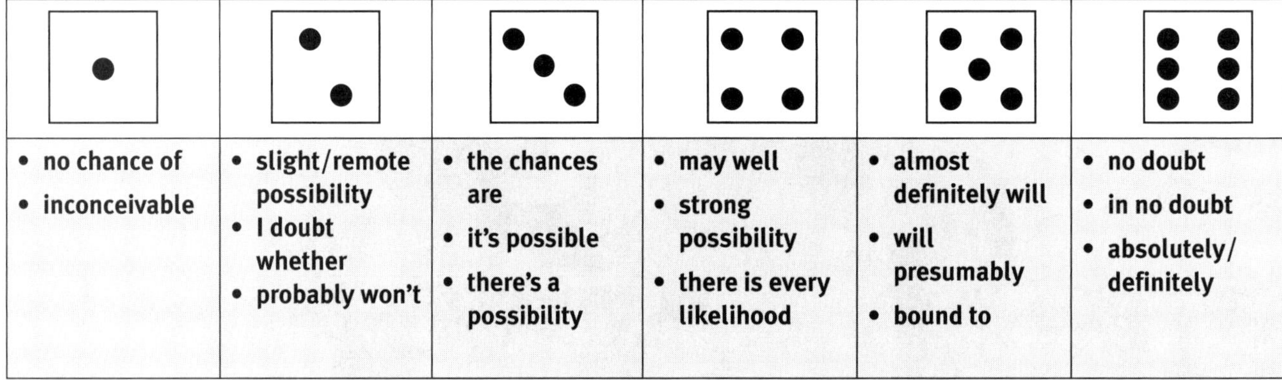

1	2	3	4	5	6
• no chance of • inconceivable	• slight/remote possibility • I doubt whether • probably won't	• the chances are • it's possible • there's a possibility	• may well • strong possibility • there is every likelihood	• almost definitely will • will presumably • bound to	• no doubt • in no doubt • absolutely/ definitely

START	see your favorite team win the championship	find a job or get a promotion this year	humans visit Mars by 2015	vote in an election this year	do a bungee jump (again)
travel to China	be sunny tomorrow	go skiing this winter	go to bed before midnight tonight	use public transportation today	hotels in space by 2025
win a contest this month	improve your English dramatically	move home this year	swim with dolphins (again)	go to the movies this week	buy a new cell phone this year
eat something later today	go to a wedding this year	see an alien in your lifetime	travel to Antarctica	rain tomorrow	read five books this year
make a speech this year	see the pyramids (again)	be ill this year	wake up early tomorrow	tell someone you love them today	have an operation in the next five years
FINISH	go to the park tonight	lose something important this month	buy a computer or car this year	take an exam this year	have a glass of milk today

Personal contract

I hereby promise myself that this time next year,

- I'll have definitely........................
- I'll probably have........................
- But I won't have ....

I can also truthfully state that in six months, two things I'll still be doing are,

- .... and ....
- And I won't be ....
- But I hope I'll be ....

I can honestly say that one day

- I'm going to ....
- And ....
- But I'm never going to ....

However, this weekend

- I'm ....
- And I'm ....

I also predict that when I retire

- I'll ....
- And I'll ....

Signed ....
Date ....
Witnessed by ....

Inversion conversion

He didn't speak to me once. *Not once did he speak to me.*	**I don't love her any longer.** *No longer do I love her.*	**He's smart but also kind.** *Not only is he smart, but he's also kind.*	**I have never seen such beauty before.** *Never before have I seen such beauty.*
I rarely go to the movies these days. *Rarely do I go to the movies these days.*	**I knew little about her family.** *Little did I know about her family.*	**I would definitely not go rock climbing.** *No way would I go rock climbing.*	**I realize I was wrong only now.** *Only now do I realize I was wrong.*
He gave me permission only when I begged. *Only when I begged did he give me permission.*	**There's no way I am apologizing.** *No way am I apologizing.*	**She didn't offer to help once.** *Not once did she offer to help.*	**We don't need that anymore.** *No more do we need that.*
It was difficult and very time consuming. *Not only was it difficult, but it was also time consuming.*	**I have never eaten such delicious pasta before.** *Never before have I eaten such delicious pasta.*	**He's rarely seen in public these days.** *Rarely is he seen in public these days.*	**We will know more about these animals only if we study them closely.** *Only if we study them closely will we know more about these animals.*
We had never had such a great vacation before. *Never before had we had such a great vacation.*	**We are beginning to understand its complexity only now.** *Only now are we beginning to understand its complexity.*	**You can leave only when you've finished your food.** *Only when you've finished your food can you leave.*	**There's no way I'm going to tell him.** *No way am I going to tell him.*

Complete these sentences so that they are true for you. Then discuss with your group.

1. Only now do I realize ________________________.
2. Never before have/had I ________________________.
3. Rarely do I ________________________.
4. No way am I ________________________.
5. Only when I am ________________________ will I ________________________.
6. Not once have I ________________________.
7. Not only am I ________________________, but I am also ________________________.

Technology crossword

Student A

1 T 2 J 3 U S
E P 4 D
5 C T N
H O
N D C
O 6 A N T I B I O T I C S 7 P
P T R
H 8 T E 9 G O
O A D
B 10 D I
E 11 G I G R G
E Y
T
12 S P A C E M I S S I O N S

Student B

1 T 2 J O 3 U R N A L S
4 D
5 C O M P U T E R N E R D O
C
U
6 A B S M 7 P
P E
8 T E C H N O L O 9 G Y N
T
10 V A
E 11 G E N E T I C E N G I N E E R I N G
R I
U E
12 S S S S

Too many superheroes

Scream and shout

Part A

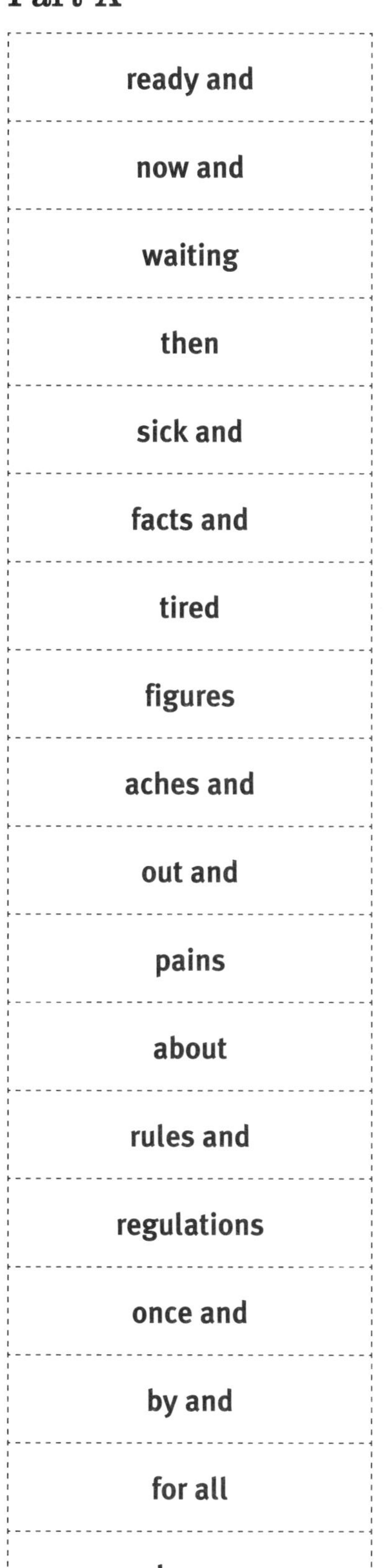

ready and
now and
waiting
then
sick and
facts and
tired
figures
aches and
out and
pains
about
rules and
regulations
once and
by and
for all
large

Part B

Sally and Justin have been on vacation and are about to check out of the hotel and go home. However, Sally disappeared for a while and Justin is angry because they are late checking out. Sally has just returned. You need to complete the dialog by filling in the blanks with word pairs that you find.

Justin: Where have you been? You're late!

Sally: None of your business. I've just been __________ and __________ (1).

Justin: What do you mean? It says here we were supposed to check out at 11:30. It's now 2:00, and we'll have to pay extra.

Sally: It's just __________ and __________ (2). It'll be fine; they won't charge us. Who cares, I was busy.

Justin: Well, I care, I'm __________ and __________ (3) of you just turning your phone off, disappearing, or showing up late.

Sally: Yeah, whatever! Don't tell me, you've been __________ and __________ (4) for three hours?

Justin: Actually, I have. So, where on earth have you been?

Sally: Gosh, you're so nosy, but if you really must know, I've been to the doctor's.

Justin: Again! I knew it! What unusual __________ and __________ (5) do you have this time?

Sally: Come on! I don't go that often, just __________ and __________ (6).

Justin: Yeah right! You mean every week!

Sally: Don't exaggerate. __________ and __________ (7), I'm quite healthy, but it's always better to be safe than sorry.

Justin: Look! For __________ and __________ (8) just admit it; you're a complete hypochondriac.

Sally: Not so! I read that 25% of the population go to the doctor's at least three times a year, so I'm completely normal.

Justin: Don't give me some of your __________ and __________ (9). It doesn't matter what you say, you are obsessed with your health.

Sally: Look, let's go and check out before they do actually charge us for another day.

Cleft sentence mingle

- What I can't stand is __________.
- What I really love is __________.
- What I really need in life is __________.
- The thing that upsets me most is __________.
- The reason I'm learning English is __________.
- The person who makes me laugh the most is __________.
- It's __________ who has helped me most in life.
- It's __________ that I most respect in people.

- What I can't stand is __________.
- What I really love is __________.
- What I really need in life is __________.
- The thing that upsets me most is __________.
- The reason I'm learning English is __________.
- The person who makes me laugh the most is __________.
- It's __________ who has helped me most in life.
- It's __________ that I most respect in people.

- What I can't stand is __________.
- What I really love is __________.
- What I really need in life is __________.
- The thing that upsets me most is __________.
- The reason I'm learning English is __________.
- The person who makes me laugh the most is __________.
- It's __________ who has helped me most in life.
- It's __________ that I most respect in people.

- What I can't stand is __________.
- What I really love is __________.
- What I really need in life is __________.
- The thing that upsets me most is __________.
- The reason I'm learning English is __________.
- The person who makes me laugh the most is __________.
- It's __________ who has helped me most in life.
- It's __________ that I most respect in people.

- What I can't stand is __________.
- What I really love is __________.
- What I really need in life is __________.
- The thing that upsets me most is __________.
- The reason I'm learning English is __________.
- The person who makes me laugh the most is __________.
- It's __________ who has helped me most in life.
- It's __________ that I most respect in people.

- What I can't stand is __________.
- What I really love is __________.
- What I really need in life is __________.
- The thing that upsets me most is __________.
- The reason I'm learning English is __________.
- The person who makes me laugh the most is __________.
- It's __________ who has helped me most in life.
- It's __________ that I most respect in people.

Conditional board game

FINISH	?	If I'd been born 50 years earlier . . .	I wouldn't be in this classroom now if . . .	I buy flowers or chocolates if . . .	I wish I had never . . .
					If it's nice weather this weekend . . .
I'll watch TV tonight if . . .	What do you wish you'd never bought?	If someone sneezes in my country . . .	What would you have done if you had been a king?	?	If the car hadn't been invented . . . (consequence now)
?					
If we turned green whenever we lied . . .	If electricity hadn't been discovered . . .	If a policeman stops me for speeding . . .	?	I always laugh if . . .	If Bill Gates hadn't been born . . . (consequence now)
					?
I wish I had . . .	What will you do when you retire?	What would you be doing now if you hadn't come to class?	?	How would life have been different if Elvis hadn't been born?	As long as you return it, I'll . . .
?					
If I had a time machine . . .	What's the first thing you're going to do after class?	What do you wish you'd never eaten?	If I think I'm getting a cold . . .	What would you do if you won the lottery?	?
					How would life be different if you'd been born the opposite sex?
START	If it hadn't been for Columbus . . .	What would you change about your appearance?	?	Do you wish you'd started learning English earlier? Why or why not?	The Titanic wouldn't have sunk if . . .

Business adverbials

Student A

fundamentally / essentially / broadly speaking / apparently / seemingly
surprisingly enough / up to a point / on the other hand / believe it or not
looking back / in hindsight / by and large

1. **Broadly speaking**, the last campaign was a success. (CORRECT)
2. Although there are differences, we are **in hindsight** talking about the same thing. (INCORRECT—*essentially*)
3. Of course there are advantages, but **on the other hand** we are taking a big risk. (CORRECT)
4. **Believe it or not**, our company was the very first one to introduce this feature. (CORRECT)
5. **Surprisingly enough** I wish I had invested in that company. (INCORRECT—*in hindsight*)
6. **Essentially,** the founder of the company left school at the age of 14. (INCORRECT—*surprisingly enough / believe it or not*)
7. **By and large**, we have excellent industrial relations. (CORRECT)
8. **Up to a point,** he has been offered a much better job by a rival company. (INCORRECT—*apparently, surprisingly enough, believe it or not*)
9. **Seemingly**, I agree with you that it would far too risky to change suppliers now. (INCORRECT—*fundamentally, essentially, by and large*)
10. **Apparently,** this computer uses a unique state-of-the-art processor. (CORRECT)

Student B

fundamentally / essentially / broadly speaking / apparently / seemingly
surprisingly enough / up to a point / on the other hand / believe it or not
looking back / in hindsight / by and large

1. What I am **essentially** saying is that it's not too late to reconsider our strategy. (CORRECT)
2. Although we only invested $2 million, **on the other hand** we made over $100 million over the next three years. (INCORRECT—*surprisingly enough / believe it or not*)
3. I think using a celebrity to endorse our campaign was, **in hindsight**, not the best option. (CORRECT)
4. There's a **seemingly** endless supply of skilled, cheap labor in the country. (CORRECT)
5. I'm not sure exactly what happened, but **by and large** the central office failed to tell the branch about the new specifications. (INCORRECT—*apparently, essentially, believe it or not*)
6. **Broadly speaking**, the key factor was that we misjudged the time it would take to build the plant. (INCORRECT—*looking back / in hindsight*)
7. **Essentially**, we are a supplier of sheet metal, but we also have plastics too. (CORRECT)
8. **Apparently**, our success is based on our knowledge of our customers' needs. (INCORRECT—*fundamentally / essentially*)
9. I agree with you **up to a point**, but I think we'll need to make a few minor modifications. (CORRECT)
10. **Looking back**, we are fairly widespread in Latin America, but we want to expand into Asia. (INCORRECT—*broadly speaking, by and large*)

Business crossword

Student A

1. Having a pension is important because you have to ______ ______ your future. (7, 3)
3. The amount I earn is based on what I sell. I'm ______ ______ ______. (4, 2, 10)
5. The place where shares are bought and sold is the ______ ______. (5, 6)
7. When banks lend money to someone, they ______ interest. (6)
9. If someone rich dies and leaves you money then you ______ ______ ______ ______. (4, 4, 1, 7)
11. When your business is not competitive there's a good chance it'll ______ ______. (2, 8)
13. The early stage of a business is the ______ ______ ______. (5, 2, 5)
15. If you have to process data and make calculations, you ______ ______ ______. (6, 3, 7)
17. If you spend a lot of money on taking clients to expensive restaurants, you entertain them ______. (8)

Student B

2. In some countries, you may have to ______ at the market. (6)
4. The Mona Lisa is ______. You can't imagine how much it's worth. (9)
6. Spending more money than you can afford is known as ______. (12)
8. If you want to own the whole company, you'll need to ______ ______ the other partners. (3, 3)
10. When life becomes difficult, ______ ______ ______ ______. (3, 5, 4, 5)
12. A business project can also be called a business ______. (7)
14. Another name for accounting is ______. (11)
16. If you need professional business advice, you might ______ ______ ______. (4, 1, 10)
18. If your business is insolvent, you'll have to ______ ______. (7, 10)

The philanthropist

Role cards

The Philanthropist
You are an extremely wealthy person who likes to use your vast personal fortune to benefit good causes. Every year you make a large donation to an organization or institution by holding a meeting where representatives present their case to you. You listen to each case in turn but like to encourage the other representatives to also ask each other questions and justify why their organization or institution's cause is the most deserving. After all the discussion has been concluded, you make your decision. You donate $5 million to the most worthy cause and $1 million to the second most deserving. The other two representatives receive nothing.

The Local Orphanage
You represent the local orphanage, which has been helping children for over 80 years. However, the orphanage is situated in a large old house with extremely high maintenance costs. Although you get some government money, you rely almost exclusively on donations to survive. If large amounts of money are not found soon, the orphanage will close. Despite the tragic circumstances in which children arrive, there are many success stories; many of your children have gone on to be successful politicians and TV celebrities. You believe this is because of the excellent level of care and guidance the children receive at the orphanage.

The Children's Hospital
You represent the local children's hospital which, over the years, has developed a reputation for excellent quality care. It has pioneered a range of treatments, especially for children with cancer and heart problems, and now helps children all over the world. Although the hospital is government funded, the present level of quality and care would be impossible to maintain without money from benefactors. The hospital is extremely popular with all of the former patients and their families and has many high-profile supporters.

The Soldier's Home
You represent a retirement home for soldiers. All the residents are elderly, retired veterans who all fought for their country in numerous wars or carried out peace-keeping missions. Many are war heroes but were disabled in the line of duty. Now, without family or relatives to look after them, are living their final years alone and in relative poverty. Although they receive retirement benefits, if it were not for this home there would be little recognition or gratitude for the sacrifice these men and women made for their country; they would die lonely and forgotten. The home gets money from the Department of Veterans Affairs, but it urgently needs modernizing.

The Animal Sanctuary
You represent a large animal sanctuary that caters to virtually all abandoned, abused, or unwanted animals in the country. There are camels and elephants from zoos that have closed, hundreds of cats and dogs, many of whom were abused by their owners, and even more exotic and difficult to care for animals like snakes and spiders. You have successfully found homes for many of the animals but many will live the rest of their lives in the comfort and safety of your sanctuary. Surviving entirely on donations, fundraising activities, and volunteers, the sanctuary is facing closure due to rising costs.

Money idioms

It was really expensive. *It cost a fortune.*	**I could sell it for a million dollars.** *It's worth a fortune.*	**I'm not very rich.** *I'm not well-off.*	**It was half price—a really good value.** *It was a bargain.*
Let's share the cost. *Let's split the bill.*	**The TV was used, so it was very inexpensive.** *The TV was used, so it was dirt cheap.*	**I don't have a lot of money.** *I'm a bit hard up.*	**The company isn't making a profit.** *The company is in the red.*
I'll pay 50%, and you pay 50%. *Let's split the bill.*	**His parents are really rich.** *His parents are worth a fortune.*	**That must have cost a fortune.** *That must have cost an arm and a leg.*	**I bought a brand new top-of-the-line computer.** *I splurged on a brand new top-of-the line-computer.*
He always owes people money. *He's always in debt.*	**It's hard to survive on $150 a week.** *It's hard to get by on $150 a week.*	**I can't come out. I have no money.** *I can't come out. I'm broke.*	**I have absolutely no money.** *I'm absolutely broke.*
My husband/wife kept all the money I won. *I didn't see a penny of the money (I won).*	**It was really, really cheap.** *It was a bargain.*	**The company has a lot of money.** *The company is worth a fortune.*	**I bought myself a new bike because it was my birthday.** *I treated myself to a new bike because it was my birthday.*

How do they do it?

Student A—*Add the correct articles. Then read aloud to Student B.*

David Blaine began his career with street magic, performing card tricks and illusions such as levitating or bringing dead flies back to life. Encouraged by his mother every step of way, he used small camera crew to record his act live in front of audience of everyday people. This act provided basis for his television specials of street magic, which defined his cool style and won him friendships with celebrities like Leonardo DiCaprio and Madonna. Magician later turned his attention to feats of endurance; these included being buried alive for week, spending 61 hours in block of ice, and standing on tiny platform at the top of 27-meter-high pole for 35 hours. Most famously, Blaine spent 44 days without food in transparent box above River Thames in London. However, stunt became the subject of much media attention due to mischievous minority. Eggs, sausages, water, beer cans, paint-filled balloons, and golf balls were all thrown at box, and he was even subjected to having hamburger flown around him by radio-controlled model helicopter. One man was arrested for climbing scaffolding supporting Blaine's box and attempting to cut power and water supply.

Student A—*Listen and check Student B's work.*

Escapologist Harry Houdini was born Ehrich Weiss on March 24, 1874 in Budapest, Hungary. He initially focused on traditional card tricks and was known as **the** "King of Cards," but he also did illusions. One of **the** most successful of these was performed in **a** London theater in 1901 with Houdini making **a** full-grown elephant vanish from **the** stage. He soon began experimenting with escape acts, and his big break came in 1899 when he met **the** showman Martin Beck. Impressed by Houdini's handcuffs act, Beck advised him to concentrate on escape acts and within months he was performing at **the** biggest theaters in **the** country. As Houdini's fame spread, he traveled to Europe and continued to develop his act, freeing himself from handcuffs, chains, ropes, and straitjackets, often while hanging from **a** rope or suspended in water, sometimes in plain sight of **the** audience. In 1913, **the** escapologist introduced perhaps his most famous act, **the** "Chinese Water Torture Cell," in which he was suspended upside-down in **a** locked glass and steel tank. Lowered into **the** water, Houdini would hold his breath for over 3 minutes before escaping from his handcuffs. Legend has it that he died from **a** punch to **the** stomach.

Student B—*Add the correct articles. Then read aloud to Student A.*

Escapologist Harry Houdini was born Ehrich Weiss on March 24, 1874 in Budapest, Hungary. He initially focused on traditional card tricks and was known as "King of Cards," but also did illusions. One of most successful of these was performed in London theater in 1901 with Houdini making full-grown elephant vanish from stage. He soon began experimenting with escape acts, and his big break came in 1899 when he met showman Martin Beck. Impressed by Houdini's handcuffs act, Beck advised him to concentrate on escape acts and within months he was performing at biggest theaters in country. As Houdini's fame spread, he traveled to Europe and continued to develop his act, freeing himself from handcuffs, chains, ropes, and straitjackets, often while hanging from rope or suspended in water, sometimes in plain sight of audience. In 1913, escapologist introduced perhaps his most famous act, "Chinese Water Torture Cell," in which he was suspended upside-down in locked glass and steel tank. Lowered into water, Houdini would hold his breath for over 3 minutes before escaping from his handcuffs. Legend has it that he died from punch to stomach.

Student B—*Listen and check Student A's work.*

David Blaine began his career with street magic, performing card tricks and illusions such as levitating or bringing dead flies back to life. Encouraged by his mother every step of **the** way, he used **a** small camera crew to record his act live in front of **an** audience of everyday people. This act provided **the** basis for his television specials of street magic, which defined his cool style and won him friendships with celebrities like Leonardo DiCaprio and Madonna.
The magician later turned his attention to feats of endurance; these included being buried alive for **a** week, spending 61 hours in **a** block of ice, and standing on **a** tiny platform at the top of **a** 27-meter-high pole for 35 hours. Most famously, Blaine spent 44 days without food in **a** transparent box above **the** River Thames in London. However, **the** stunt became the subject of much media attention due to **a** mischievous minority. Eggs, sausages, water, beer cans, paint-filled balloons, and golf balls were all thrown at **the** box, and he was even subjected to having **a** hamburger flown around him by **a** radio-controlled model helicopter. One man was arrested for climbing **the** scaffolding supporting Blaine's box and attempting to cut **the** power and water supply.

Whatever checkers

A				B
however much/many	on vacation	whatever	forget a name	whenever
get bored	wherever/whoever	lose weight	wherever/whoever	lose something important
whenever	go shopping	however + adjective or adverb	retire	whenever
celebrate my birthday	whatever	try to learn English	whatever	meet new people
whenever	wake up	however + adjective or adverb	miss someone	whenever
fall in love	wherever/ whoever	forget something important	wherever/ whoever	sing
whenever	fall asleep	whatever	laugh a lot	however much/many
C				D

Life on the edge

Student A

1. While descending Siula Grande in Peru, Joe and Simon, experienced climbers and best friends, had a dramatic, life-changing experience. **On reaching (1st line)**
2. he had managed to compose himself again, Simon, deeply traumatized, continued the down the mountain alone. **On reaching**
3. feeling very upset, Simon was absolutely exhausted and could do nothing but sleep. Three days passed, **by which time**
4. Simon and Richard were leaving, they heard a voice. It was Joe's. Were they imagining it? **As soon as**
5. cutting it would mean he would survive, it would mean certain death for his friend. **Impossible as**
6. Simon had cut the rope, Joe wasn't angry. **Hard as**
7. that disaster struck—Joe fell and broke his leg. Simon had to make a very difficult decision. **While**
8. it was, Simon decided to risk lowering Joe down the mountain single-handedly. **During (7th line)**
9. they were heading back down the mountain, they encountered a massive storm. **Despite**
10. this happened when Simon realized he was being pulled toward the crevasse too. **At this point**

Discuss: *How did Joe survive? Would you have cut the rope?*

Student B

a. Simon was feeling strong enough to leave base camp and return home. However, **just as**

b. they realized it was really him, they ran, overjoyed, to find their friend, who was in horrible shape, but alive. **Although**

c. the base camp, Simon told Richard, another climber, the bad news. **Despite (14th line)**

d. it would be easy for him to go on and get help, leaving Joe would probably kill him. **Hard as**

e. the summit a few hours earlier, the weather had looked fine, but **just as**

f. the now even more hazardous descent, disaster struck again when Joe fell into a crevasse. **Hardly had**

g. he had to make a split-second life or death decision to cut the rope or not. **Even though**

h. it was, Simon cut the rope, and Joe fell into the crevasse. **When**

i. the freezing temperatures, driving snow, and zero visibility, they continued slowly down the mountain. It was **at this point**

j. it was to believe, they had both survived and lived to tell this remarkable story. **(20th line)**

Discuss: *How did Joe survive? Would you have cut the rope?*

Ex-Presidents

Student A	Student B
 **Abraham Jones 1879-85** trustworthy, dignified, inspirational Jones was a reliable, honest, and sincere president who always conducted himself in a calm and serious manner and was deserving of his people's respect. He filled his people with passion and exciting new ideas.	**Abraham Jones 1879-85** 1. t..................................y 2. d................................d 3. i..................................l 
Rupert Mathias 1901-11 1. a...f 2. t..s 3. i...c 	 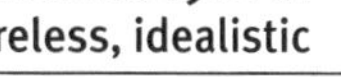 **Rupert Mathias 1901-11** aloof, tireless, idealistic Mathias was not the most popular president. He seemed to be an unfriendly and distant man. However, he never stopped working to improve the lives of his people. Critics say his beliefs and perfectionism were unrealistic.
Michelle Montague 1978-81 approachable, corrupt, down-to-earth The country's first female president was friendly and easy to talk to, but she accepted large amounts of money illegally from powerful people. Despite this, she'll be remembered for being sensible, practical, and easy to be with.	**Michelle Montague 1978-81** 1. a...e 2. c...t 3. d......... - .... - ....h  
Lucas Lopez 1956-59 1. n.....................................t 2. l.............. ....e 3. l.............. ....s 	 **Lucas Lopez 1956-59** nondescript, lacked drive, lacked gravitas Rather unkindly remembered as the dullest, most uninteresting president of the republic, Lopez also didn't seem to have much energy or desire to achieve great things. As a public speaker, what he said didn't carry enough weight or seriousness.
 **Serge Kozlow 1973-78** inspirational, untrustworthy, wavered in the face of problems Possibly the most unpopular president. Although he certainly excited people and gave them new ideas, he was fundamentally dishonest and unreliable. He was famous for hesitating and being indecisive when there were difficulties.	**Serge Kozlow 1973-78** 1. i......................................l 2. u......................................y 3. w......... in the .... of ....s 
Martin Duval 1959-68 1. c.......................................c 2. r.......................................e 3. u.......................................d 	 **Martin Duval 1959-68** charismatic, resolute, undignified The republic's longest-serving president had a powerful attraction and ability to impress people with extreme strength and determination. Often his behavior made him look silly, and he lost the respect of some people.

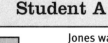

Manifesto

THE ____________________ PARTY'S TEN PROMISES

1

2

3

4

5

6

7

8

9

10

REMEMBER: VOTE ____________________

(SLOGAN) ____________________

Body idioms

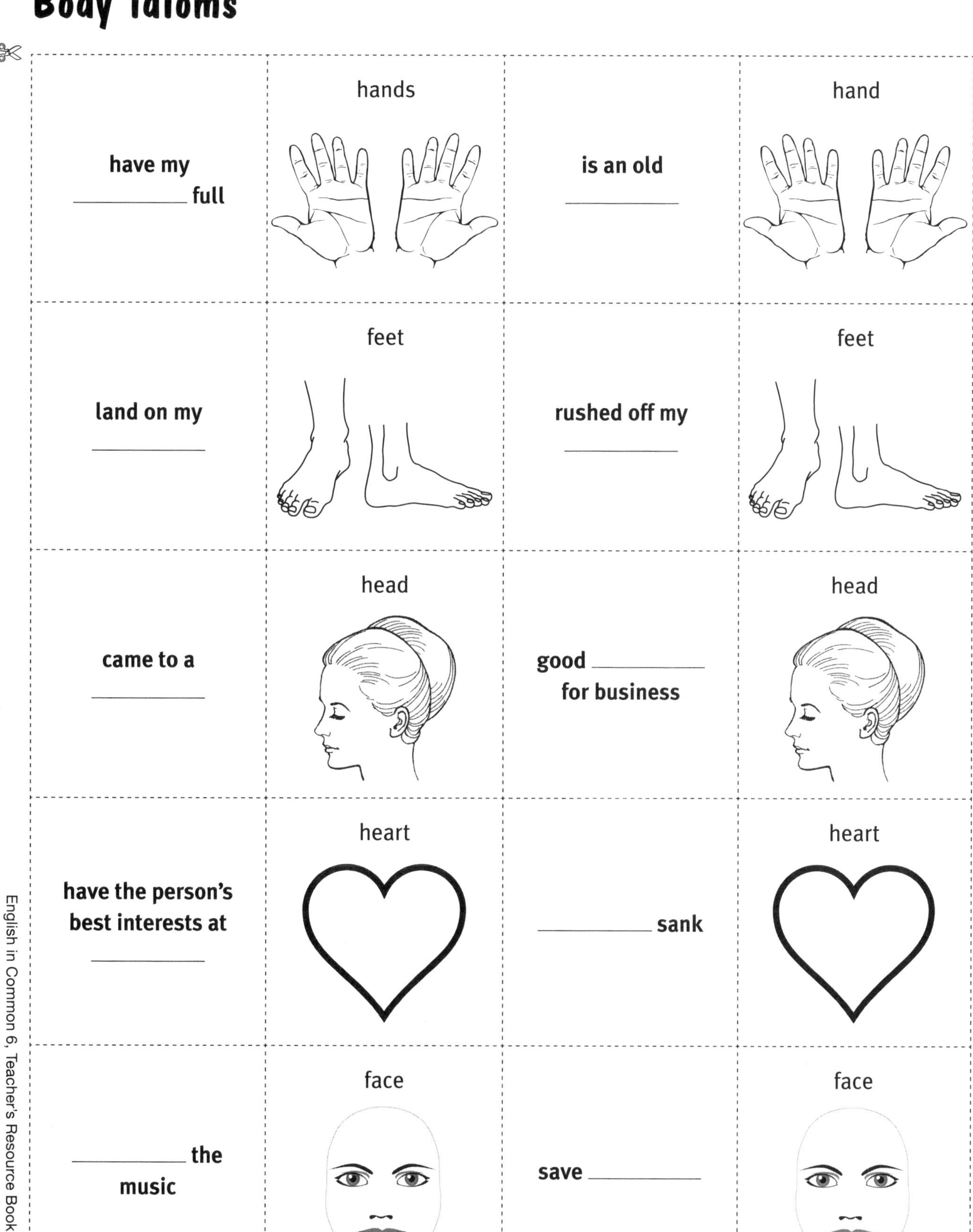
have my
_______ full
hands
is an old
____
hand
land on my
____
feet
rushed off my
____
feet
came to a
____
head
good _______
for business
head
have the person's
best interests at
____
heart
_______ sank
heart
_______ the
music
face
save _______
face

Amazing animal fact or fiction

	T	F	✔/✘
1. The blue whale has a heart that is as big as a large van.			
2. Mice that are kept in laboratories will run up to two miles a night on their wheels.			
3. The ancient Japanese thought that earthquakes were caused by a giant spider on which the Earth rested.			
4. Polar bears, who live in the Arctic, have black skin.			
5. Bats, who are very clean animals, groom themselves almost constantly.			
6. Male emperor penguins, which are responsible for incubating the egg, will fast for up to 130 days.			
7. Crocodiles have digestive juices that are so strong they can digest a steel nail.			
8. There are a number of animals whose tongues are blue, including the polar bear, giraffe, and chow chow dog.			
9. Hummingbirds are the only birds that can fly backwards.			
10. Beavers, which have recently been reintroduced to the UK, can hold their breath for 60 minutes.			
11. There are some species of salamander that can grow new limbs in place of ones that are lost.			
12. China and Vietnam are the only places in the world where you can find giant pandas in the wild.			
13. Giraffes, every one of whom has a unique pattern, stand up when they are sleeping.			
14. Butterflies, whose feet contain tiny sensors, taste their food by standing on it.			
15. There are some species of animal, like armadillos, opossums, and sloths, that spend up to 60 percent of their lives sleeping.			
16. Elephants are the only animal that can't jump.			
17. Reindeer eat moss because it contains a chemical that stops their body from freezing.			
18. The strongest animal in the world is the rhinoceros beetle, which can lift 850 times its own weight.			
19. The chameleon has a tongue that is twice as long as its body.			
20. A cockroach that has lost its head can live for up to nine days.			
21. Baby amarobia spiders eat their fathers when they are born.			
22. The ostrich has an eye that is bigger than its brain.			
23. It's only male mosquitoes that bite; female mosquitoes are vegetarians.			
24. Chimpanzees are one of the few mammals who can go bald as they age.			

Infinitive or gerund?

A GOAL!		START		B GOAL!

Student A	Student B
• I must remember calling my mom tonight. It's her birthday. ✘	• I tried not drinking coffee before going to bed, but I still couldn't sleep. ✔
• I really regret to get married when I was so young. ✘	• I was tired of driving, so I stopped getting a coffee. ✘
• Could you please stop tapping your finger? ✔	• I'll never forget to see the pyramids for the first time. ✘
• Working for us will mean to live abroad for at least three years. ✘	• She just didn't stop. She went on talking about her boyfriend all night. ✔
• I'm sorry I forgot to send you the information. ✔	• I meant to tell you but it just slipped my mind. ✔
• As I was driving home I saw Joe walk down the street. ✘	• As we stood there in the jungle, I could feel something to crawl up my leg. ✘
• After he finished college he went on getting a job in the city. ✘	• I dread thinking what might have happened if I hadn't found him. ✘
• I tried to call you, but your phone was turned off. ✔	• We regret to inform passengers that there will be delays to all services. ✔
• I hate telling you, but your work is simply not up to our standards. ✘	• We're busy, but we will try coming to your party. ✘
• I dread going to the dentist more than anything else. ✔	• The lights went out, and I remember falling on the floor, but nothing else. ✔

"As" board game

as little as	not as . . . as he expected	as large	**A** as much as $10	as hungry	as friendly	
as easy as				as possible	as	as many as
as often	as possible	as late as 2:00 A.M.	as little as	as strong		as few as
B as many as		not as . . . as he intended	**AS**	as little as $1		**C** as free
as few as three times		as many as	as possible	not as . . . as he wanted	as possible	not as . . . as they remembered
as high	as blind as	not as . . . as she used to be				as many as
	as few as	as possible	as many as **D**	as early as 6:00 A.M.	as funny	as heavy as

Animal jumble

1. These are animals with warm blood. ***slammma*** □□□□□□□

2. This happens when there's too much exploitation of the ocean's resources. ***ginovreshif*** □□□□-□□□□□□□

3. This is the trapping of animals and the use of their coats to make clothes. ***fuetrrathed*** □□□ □□□ □□□□□

4. This is the name for an animal that kills and eats other animals. ***reprotad*** □□□□□□□□

5. This is the name for an animal that eats meat. ***revoranic*** □□□□□□□□□

6. This is the place where animals are found in the wild. ***lathitabnurata*** □□□□□□□ □□□□□□□

7. This is a political movement that wants to defend animals from exploitation. ***limtganrhias*** □□□□□□ □□□□□□

8. This is the place where you keep some animals, for example, in zoos. ***gace*** □□□□

9. This is what animals do when they reproduce. ***dereb*** □□□□□

10. This describes animals and plants which are exciting and unusual, maybe because they are from a different country. ***citoxe*** □□□□□□

11. This is when certain animals like bears spend the winter in a deep sleep. ***rienbathe*** □□□□□□□□□

12. This is an area where wild animals or birds are protected and encouraged to breed. ***cranuasty*** □□□□□□□□□

13. This is an area where wild animals and plants are protected. ***presetanurerev*** □□□□□□ □□□□□□□□

14. This is the use of animals by companies who want to see the effects their products might have on people. ***leminnistagat*** □□□□□□ □□□□□□□

15. This describes a very rare animal or one that is perhaps on the verge of extinction. ***degerendan*** □□□□□□□□□□

16. This is an egg-laying, cold-blooded, animal like a snake or lizard. ***peliret*** □□□□□□□

Save our species

Ecologist A—The Baiji
China—Total Population 9

The Baiji is a type of freshwater dolphin. The distribution of the Baiji originally included not only the whole of the Yangtze River right down to the river's mouth, but also lakes. It's a graceful animal, with a long, narrow and slightly upturned beak. It is bluish-gray on top and ashy-white on its stomach. It weighs up to 440 lbs (200kg) and measures up to 8 ft (2.5m) in length. Groups congregate in small pools for five or six hours to catch small fish. They generally live in groups of three or four.

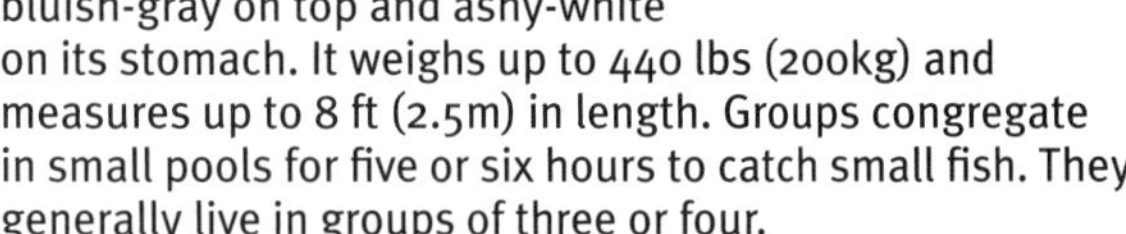

Recently found in one location, deaths from entanglement in or electrocution by fishing gear, collisions with ships and illegal hunting are partially responsible for the Baiji's decline. However, the damming of rivers, over-fishing of its prey and the increasing degradation of its environment by heavy river traffic are also important factors.

In the past, the Baiji had been protected by tradition, since the Chinese considered it to be an incarnation of a drowned princess. However, further planned dam projects leave it on the edge of extinction. You've studied these beautiful creatures for 5 years and have even had the awful experience of finding dead specimens that had been caught in nets.

Ecologist B—The Ivory-Billed Woodpecker
US—Total Population unknown/possibly extinct

The Ivory-billed woodpecker was once widespread in virgin forests throughout much of the southeastern United States and up the Mississippi and Ohio Rivers. However, little is known about this rare bird; it is one of the largest woodpeckers, 1½ ft (50cm) in length with a distinctive red crest. It strips the bark off dying trees with its powerful beak to get to insects and grubs underneath.

Truly on the verge of extinction, the bird had been declared extinct, as it hadn't been seen in the US since a 1944 sighting in Louisiana. However, in the 1980s sightings of the bird were made, and as recently as 2004 and 2005 there have been various unconfirmed reports in the Mississippi basin.

Decimation of its habitat by logging and the subsequent collecting of specimens have led to its current status as the rarest bird in the world and has inspired many people to prove either its existence or extinction. You have led two unsuccessful expeditions to find it but passionately believe it is still exists and can be saved. Indeed, the prospects for survival are good, because there is still suitable habitat.

Ecologist C—The Javan Rhino
Java / Vietnam—Total Population 25

The Javan rhino used to be widespread across most of Southeast Asia, but now there are only two known populations, both in national parks on Java and in Vietnam. Covered in thick gray skin with one 1 ft (25cm) horn, they are hairless except for their ears and tail tip, weigh 3,000–4,000 lbs (1500–2000 kg) and have a length of 10–11 ft (3–3.5m). Preferring tall grass and reeds in wet lowland rainforests near rivers, their diet consists of young plants and fallen fruit.

There are two major reasons for its decline. The first is the poaching of the rhino for its horn, which is highly valued in Eastern medicine and in the carving of traditional dagger handles in Yemen. The second reason is habitat loss due to clearing of lowland forest to provide agricultural land for a growing Javanese population.

The Javan rhino can actually tolerate disturbed forest. Despite this fact, the few surviving rhinos have been forced to retreat to less desirable upland habitats because of the intense pressure from human settlement in their preferred lowland habitat. You've been studying their habitat in Vietnam and know they can be saved if more are protected.

Ecologist D—Queen Alexandra's Birdwing
Papua New Guinea—Total Population 500

The largest butterfly in the world was once widespread in the rainforests of Papua New Guinea but is now confined to just the Owen Stanley Mountains in the north. Females are larger than males and can have a wingspan of 1 ft (28cm) and a body length of 3 in (7.5cm). They have brown wings with white markings, whereas the males have brown wings with blue and green markings and a bright yellow abdomen.

The female lays about 27 eggs on a species of toxic vine, and when the caterpillar (larva) hatches, it will only eat leaves from that plant. Fully grown from egg to adult in only one month, the butterfly has an average life span of three months. They protect themselves with a poison that comes from the vine plant.

The larva's dependency on one single food plant means this species has become especially vulnerable due to the habitat destruction caused by oil palm plantations. Collectors who prize the butterfly's size, beauty, and coloration are also playing a part in its disappearance, and it is now extremely rare. You've played a leading role in encouraging the local government to penalize those involved in collecting these butterflies.

Word formation race

Make people	Make abstract nouns	Make verbs	Make adjectives
impression *impressionist* **garden** *gardener* **apply** *applicant* **business** *-man/woman/person*	**possessive** *possessiveness* **realize** *realization* **embarrass** *embarrassment* **diplomat** *diplomacy*	**motive** *motivate* **broad** *broaden* **note** *notify* **critical** *criticize*	**self** *selfish* **tolerate** *tolerant* **hope** *hopeful* **practice** *practical*
Make people	**Make abstract nouns**	**Make verbs**	**Make adjectives**
economy *economist* **create** *creator* **defend** *defendant* **door** *doorman*	**clarify** *clarification* **kind** *kindness* **enjoy** *enjoyment* **literate** *literacy*	**straight** *straighten* **emphasis** *emphasize* **terminal** *terminate* **intense** *intensify*	**child** *childish* **please** *pleasant* **deceit** *deceitful* **history** *historical*
Make people	**Make abstract nouns**	**Make verbs**	**Make adjectives**
burgle *burglar* **assist** *assistant* **social** *socialist* **chair** *-man/woman/person*	**ruthless** *ruthlessness* **settle** *settlement* **moderate** *moderation* **accurate** *accuracy*	**sympathy** *sympathize* **simple** *simplify* **long** *lengthen* **regular** *regulate*	**magic** *magical* **dominate** *dominant* **fool** *foolish* **tear** *tearful*
Make people	**Make abstract nouns**	**Make verbs**	**Make adjectives**
inhabit *inhabitant* **perform** *performer* **gun** *gunman* **feminine** *feminist*	**agree** *agreement* **empty** *emptiness* **efficient** *efficiency* **modify** *modification*	**short** *shorten* **apology** *apologize* **donor** *donate* **horror** *horrify*	**green** *greenish* **respect** *respectful* **office** *official* **permanence** *permanent*
Make people	**Make abstract nouns**	**Make verbs**	**Make adjectives**
immigration *immigrant* **crafts** *craftsman/craftsperson* **illustrate** *illustrator* **piano** *pianist*	**redundant** *redundancy* **employ** *employment* **explain** *explanation* **dark** *darkness*	**category** *categorize* **light** *lighten* **differ** *differentiate* **class** *classify*	**help** *helpful* **snob** *snobbish* **distance** *distant* **economy** *economical*

People	Abstract Nouns	Verbs	Adjectives
-er / -ar / -or -ant / -ent -ist -man / -woman / -person	-cy -ation / -ization -ment -ness	-ate -ize -ify -en	-al / -ical -ant / -ent / -ient -ful - ish

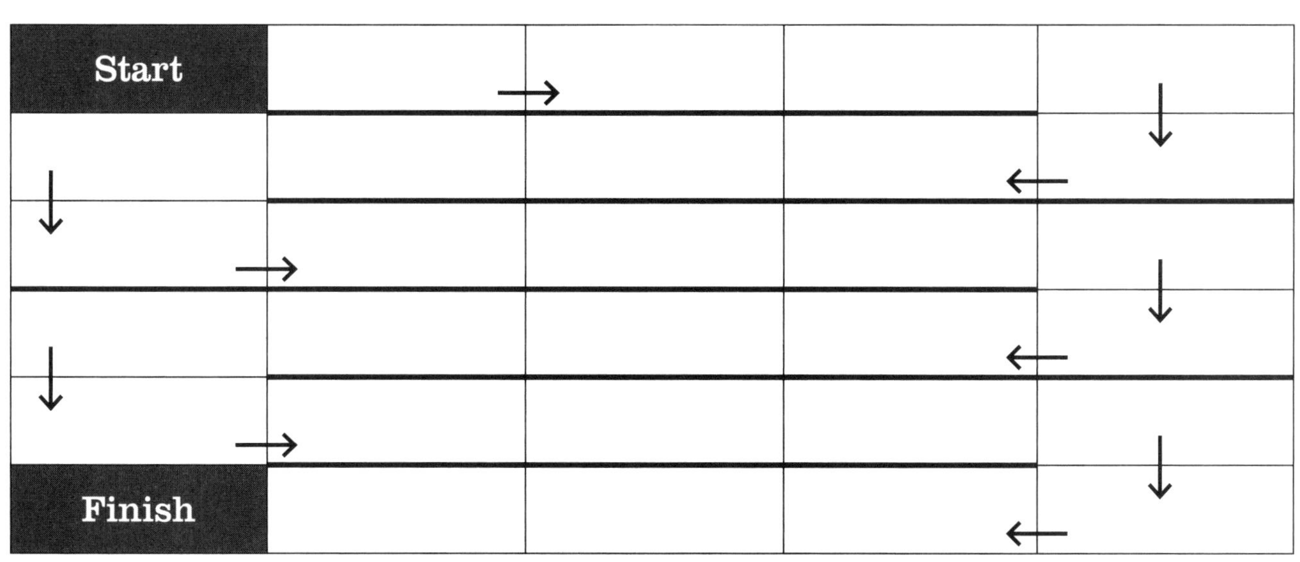

Fox and hound verbs

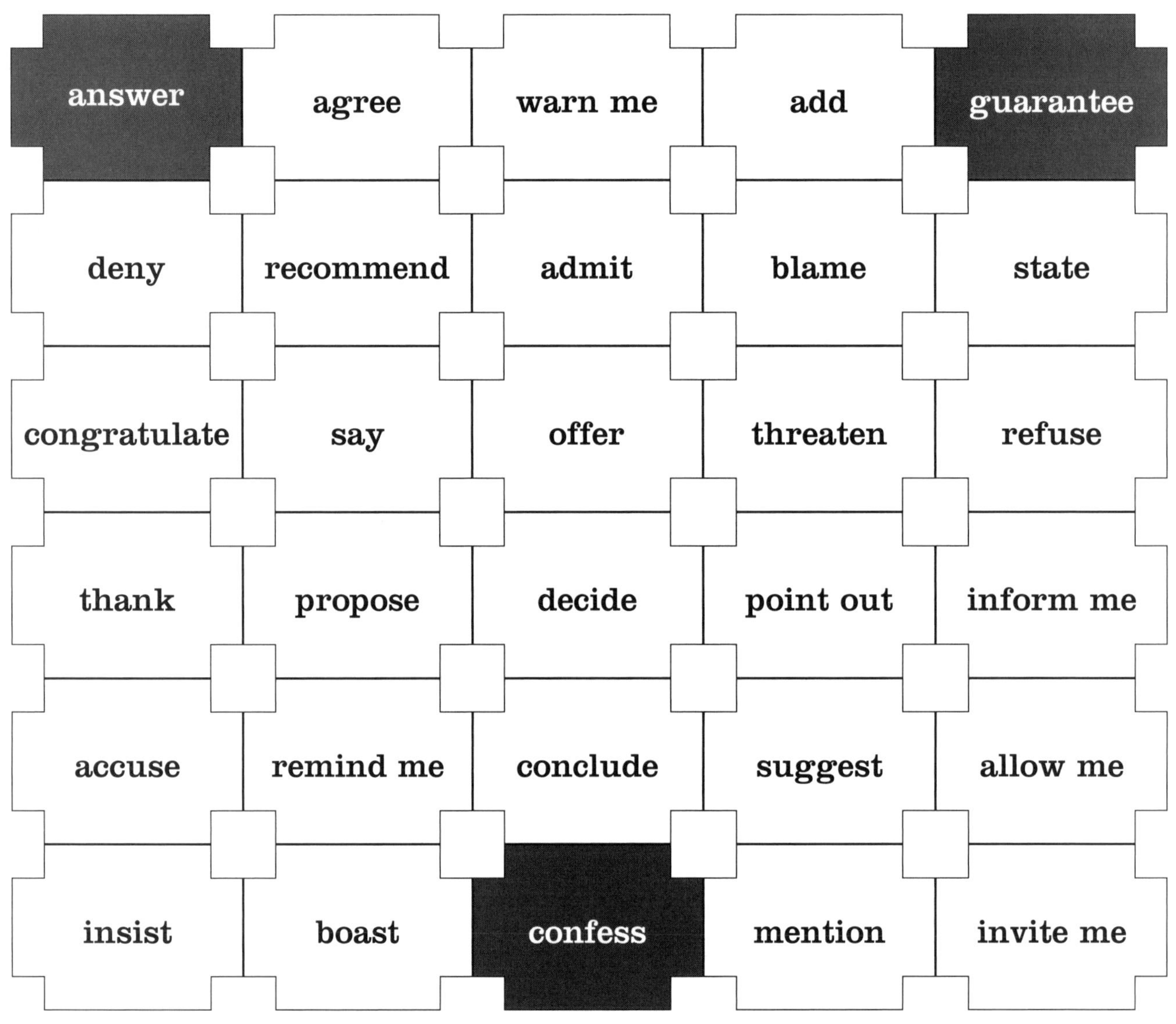

answer
agree
warn me
add
guarantee
deny
recommend
admit
blame
state
congratulate
say
offer
threaten
refuse
thank
propose
decide
point out
inform me
accuse
remind me
conclude
suggest
allow me
insist
boast
confess
mention
invite me

Referee's answers

answer **+ that**	agree **+ that/+ inf.**	warn me **+ that/+ inf.**	add **+ that**	guarantee **+ that**
deny **+ that**	recommend **+ that**	admit **+ that**	blame **for + gerund**	state **+ that**
congratulate **on + gerund**	say **+ that/ something to me**	offer **+ inf.**	threaten **+ that/+ inf.**	refuse **+ inf.**
thank **for + gerund**	propose **+ that/+ base form/+ gerund**	decide **+ that/+ inf./on + gerund**	point out **+ that**	inform me **+ that**
accuse **of + gerund**	remind me **+ that/+ inf.**	conclude **+ that**	suggest **+ that/+ gerund**	allow me **+ inf.**
insist **+ that/on + gerund**	boast **+ that/about + gerund**	confess **that/to + gerund**	mention **+ that/+ gerund to me**	invite me **+ inf.**

Continuous gamble

Decide if the following sentences are grammatically correct or incorrect and bet between $1 and $5 in the second column—leave the third column empty.	✓/✗	Bet	$
1. When I was hearing the noise, it was right outside the door.			
2. I wasn't believing anything he said in the meeting.			
3. I've been jogging every day for the past year.			
4. I tell you, life is getting harder every day.			
5. I'm disliking all the work I have to do.			
6. She's answering the phones today.			
7. You need to add some salt; it's tasting really bland.			
8. Changes are occurring.			
9. While I was watching TV, he was cooking in the kitchen.			
10. When I woke up this morning, it had been snowing.			
11. The ferry to the mainland is always leaving at 6:00 A.M.			
12. I was wondering if you could babysit for me this weekend?			
13. She was liking the job for the first month.			
14. I've been belonging to that club for a year.			
15. I've been meaning to call him but I haven't done it yet.			
16. People are asking for a better level of service these days.			
17. This box is containing new state-of-the-art navigational equipment.			
18. I'll have been working here six years tomorrow.			
19. I'm sorry, I'm doubting my ability to do this task.			
20. The thunderstorm is getting worse.			
21. I was studying German in Munich when I met Marlene.			
22. I'm finding the course really difficult and I may drop out.			
23. Sorry, I've been completely forgetting your name.			
24. I can't go. I'll be working on Saturday afternoon.			
25. He'll be appearing as Macbeth in the production.			
	Total $		

Fronting jumble

Student A

Put the words in the correct order and read them to your partner.

1. a | is | never | say | **The** | **trouble** | she | to | listens | word | I | . | ,
2. isn't | gentleman | **A** | **genius** | a | he | may | but | he | be | . | ,
3. he | couldn't | might | as | **Try** | her | to | he | persuade | leave | . | ,
4. I | though | asked | for | **Reluctant** | was | still | his | I | help | . | ,
5. is | matter | always | ask | you | of | **The** | **fact** | should | the | first | . | ,
6. like | wanted | never | do | I'll | something | **Why** | that | he | to | know | . | ,
7. fact | me | **What** | is | lied | I | can't | the | to | forgive | he | that | .
8. time | be | in | **The** | **question** | will | everything | ready | is | ? | ,
9. remains | no | **The** | **fact** | that | alternatives | are | other | there | .

Student B's answers

1. The problem is, there isn't enough room to sleep four people.
2. The question is, will they really believe my story?
3. The fact remains that I simply don't have the money.
4. What they told him I've absolutely no idea.
5. Hungry though they were, they continued working.
6. Try as she might, she couldn't forget what he had said.
7. Funny he may be, but mature he isn't.
8. Where they disappeared to nobody knows.
9. The fact of the matter is, your car was parked illegally.

Student B

Put the words in the correct order and read them to your partner.

1. is | **The** | **problem** | people | room | to | there | sleep | enough | four | isn't | . | ,
2. believe | they | my | **The** | **question** | really | is | will | story | ? | ,
3. money | the | don't | that | have | **The** | **fact** | I | remains | simply | .
4. absolutely | I've | idea | **What** | him | they | no | told | .
5. they | **Hungry** | though | were | working | they | continued | . | ,
6. as | forget | she | **Try** | might | had | what | he | she | said | couldn't | . | ,
7. mature | he | **Funny** | but | be | he | isn't | may | . | ,
8. disappeared | they | knows | to | nobody | **Where** | .
9. car | the | your | illegally | **The** | **fact** | is | was | matter | of | parked | . | ,

Student A's answers

1. The trouble is, she never listens to a word I say.
2. A genius he may be, but a gentleman he isn't.
3. Try as he might, he couldn't persuade her to leave.
4. Reluctant though I was, I still asked for his help.
5. The fact of the matter is, you should always ask first.
6. Why he wanted to do something like that, I'll never know.
7. What I can't forgive is the fact that he lied to me.
8. The question is, will everything be ready in time?
9. The fact remains that there are no other alternatives.

Have your say!

ONE	TWO	THREE	FOUR	FIVE	SIX
• It/They have had an influence on . . . • We can do without it/them.	• It's/They're a waste of space. • It's/They're underrated.	• It's/They're overrated. • It's/They've had big benefits for humanity.	• It's/They're a major source of . . . • It's/They're indispensable.	• It's/They've been disastrous for humanity. • It's/They've resulted in . . .	• It's/They've brought about . . . • We can't do without it/them.

the automobile	**the airplane**	**the bicycle**	**giant corporations**	**biotechnology**
censorship	**the internet**	**ID cards**	**the washing machine**	**immigration**
freedom of speech	**the vacuum cleaner**	**aspirin**	**democracy**	**the right to vote**
global warming	**the telephone**	**globalization**	**the computer**	**penicillin**
space exploration	**the TV**	**cloning**	**the radio**	**multiculturalism**

What's the big issue?

Part One

With your group discuss:

- What are the issues illustrated here, and what are their causes?
- What are the possible consequences and effects of the issues shown here?

1.

2.

3.

4.

5.

6.

7.

8.

9.

Part Two

Discuss with your group:

- Which of these things are an issue in your country?
- What can be done regarding these issues to make the situation better? Make a list of practical suggestions.

Academic crossword

Across

1. Produce or create ideas or interest *(1, verb)*
3. Suggest something without saying it directly *(1, verb)*
6. Emphasize something so people give it more attention *(1, verb)*
11. Emphasize something and show its importance *(1, verb)*
12. Present the other side of the argument *(4, adv. phrase)*
15. To be very exact *(3, adv. phrase)*
16. State the main points in short and clear form *(3, adv. phrase/verb)*
17. Introduce exact and detailed information *(1, adv. phrase)*
18. Introduce a good or important example *(1, adv. phrase)*
19. Introduce more information about what's been stated *(1, adv. phrase)*
20. Say something indirectly to subtly show what you're thinking *(2, verb)*

Down

2. Refer to a subject *(1, adv. phrase)*
4. Mention something in order to give someone more information *(2, verb)*
5. Carefully form an opinion about the amount, value, or quality of something *(1, verb)*
7. Finally consider all the information *(2, adv. phrase)*
8. Reach an opinion on the basis of information available *(1, verb)*
9. Judge something's quality or nature, can be similar to test *(1, verb)*
10. Emphasize a specific point *(2, adv. phrase)*
13. Emphasize another related point *(3, adv. phrase)*
14. Create or prepare something carefully, for example, an idea *(1, verb)*

Lots of prepositions

Part One

Place the following prepositions in the text below.

in in in in in in in in in for for for of of of of of of of of of without to to to with with with on by at at at at as

Charles Babbage was born ____________ (1.) Walworth, London in 1792. Known ____________ (2.) some ____________ (3.) the "Father ____________ (4.) Computing" for his contributions ____________ (5.) the basic design ____________ (6.) the computer, he died a largely forgotten man, disillusioned ____________ (7.) life. Educated ____________ (8.) Cambridge, Babbage was seriously disappointed ____________ (9.) the mathematical instruction available there and ____________ (10.) the end failed to graduate. However, he had tremendous ability and vision, excelling ____________ (11.) a variety ____________ (12.) fields including politics and philosophy. ____________ (13.) Babbage's time, complex calculations were done ____________ (14.) humans called "computers" who used numerical tables. ____________ (15.) Cambridge he saw the high error rate ____________ (16.) the people computing the tables and thus started his life's work in trying to calculate the tables mechanically. He began in 1822 ____________ (17.) the "Difference Engine," and ____________ (18.) completing it in 1832 he conceived ____________ (19.) an even better idea; a machine that could perform not just one mathematical task, but any kind ____________ (20.) calculation. This was the "Analytical Engine," which had some ____________ (21.) the characteristics ____________ (22.) today's computers. In spite of receiving much funding ____________ (23.) the project, he did not complete it, and this ultimately cost him his reputation. Babbage was an eccentric man who took pleasure ____________ (24.) counting even the most boring things. Obsessed ____________ (25.) fire, he once baked himself ____________ (26.) an oven ____________ (27.) 266°F (130°C) ____________ (28.) four minutes "without any great discomfort" to "see what would happen." Despite his many achievements, the failure to construct his calculating machines, and ____________ (29.) particular the failure ____________ (30.) the government to lend support ____________ (31.) his work, left Babbage ____________ (32.) his declining years a disappointed man ____________ (33.) the recognition ____________ (34.) brilliance that he deserved. He died ____________ (35.) his London home in 1871.

Final Score: ____________ out of 35

✂ -

Answers:

1. in 2. to 3. as 4. of 5. to 6. of 7. with 8. at 9. in (with) 10. in 11. in 12. of 13. in 14. by 15. at 16. of 17. with 18. on 19. of 20. of 21. of 22. of 23. for 24. in 25. with 26. in 27. at 28. for 29. in 30. of 31. to 32. in 33. without 34. for 35. at (in)

✂ -

Part Two

Without looking at the text, fill in the missing prepositions in these phrases from the text.

verb + preposition	verb + object + preposition	noun + preposition	adjective + preposition	prepositional phrases (beginning with a preposition)
excel ____________ conceive ____________	lend support ____________ take pleasure ____________	contributions ____________ recognition ____________	disillusioned ____________ obsessed ____________	____________ particular ____________ the end (eventually)

Look at the text again. Add other phrases to these categories.

Making small talk

Student A

You and your partner, Student B, have just met for the first time and are about to board a plane, but you have just heard that it's going to be delayed for a few hours. You are tired of reading your book and want to have a conversation with someone. Talk to your partner and try to keep the conversation going for as long as possible by discussing the following topics. Start with *travel*. Your teacher will tell you when to change to the next topic. You must use the phrases listed below. You should use them in as many conversations as possible, and as naturally as possible, so your partner doesn't notice you using them. Your partner has to do the same, so try and listen for the phrases they are using.

Conversation Topics

- **Travel:** the current trip, past trips, future travel plans, the price of travel, airport security
- **Weather:** recent bad or extreme weather, the weather when you were younger, climate change and pollution, favorite climate or weather
- **Crime:** young people's behavior, friends' experiences, recent news stories, punishments

Phrases:

- Regarding, . . .
- At any rate, . . .
- And yet, . . .
- In fact, . . .
- . . . kind of . . .
- As I was saying, . . .
- As far as . . . is concerned, . . .
- As a matter of fact, . . .
- . . . more or less . . .
- Anyhow, . . .

Student B

You and your partner, Student A, have just met for the first time and are about to board a plane, but you have just heard that it's going to be delayed for a few hours. You are tired of reading your book and want to have a conversation with someone. Talk to your partner and try to keep the conversation going for as long as possible by discussing the following topics. Start with *travel*. Your teacher will tell you when to change to the next topic. You must use the phrases listed below. You should use them in as many conversations as possible, and as naturally as possible, so your partner doesn't notice you using them. Your partner has to do the same, so try and listen for the phrases they are using.

Conversation Topics

- **Travel:** the current trip, past trips, future travel plans, the price of travel, airport security
- **Weather:** recent bad or extreme weather, the weather when you were younger, climate change and pollution, favorite climate or weather
- **Crime:** young people's behavior, friends' experiences, recent news stories, punishments

Phrases:

- On the other hand, . . .
- Anyway, what I was going to say was . . .
- Regarding . . . ,
- . . . sort of . . .
- As for . . .
- Actually, . . .
- Still, . . .
- At any rate, . . .
- To be honest . . .
- Mind you, . . .

It's all unreal

START	You prefer listening to opera and not hip hop.	Your wife or husband has to go away on business when it's your birthday.	You prefer to travel alone and not with others.	Your child is very late going to bed.
What if you can't get home tonight?	You regret the fact you had plastic surgery and it went wrong.	Suppose you went blind?	You regret the fact you weren't taught Spanish in school.	Suppose you'd been born in the United States?
You regret the fact you didn't visit the Louvre when you were in Paris.	What if it's raining all weekend?	You regret the fact you went to prison for not paying taxes.	What if you went deaf?	You regret the fact you didn't remember your anniversary (again).
Someone you like asks you to go dancing, but you can't dance.	Your best friend is getting married, but you are away and can't go to the wedding.	You prefer to arrive really early and not risk being late.	You've lost your glasses and can't find them anywhere.	You work too much and never see your family.
Your best friend always does embarrassing things at parties.	Your friend hasn't washed his hair for two weeks.	You fell in love and married the wrong person.	Your co-worker never does any work.	Sitting on a plane, the person behind you keeps kicking your seat.
Your friend wants to smoke in your house, and you don't want her to.	You are annoyed because your partner never listens to your advice.	The person sitting next to you on the train is talking loudly on his or her cell phone.	Your sister always tells totally unbelievable lies to impress people.	It's really late. You want your friend to go home, but he or she wants to stay.
Your spouse has been unemployed for 18 months.	What if you could really hypnotize people?	What if you'd been born 100 years ago?	You are late for a plane, and your spouse is still packing his or her suitcase.	FINISH

wish or *if only* + past tenses	*wish* or *if only* + object + *would*	*wish* or *if only* + past perfect	*It's high time* or *about time* + past tenses	*would rather* + simple past	*What if* or *Suppose* + past tenses

The gallery

1.

"Palette"
Sean Sweeney
1981

2.

"David and Lamp post"
Celia Holme
1990

3.

"Church on Hill"
Nora Musa
2011

4.

"Psycho"
Cameron Black
1993

Student A

You like the first and third painting, but you don't like the second and the fourth.

You must use these adjectives:

- figurative
- tranquil
- colorful
- disturbing
- spectacular
- stunning

You must use these phrases:

- It's not my kind of thing at all.
- I'm really/not really into his/her work.
- It's not my cup of tea.
- I've always admired his/her work.

Student B

You like the second and fourth painting, but you don't like the first and the third.

You must use these adjectives:

- abstract
- striking
- avante-garde
- traditional
- awful
- dull

You must use these phrases:

- It's not really my taste.
- I'm a big fan/not a big fan of his/her work.
- I can't relate to this kind of thing.
- He's/She's one of my all-time favorites.

Get me out of here!

1 START You lose your job in IT but get $5000 severence pay. Do you . . . go on vacation? **Go to 8** spend the money on getting retrained? **Go to 4** start your own business? **Go to 13**	**2** Although in the short term this solution works, there are too many people trying to steer the company, and its lack of direction results in it becoming unprofitable and going out of business. Bad luck! **Go to 1**	**3** The bank likes your business plan and is willing to give you a substantial loan, but the interest is high. Do you . . . take the loan? **Go to 9** try going into partnership with some friends? **Go to 6**	**4** You get retrained and find a new job quickly, but the salary isn't that great. Do you . . . take it? **Go to 7** wait for a better one? **Go to 12**
5 The job is challenging, and the money is better, but you don't like being away from your family. Do you . . . continue and hope it gets easier? **Go to 12** leave and start your own business? **Go to 13**	**6** The partnership seems to be working well. You have some lucrative contracts, but you need more office space and some more money. Do you . . . take a high interest bank loan? **Go to 9** involve more partners? **Go to 2**	**7** Things seem to be going OK, and you're offered a promotion in another branch, but this means only seeing your family on weekends. Do you . . . take it? **Go to 5** stay where you are? **Go to 12**	**8** While on vacation you have some ideas for new businesses. The options are . . . an IT company. **Go to 13** a hotel at the bottom of the ocean. **Go to 10** a gourmet pet food company. **Go to 11**
9 Although the business does win contracts and make money, the high interest payments are crippling, and you are eventually forced to close. You are totally broke. **Go back to 1 and try again.**	**10** Don't be ridiculous! How could that ever work? **Go back to 1 and try again.**	**11** Good choice. There's a growing market for gourmet pet food, but you need money. Do you . . . go to the bank and get a high interest loan? **Go to 9** ask your rich father whom you don't get along with? **Go to 20**	**12** Your branch experiences severe financial problems and is forced to close. **Go to 1**
13 You've always wanted to be the boss of your own IT company, but how do you finance it? Do you . . . get a bank loan? **Go to 3** use all your severance money and start a partnership with some friends? **Go to 6**	**14** This is a huge market, and your company soon develops a good reputation. Orders are flooding in. Do you . . . now diversify into other gourmet pet foods? **Go to 10** consolidate what you're doing in the dog food market? **Go to 27**	**15** This isn't a good strategy. You need more money, and your father is offering some, but he wants 51% of the business. "Yes!" **Go to 24** "No, I'm going to speak to the bank." **Go to 18**	**16** You're an established name in the pet food world, so maybe you'll be able sell gourmet pet food to the US market (again). "USA here we come!" **Go to 22** "No thanks." **Go to 24**
17 Congratulations! You've reached the end of the maze. It's been a long and difficult road, but you're now rich, retired, and extremely happy. But maybe you'd like to start another business? Tempted? **Go to 1** (Just kidding!) **THE END**	**18** The bank is very helpful and loans you the money at a reasonable rate of interest. This gets the business back on track, and you have now decided just to concentrate on gourmet dog food. **Go to 27**	**19** The public doesn't forget about all those news stories, and you have no time to diversify now. The business goes bankrupt, and you're left with nothing. **THE END**	**20** Dad listened to you and liked your idea. He loans you the money you need at a low interest rate. Do you . . . specialize in just gourmet dog food? **Go to 14** produce a variety of pet food for different animals? **Go to 15**
21 He's not an easy person to work with, but the business is now thriving. However, you're bored with dog food. Do you . . . keep going and try and make even more money? **Go to 23** sell and get a good price? **Go to 17**	**22** If you've already been to **26**, you know it didn't work the first time. Why would it work the second time? If you haven't been to **26** before, the Americans don't understand gourmet pet food. Anyway, **go back to 16** and choose the other option.	**23** Disaster! Sales slump after top vets announce that gourmet dog food is dangerous to dogs' health. Do you . . . wait for people to forget about this? **Go to 19** decide now is the time to diversify? **Go to 16**	**24** The business keeps going, but working with your father creates unimaginable tensions. You end up having a heart attack and selling him your share of the business for virtually nothing. **THE END**
25 Europe loves your gourmet dog food, and you can't keep up with demand. You are tired and stressed, and you need help running the company. Do you employ . . . your dad? **Go to 21** someone else? **Go to 28**	**26** Americans don't really understand the "gourmet" concept, and you find it difficult to achieve any kind of success there. We'll pretend you said "Europe." **Go to 25**	**27** Good decision. The business starts to do really well. Dog food is the biggest and strongest market. It's now time to expand. Europe? **Go to 25** USA? **Go to 26**	**28** Good choice. Madeline, your new manager, does really well. But you're bored with the gourmet dog food market. Do you . . . keep going and try and make even more money? **Go to 23** sell and get a good price? **Go to 17**

Name that word

My boss called a very early morning BEEP to discuss the fate of the company. *meeting*	The seminar will give you the BEEP to meet important professors in the field. *opportunity*	The company spent a lot of money on BEEP in order to sell their product. *advertising*	I was BEEP to my friend when she lost her dog. *sympathetic*
Our job was to make people feel comfortable, so when the new students arrived we were very BEEP. *friendly*	The weather forecaster predicts a BEEP of snow tomorrow. *possibility*	My friends couldn't get a room at the hotel—there were no BEEP. *vacancies*	The book received terrible reviews from the critics, but BEEP some people said it was quite good. *actually*
BEEP of the mystery novel the author resolved all of the loose ends. *at the end*	During the war, the government produced a lot of BEEP. *propaganda*	The final exam will BEEP your command of the language. *test*	After ten years, all of my family gathered for a BEEP in my home town. *reunion*
Frankenstein is a BEEP horror story written by Mary Shelley in 1818. *classic*	He gets his feelings hurt so easily. He's so BEEP. *sensitive*	After debating for hours, BEEP nobody won. *in the end*	The kids enjoyed a nice long summer BEEP. *vacation*
The actor wanted to BEEP to everyone that he could memorize his lines. *prove*	The orchestra only plays BEEP music such as Mozart and Beethoven. *classical*	I'm so busy; I have no time for you BEEP. Maybe later. *at the moment*	She was BEEP because she wore her raincoat and rain boots in the storm. *sensible*

Modal hat-trick

I took my umbrella and it didn't rain. *need*	You can wear a helmet if you want to, but it's your choice. *have to*	You don't think your age will affect your employment. *should*	You've missed the last bus home, and there's no choice but to get a taxi. *might*	You called for a taxi. It's expected soon at your home, but your spouse is still getting ready. *will*
The new employee was told to start at 8:00 A.M. It's now 9:00 A.M., and he or she is not at work. *suppose*	Arriving at the airport, your friend tells you that there was no food on their long flight. *must*	The Brazilian soccer team is going to play Chile. You think Brazil will win. *bound*	You offer to help a friend with his homework. *will*	Your father takes your mother for granted. *shouldn't*
It's a cold morning, and you can't get the car to start. *will*	You know your boss's routine and are sure that she is in her office. Someone asks where she is, and you say . . . *bound*	You are lost and are sure that this isn't the right street. *can*	The vaccination wasn't absolutely necessary, but you got it anyway. *need*	It is customary to take a present to a wedding if you're a guest. *suppose*
Sometimes living with other people is difficult. *can*	The notice said that it's not a good idea to leave bags unattended. *should*	Your friend is talking really loudly in the library. *must*	You want to know if it's OK to park here. *can*	There's a strong probability that your friend will win the contest. *likely*
Your friends are late and you expected them an hour ago. *should*	Your friends tell you that they are driving to California, and you want them to be safe. *must*	A visa isn't required to enter the country, so you didn't get one. *need*	You are uncertain about how safe an area is and ask about taking a taxi. *should*	You can arrive any time before noon. *have to*

✂ -

Referee's Answers

I didn't need to take my umbrella.	*You don't have to wear a helmet.*	*Your age shouldn't affect your employment.*	*I might as well get a taxi.*	*Hurry up! The taxi will be here soon.*
The new employee was supposed to start at 8:00 A.M.	*You must be hungry/ starving.*	*Brazil is bound to win.*	*I'll help you with your homework.*	*You shouldn't take Mom for granted.*
The car won't start.	*She's bound to be in her office.*	*This can't be the right street.*	*I didn't need to get the vaccination.*	*You're supposed to take a present.*
Living with other people can be difficult.	*Bags should not be left unattended.*	*You mustn't talk so loudly.*	*Can I park here?*	*You are likely to win the contest.*
They should have been here an hour ago.	*You must be safe/ careful.*	*I didn't need to get a visa.*	*Should I take a taxi?*	*You don't have to be/arrive there until noon.*

What's the story?

Part A

With your group, think about the stories behind the pictures below. Try to make at least three deductions about what happened in each case.

1.

2.

3.

4.

5.

6.

Part B

With your group, think about the stories behind the headlines below. Try to make at least three deductions about what happened in each case.

1. **Brazil 0 - Costa Rica 4**
2. **Explorers reach South Pole despite extreme weather**
3. **Candidate in dramatic election loss**
4. **Celebrity hits photographer**
5. **Top-rated company's profits drop sharply**
6. **Police say bank robbers disappeared into thin air**

Would you believe it?

Student A

1 (like/hear/story? meet/beautiful girl/train in Italy/ last summer.)

____

____

3 (return home/email/every day/a while. hope/see/again.)

____

____

2 (just/set up/courage/tall man/come over./judging/ ring on finger/fiancé)

____

____

4 (end up/talk./ask/give/email address.)

____

____

Student B

a (year /later/new neighbor/move in. believe it? same girl/train in Italy.)

____

____

c (wish/ask/meet/year ago. maybe/move in/ my house.)

____

____

b (see/struggle/luggage/ask/like/help.)

____

____

d (agree,/and/take/photo/not forget.)

____

____

Feeling faces

Student A
thrilled
miserable
down in the dumps
indifferent
surprised
terrified
taken aback
at wits end
furious
ecstatic
upset
uninterested
petrified
wound up
flabbergasted
outraged
pleased
dumbstruck
livid
delighted
Student B

English in Common 6, Teacher's Resource Book

Feeling lucky

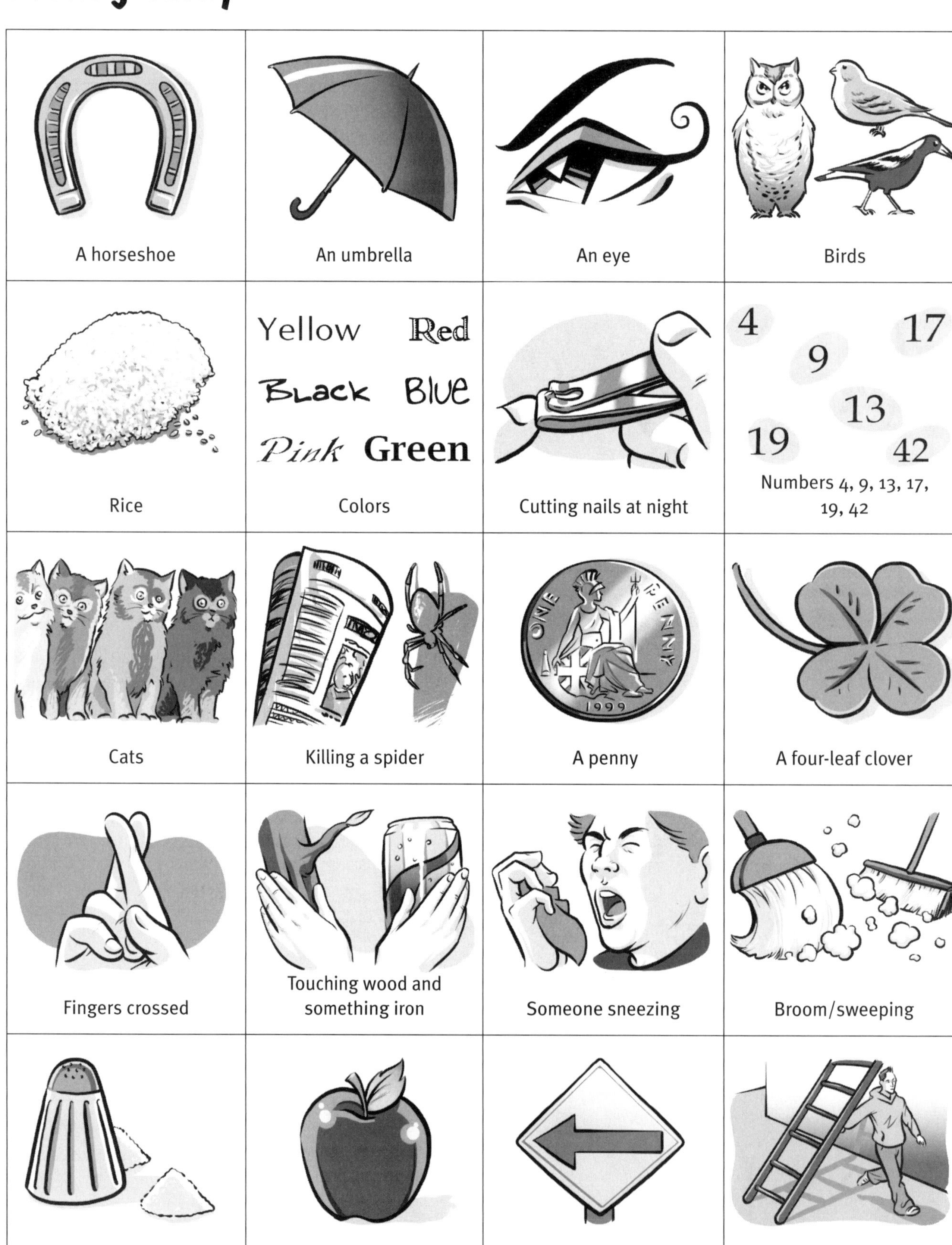
A horseshoe
An umbrella
An eye
Birds
Yellow Red
Black Blue
Pink Green
Rice
Colors
Cutting nails at night
4 9 17 13 19 42
Numbers 4, 9, 13, 17, 19, 42
ONE PENNY
1999
Cats
Killing a spider
A penny
A four-leaf clover
Fingers crossed
Touching wood and something iron
Someone sneezing
Broom/sweeping
Salt
An apple
Left/Right
Walking under a ladder

What's the phrasal verb?

								1		2		
3		4				5						
				6			7		8			9
						10						
									11			
	12			13				14				
						15	16					
	17	18				19						

Across

3. This boomerang won't come down.
5. We had nothing to do so we just hung up.
6. Stop messing off, you'll break something.
10. When I tried to talk to him he just clammed down and wouldn't speak.
11. They struggled for years, but eventually the business passed under.
12. It was a hot day, so we faced for the beach.
14. It was hard work, but we soldiered along.
15. I got up too quickly and passed up.
17. Slow up! You'll get us killed.
19. The manager counted down the money and left.

Down

1. I need to cut up on the amount I eat.
2. The walking trail became difficult, but we continued out.
4. They climbed on with their party plans, despite the bad news.
5. We lounged under at home, waiting for him to return.
7. The lake has completed dried out.
8. During the lecture it's important you write up some notes.
9. I always take off for work at 8:00 P.M.
13. Just relax, would you? You need to calm away.
14. The teacher handed in the students' assignments.
15. I can't do any more. I'm worn in.
16. The three friends drank down and left the restaurant.
18. I hit my head and knocked myself down.

Teacher's notes

Activity Worksheets

Activity Worksheets, pp. 103–106

Teaching Notes

Grammar 1

verbs and adjectives with prepositions

Procedure

Use after Lesson 1.

Divide the class into pairs or groups of four. Give each group one set of cut up cards and the list of sentences. Place the cards facedown and spread out across the table in front of the students. Tell students to take turns turning over a matching pair, for example the *opt* and *for* cards. They can turn over only two cards at a time, and if they are not a pair, they have to put them back facedown in the same place. If the two cards are a pair, then they have to find the correct sentence to write them in, though they may need to change the tense. If the others agree, then they win that sentence, keep the cards, and get a point. This continues until all the pairs have been made and the correct sentences formed.

Answers

1. opted for **2.** lacking in/short of **3.** lacking in/short of **4.** bothered about **5.** nervous about **6.** distinguish from **7.** stem from **8.** rely on **9.** appeal to **10.** riddled with **11.** benefit from **12.** succeeded in

Grammar 2

passives

Procedure

Use after Lesson 2.

Divide the class into pairs (Reporter A and Reporter B). Starting at the top, Reporter A converts the sentence in bold to a passive form using the clue word in brackets. If the word is *not* in the original sentence, it must be used in the converted sentence.The statement is then read to Reporter B, who has the answer. For example, Reporter A says, "*It is believed that Jonny Star has checked into an exclusive clinic.*" If it is correct, then Reporter A moves on, and Reporter B has to convert his or her next sentence in bold. This continues until the conversation is complete. Reporters can give each other extra clues if their partner is having difficulty. Note that some sentences can be converted to the passive in more than one way.

Grammar 3

perfect forms

Procedure

Use after Lesson 3.

Tell students that they are sports stars and they are going to interview another famous sports star. Have students work in pairs and give one partner the soccer player worksheet and the other the ice-skater worksheet. Then have them take turns interviewing each other, asking the questions in order. Explain that they have to choose the correct answer from the answer options. All of the answers use perfect tenses.

Answers

Student A (Adam's questions, Tanya's answers): 1. b **2.** g **3.** f **4.** h **5.** a **6.** e **7.** c **8.** d

Student B (Tanya's questions, Adam's answers): 1. c **2.** a **3.** f **4.** b **5.** g **6.** e **7.** h **8.** d

Vocabulary

unit vocabulary

Procedure

Use after Lesson 3.

Divide the class into pairs and give each pair a maze. Starting in the top left-hand corner as indicated, ask them to find collocations. These can be adjective-noun or verb-noun combinations, but all relate to the theme of challenges and achievements. Once students have found a collocation they then can move either horizontally or vertically to another square, where they have to find another collocation. Collocations run horizontally and vertically but not diagonally. After moving through most of the maze, students will eventually arrive at the finish.The first pair to get to the finish are the winners.

Answers

set achieveable goals; deal with problems; face challenges; make a difference; have the right attitude; paid off; rise to the challenge; ultimate ambition; look forward; an element of risk; have the potential; a learning experience; exceed expectations; pursue a dream; take on an opponent; believe in yourself; head for the top

Activity Worksheets, pp. 107–108

Teaching Notes

Speaking

discuss experiences

Procedure

Use after Lesson 4.

Divide the class into groups of three or four. First ask students to discuss which of the things on the list they have done and whether or not they would ever consider doing the others. Encourage them to explain why or why not. Ask the class for feedback. Then have the students work in the same groups to complete the list with another "20 things to do." Have them include one thing you should **never** do in your life. When this is complete tell students to exchange lists with other groups. Now have students discuss which things they have done and whether or not they would consider doing any of the other things. Encourage them to explain why or why not.

Extra Vocabulary

prefixes

Procedure

Use after Extra Vocabulary Study in ActiveBook.

Divide the class into groups of three or four. Divide the cards equally and place them face up in front of the players. The first player puts a card down in the middle of the table and the other players take turns placing the correct responses to the comments on the right-hand side of the cards or correct comments for the responses on the left-hand side. There needs to be unanimous agreement in the group before the next player can take his or her turn. If a player can't place a card, they miss a turn. The first player to put down all of their cards is the winner. Students can check with the teacher if they are not sure. As an alternative, ask one student to act as referee by checking the worksheet as it appears in the book. In this way, there is less chance of incorrect cards being put down, and the students can continue without needing to consult the teacher.

Activity Worksheets, pp. 109–111

Teaching Notes

Grammar 1

gerund and infinitive review

Procedure

Use after Lesson 1.

Divide the class into pairs and give them a worksheet each. Have them read the profile at the top of their worksheet and explain their situation to their partner. Students have to work their way down the worksheet, exchanging comments about their situations. Student A starts and makes a statement which Student B has to echo in a "conversational" way, using a verb from the top of their worksheet. The other student has the correct echo response on their worksheet and has to elicit a correction if there are any mistakes. Do the first one as an example:

Student A

(gives prompt) *I'm really excited about moving home.*

Student B

Oh really! You're looking forward to moving home.

(gives prompt) *We still haven't managed to sell our house in the United States.*

Student A

Oh, you still haven't succeeded in selling your house in the United States.

Have students continue in this manner, taking turns and eliminating verbs from the boxes at the top of their worksheets as they go.

Grammar 2

comparisons

Procedure

Use after Lesson 2.

Divide the class into groups of three or four and give each group one board, counters or small objects, and a die. Ask students to take turns moving around the board. In order to stay on the square they have moved to, they have to make a comparison between the two words or phrases in the square. The structure they have to use depends on the number they throw; if for example, they throw a five, they have to use one of the structures in the "five" box on the right. For example, "*I'd rather travel by ship than by airplane if I had a lot of time.*" If the others in the group think this is a sensible comparison, the student can stay on that square. The next player rolls the die, moves that many squares, and then makes the comparison. Players should be encouraged to use all the different structures in the boxes if possible. The winner is the first player to reach the finish.

Vocabulary

unit vocabulary

Procedure

Use after Lesson 3.

Divide the class into pairs. Give students the appropriate worksheet (A or B) and ask them to take turns describing the word or phrase in bold on their worksheet without using any of the three words below. If they accidentally say one of the words they are not supposed to say, they declare it to their partner, and they receive a penalty point. Students must not use any forms of the "taboo" words listed. For example, if one of their "taboo" words is *attract* they can't say *attractive*. The activity continues until all of the words have been described. Then review the words with the class and see who received the least penalty points. Emphasize that students must not show their worksheet to their partner.

Activity Worksheets, pp. 112–113

Teaching Notes

Speaking

compare experiences

Procedure

Use after Lesson 4.

Give each student a worksheet and ask them to rank the 15 vacation scenarios in order of how bad they are, number one being the worst. Then ask them to compare their rankings with their partner and come to a consensus about the five worst ones. After that, put students into larger groups and then ask them to agree on a top three. Finally, if there is time for further discussion, ask the class as a whole to agree on the worst one. Students should explain why they think something is particularly bad or not. Here are some additional questions to be discussed in small groups:

Has anything like this ever happened to you? If it has, tell your partner or group about it. What other disastrous things can happen on vacation? What would you do in these situations?

Extra Vocabulary

phrasal verbs

Procedure

Use after Extra Vocabulary Study in ActiveBook.

Divide the class into pairs and give them the appropriate worksheet. Ask them to take turns reading the sentences in bold to each other. Have their partner restate the sentence using the phrasal verbs from their chart. Their partner will tell them whether the restated sentence is correct. If it is, the phrasal verb can be crossed out of the chart, making subsequent sentences easier to make. If there is a sentence that a student can't make, it can be passed over and returned to later when there are fewer words in the chart to choose from.

Activity Worksheets, pp. 114–116

Teaching Notes

Grammar 1

review of past forms

Procedure

Use after Lesson 1.

Divide the class into two separate groups, A and B. Within each group, students work in pairs and are given a story with the lines of the story in the wrong order. Ask the students to number the order of the lines; the first is already indicated. When this has been done, the answers can be given to each group so that students can check their answers.

Then give students a few minutes to reread their story and ask them to remember as much as they can. Reorganize the class so a student from group A is now working with a student from group B. Tell the new pairs to tell their stories to each other, paying attention to past forms and without looking at the original story. After this, ask students to report what they heard to the rest of the class. Any gaps in the story can be filled in by the other students. Then have them discuss the following questions:

Why was one hoax so much more successful than the other? Would you have believed either hoax? If you had worked for *Stern* magazine, would you have been so eager to publish the diaries? Can we believe any of the images of UFOs, monsters, etc. that people sell to the media? What makes a good hoax? What other hoaxes do you know about? Tell the group.

Answers

The Surgeon's Photo: **1.** h **2.** c **3.** m **4.** e **5.** j **6.** a **7.** o **8.** f **9.** b **10.** l **11.** i **12.** n **13.** d **14.** g **15.** k

The Hitler Diaries: **1.** d **2.** i **3.** m **4.** a **5.** f **6.** k **7.** o **8.** e **9.** b **10.** h **11.** j **12.** c **13.** n **14.** g **15.** l

Grammar 2

compound adjectives

Procedure

Use after Lesson 2.

Divide the class into pairs and give them an individual worksheet and a plan of the office to share. There are nine desks in the office. Ask students to take turns reading their information to their partner so that they can find out the names and characters of the nine office workers. For students to do this effectively they need to listen for synonymous words and expressions about the workers. For example, if Student A says, "*The person who can take criticism is next to the door*," Student B looks for related information and reads, "*The thick-skinned person is Mark*." The office workers' names can then be filled in on the office plan. To help students think of the compound adjective, they can look at the reference box to the right of the plan, which also has the names of the office workers. It is only through sharing the information that the task can be completed. Students should not fill in any names unless they are absolutely certain they are correct. Tell students not to show each other the information during this activity.

Answers

1. Sara: level-headed
2. Teresa: hard-working
3. Paulina: absent-minded
4. Joe: self-sufficient
5. Martin: fun-loving
6. Maria: career-oriented
7. Claire: single-minded
8. Ann: stand-offish
9. Mark: thick-skinned

Grammar 3

phrases with participles and gerunds

Procedure

Use after Lesson 3.

Divide the class into pairs and give them the appropriate handout. Have students take turns reading the sentences in bold, which their partner has to convert using a phrase with a participle or a gerund. If the second student has trouble, the first student can read the first word of the converted sentence (in italics) as a hint. Students must not show each other the unconverted sentences; they must be dictated.

Vocabulary
unit vocabulary

Procedure
Use after Lesson 3.

Divide the class into pairs and tell them that they are literary critics who will be discussing some books. Give a handout to each student.The goal of the activity is to put the conversation in the correct order. Student A begins and reads START, then Student B has to find the reply. Student A then finds the correct response to Student B's comment, and so on. Point out that students have to look for synonymous expressions and words, as well as connectors and appropriate answers to questions to complete the activity. They must not show each other their handouts or look at their partner's handout.

After the conversation is completed give both students the discussion questions on the bottom of the page. Have them work in pairs or small groups and report any interesting conclusions to the whole class.

Answers

d - 3 - h - 1 - a - 8 - c - 7 - b - 4 - f - 5 - g - 6 - e - 2

Speaking
ask questions

Procedure
Use after Lesson 4.

Divide the class into teams of three. Give two "It's true" cards and one "I'm lying!" card per team. These cards are divided among the team. Have each team pair up with another team. Place the situation cards facedown in the middle. One member of the team picks up a card and reads the situation. Each member has to answer the question either truthfully if they have an "It's true" card, or if they have an "I'm lying" card, lie and say the opposite of what they would do. The other team is allowed to ask further questions to try to figure out who the liar is. After a brief discussion the team asking the questions guesses who is lying, and the person they accuse has to show them their card. If they have identified the liar correctly, they win that question card. If they are incorrect, the team answering the questions wins the card. Then the other team picks a card and answers the question. The team with the most cards at the end wins. It's important that just before teams are asked the next question they discretely switch their truth or lie cards so the other team doesn't know who is lying. In the event of there being an unequal number of students, students can take turns answering questions.

Extra Vocabulary
metaphors

Procedure
Use after Extra Vocabulary Study in ActiveBook.

Divide the class into groups of four, with two students on each team. One team has the picture cards, and the other team has the phrase cards. Tell students to turn over the cards simultaneously and place them in the middle. If the cards match, the first team to say "Snap" has to make up an appropriate sentence that uses the metaphor on the picture card with the sentence on the phrase card. For example, the picture of someone following in someone's footsteps and the card that says *I'm going to become a doctor like my dad* would require something like *I'm going to follow in my father's footsteps.* If the students agree that the sentence is appropriate, the team wins that pair of cards and the game continues. When all of all the cards have been turned over, the cards are reshuffled so that the game can continue. This goes on until all the cards have been won. The winning team is the team with the most pairs at the end.

Depending on the level of the class and when the student book activities were done, students could be given just the picture cards and asked to remember the metaphor before doing the activity.

Answers

(Tenses may vary.)

I'm going to follow in my father's footsteps./I've reached a crossroads in my life./My career is taking off./I don't want a dead-end job./He gave me a frosty reception./I've been feeling under the weather recently./He's got a warm personality./He has his sights set on a new job./We have a stormy relationship.

Grammar 1
future probability

Procedure
Use after Lesson 1.

Divide the class into groups of two, three, or four and give them a counter each, one die, and a board. The counters are placed at the start. The first player moves to the first square. They do not roll the die yet. The square says, "See your favorite team win the next championship." The student makes a prediction using any one of the prompts from the six boxes above. For example, the player decides, "*My team may well win the next championship*," choosing to use a prompt from box 4. The next player must now roll the die to see if their prediction comes true or not. If the player rolls a four, the prediction has come true, and the player who made the prediction can move the number of spaces indicated (4). If the player rolls any other number, then the prediction doesn't come true, and they stay on the same square, only moving to the next square when it's their turn again. (Players always move forward one square when it's their turn, regardless of whether their last prediction came true or not). Then it is the next player's turn.

Students should be encouraged to make sensible predictions but also to use all three prompts in each box if possible.

Grammar 2
future forms

Procedure
Use after Lesson 2.

Give each student a contract to fill in. Remind weaker students beforehand or during monitoring that in the second section they need to use the future continuous, and in the final section just *will* plus base form. After the contracts have been completed, students sign them in front of a "witness." Then in pairs, or groups of three or four, ask the students to present their contracts to each other, justifying and explaining decisions made.

Grammar 3
subject/verb inversion

Procedure
Use after Lesson 3.

Divide the class into groups of three and give each group a set of cut-up cards. Tell the first player to pick up a card and read the sentence in bold to the player on their right, who then has to invert it. This is checked by the player reading the sentence. (The answer is in italics underneath.) If it is incorrect, the next player has a chance to invert it, and if they don't get it right, it goes back to the first player. After the card has been won, the next player picks up a card and reads it to the player on his or her right. The goal of the activity is to win as many cards as possible.

Students stay in the same groups, and each are given the second handout, which they will have to fill in. Then they tell the other students their ideas. Those listening should be encouraged to ask questions about what has been said.

Vocabulary
unit vocabulary

Procedure
Use after Lesson 3.

Divide the class into pairs and give them the appropriate handouts. Student A describes the completed words and phrases in his or her puzzle, and Student B describes the completed words and phrases in his or her puzzle. Student A asks student B for a word first, which B describes, giving clues and hints if A cannot remember the word. It's important that the answer is not just given if the student cannot remember it, and students should be encouraged to be creative, so that their partners can eventually guess the word. Handouts must not be shown to partners.

Activity Worksheets, pp. 124–125

Teaching Notes

Speaking

describe a scene

Procedure

Use after Lesson 4.

You will need at least two sets of the 12 pictures.Divide the class into two groups of six. Give one complete set to each group, two pictures per student. If there are more or fewer than six students, then some can have three pictures or just one. Explain to the students that they will put the superhero picture story in order by describing the pictures to each other. Students must not look at each others' pictures. Explain that they must listen to each other and be able to describe their picture in detail but quickly. Tell students that the story begins with Picture E and ends with Picture F. When students think they have the right order, they have to retell the story to you so you can check it. If it's not right, they have to try again. The first team to order the pictures correctly wins.

Answers

E I L A J B H D G C K F

Extra Vocabulary

two-part expressions

Procedure

Use after Extra Vocabulary Study in ACTIVEBOOK.

Divide the class into pairs or fours (two on each team). Give them one set of cut-up cards (in Part A), and either one or two copies of the dialog (in Part B). The cards are placed facedown and spread out across the table in front of the students. Then have them take turns turning over a matching pair, for example the "sick and" and "tired" cards. They can turn over only two cards at a time, and if they are not a pair, they have to put them back facedown in the same place. If the two cards are a pair, then they have to find the correct part of the conversation in which to put to put the expression. If the others agree, then they keep the cards and get a point. The winners are the pair or team with the most points. This continues until all the pairs have been found and the conversation is complete. After the activity, students can practice the completed conversation in pairs, though guidance might be needed on intonation and tone because a lot of remarks are sarcastic or scornful.

Answers

1. out and about **2.** rules and regulations **3.** sick and tired **4.** ready and waiting **5.** aches and pains **6.** now and then **7.** by and large **8.** once and for all **9.** facts and figures

Activity Worksheets, pp. 126–129

Teaching Notes

Grammar 1

emphasis

Procedure

Use after Lesson 1.

Give each student a card to fill in. After everyone has filled in their card, students mingle and ask each other questions related to the statements they have just completed. For example, the question for the first statement is "*What can' t you stand*?" The student should reply using what they have written. Then the person who asked the question should be encouraged to ask further questions—for example, "*Why*?" Students can either be asked to find as many other students with the same or similar answers as they have, or they can talk to at least four other students.

Grammar 2

conditionals

Procedure

Use after Lesson 2.

Divide the class into groups of four and give them a board, counters, and a die. It's a good idea to enlarge the board if possible. Have students take turns rolling the die and moving around the board, either finishing the conditional prompts, adding the main clause, or answering the question. If a student lands on a question mark, they have to think of a question (using the target language) to ask the student to their right. The winner is the first player to the finish. Students should try to settle disagreements about correct answers among themselves but check anything they are not sure about with the teacher.

Grammar 3

sentence adverbials

Procedure

Use after Lesson 3.

Divide the class into pairs and give each pair the appropriate handout. Have them take turns reading sentences to each other. The student who is listening says whether the sentence adverbial is used correctly or not. If they think it is incorrect, they need to say which adverbial from the box could be used instead. Tell students that more than one adverbial may be possible. They get a point for successfully identifying correct or incorrect sentences and an extra point for a successful correction. The winner is the student with the most points.

Vocabulary

unit vocabulary

Procedure

Use after Lesson 3.

Divide the class into pairs and give them the relevant handout and a copy of the crossword puzzle. The goal is to fill in the puzzle and eventually find the vertical phrase, 18 down, *declare bankruptcy*. Have students take turns reading their clues to their partner, who then gives the answer. If students don't know or remember the word, then they have to try to figure out the answer together before filling in the puzzle. It's important to emphasize that students must try to guess each other's clues rather than just look at their own clues and fill them in. It's also helpful if the student who is listening is told if the word is divided into two or more words, and how many letters are in each word. Note that the numbers in parentheses refer to the number of letters in each word.

Answers

1. provide for **2.** haggle **3.** paid on commission
4. priceless **5.** stock market **6.** extravagance
7. charge **8.** buy out **9.** come into a fortune
10. the going gets tough **11.** go bankrupt **12.** venture
13. start–up phase **14.** bookkeeping
15. crunch the numbers **16.** hire a consultant
17. lavishly **18.** declare bankruptcy

Speaking

make choices

Procedure

Use after Lesson 4.

First put the students in groups of five. Give each student a role card. If necessary, two people can share a role or one role could be skipped. Tell the students that they each represent an organization or institution that needs money, and are meeting with a rich philanthropist in order to persuade him or her that their cause is the most deserving. The philanthropist is the chairperson and will invite each representative to speak and present his or her case, but the other representatives are also encouraged to ask questions. The situation is a competitive one, because the money will ultimately be awarded to the representative who presents the strongest case.

It's important to give students a few minutes to prepare for the activity in addition to reading time. Encourage them to take notes on the main points that they want to raise. It's also important to explain to the philanthropist that as the chairperson he or she must be impartial and firm with anyone who interrupts others during the meeting. It's a good idea to encourage the philanthropist to prepare questions to ask the representatives about their causes.

Extra Vocabulary

idioms 1

Procedure

Use after Extra Vocabulary Study in ActiveBook.

Divide the class into groups of three and give them a set of cards per group. Have students place the cards facedown. The first player draws a card and reads the prompt in bold to the other two. The first one to give the correct response, written in italics, wins the card. The next player picks up a card and reads the prompt to the other players. The winner is the student with the most cards in the end. In some cases there could be more than one possible answer, but students must give the exact phrase on the card.

Activity Worksheets, pp. 132–134

Teaching Notes

Grammar 1

articles

Procedure

Use after Lesson 1.

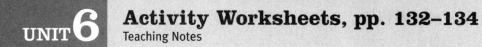

Divide the class into pairs and give each student a handout. The top paragraph on each sheet has the articles missing. Give students a few minutes to add the articles to their top paragraph. Then Student A begins and reads the sentences aloud correctly, with the appropriate articles inserted. Student B follows what's being read by looking at his or her bottom paragraph. It's important that the student who is listening says *correct* or *incorrect* only when the **whole** sentence has been read, not as they go along. If it isn't right, the sentence must be reread. Student B then reads his or her top paragraph. It is important that students don't show their handouts to their partner.

Grammar 2

clauses with *whenever, whoever,* and *whenever*

Procedure

Use after Lesson 2.

Divide the class into groups of three or four and give each group one board and a counter (coin or small object). Ask students to put their counter on a letter. The object of the activity is to visit two other letters by moving across the board, before returning home to the original letter. For example, A could go to D and then C before returning back to A. Have students take turns moving by making correct sentences using a white *however much/many, whenever, wherever, however, whoever* word and a prompt from a dark square. For example, A has to choose *however much/many* but could move to *on vacation* or *get bored*. If A chooses *on vacation*, he or she could say, "*However many things I bring on vacation, I always forget something.*" If the other students agree that the sentence is grammatically correct, then A can stay on the *on vacation* square. Students cannot be on the same square at the same time or move diagonally. The winner is the first player to return to his or her starting letter, having visited two other letters.

Grammar 3

logical connectors of time and contrast

Procedure

Use after Lesson 3.

Divide the class into pairs and give them the appropriate handout. Explain that they are going to piece together an incredible true story, based on a movie titled *Touching the Void*. Student A starts and reads the first sentence to Student B, who has to find the next one. Students find alternating lines of the story until it is complete. There are some numbers given to help students with the ordering.

Students are then asked to speculate on how Joe survived and what they would have done in the same situation. In this case, Joe landed on an ice-shelf half way down the crevasse, and, dragging his body, managed to find a path that led to base camp. However, he barely survived. Despite what happened, the two remained friends and continued to climb together.

Answers

1, e, 9, i, 7, d, 8, f, 10, g, 5, h, 2, c, 3, a, 4, b, 6, j

Activity Worksheets, pp. 135–137

Teaching Notes

Vocabulary

unit vocabulary

Procedure

Use after Lesson 3.

Divide the class into pairs and give them the relevant handout that they must not show to their partner. Students read the descriptions of their presidents to their partner, but not the personal characteristics under the name. Their partner then guesses the three personal characteristics being described and writes them in the appropriate blanks. These can be individual adjectives or adjective phrases. The first and last letter of the word or phrase is given. If necessary, the student reading the description can reread any parts the listener wants to hear again. When both students have filled in all the adjectives and phrases, they can look at each other's handout and check their answers. The correct adjectives and phrases are written under the pictures. Students can then discuss the following questions in pairs or small groups: Which of the characteristics on the handout are the most desirable in a president? Which are the least desirable? Which characteristics would you use to describe the president of your country?

Answers

Jones trustworthy, dignified, inspirational **Mathias** aloof, tireless, idealistic **Montague** approachable, corrupt, down-to-earth **Lopez** non-descript, lacked drive, lacked gravitas **Kozlow** inspiring, untrustworthy, wavered in the face of problems **Duval** charismatic, resolute, undignified

Speaking

present ideas

Procedure

Use after Lesson 4.

Divide the class into groups of three or four and give each group a worksheet. Tell the students that the context is a local election, and each group is a political party trying to win. Students need to choose a party name, a slogan, and ten realistic promises or policies that they will have five years to implement. Once the promises have been written, they can be placed around the class for the other students to read. The "political parties" can then present their policies to the class and answer questions. A vote can be taken to choose which party is going to govern. Students are not allowed to vote for their own party.

Extra Vocabulary

idioms 2

Procedure

Use after Extra Vocabulary Study in ACTIVEBOOK.

Divide the class into pairs. Give them one set of cut-up and shuffled cards per pair. Have students spread out each card facedown across the table between them. Ask students to take turns turning over two cards at a time, looking for a match. Each card is either a picture of a body part or an idiom with a blank for the body part. Students try to match the idiom to the correct picture card. If the cards do not match, make sure the students put them back in the same place. When the student makes a match they take the cards. The activity continues until all of the cards have been matched. The winner is the player with the most cards at the end of the game.

Activity Worksheets, pp. 138–139

Teaching Notes

Grammar 1

adjective clauses

Procedure

Use after Lesson 1.

Divide the class into pairs and tell them to decide if the statements are fact or fiction. Have them check the appropriate box and then pass their handout to another pair to mark. The teacher reveals the answers and the worksheets are corrected and then returned. Students should mark each answer correct (✓) or incorrect (✗) in the right-hand column. Discuss with the students which facts they find surprising. Point out the statements that can have the relative clause reduced. For example, "*The blue whale has a heart that is as big as a large van*" could be "*The blue whale has a heart as big as a large van.*"

Answers

All of the statements are true except:

1. The blue whale's heart is as big as a car.

10. They can hold their breath for 15 minutes.

12. Pandas are only found in China.

15. They spend 80% of their lives sleeping.

16. There are several animals that can't jump, including elephants, rhinos, and mollusks, among others.

19. It's the same length as its body.

21. They eat their mothers.

23. It's the females that bite; the males are vegetarian.

Grammar 2

verbs followed by infinitives or gerunds

Procedure

Use after Lesson 2.

Divide the class into pairs (Student A and Student B) and give them the relevant sheet and the start/goal handout at the top of the page. They will also need a counter, such as a coin. Then have students take turns reading each of their sentences to their partner, who says whether they are correct or not. If they answer correctly, they move the coin or small object one space toward their goal (A goal or B goal). Two moves either right or left of the start square will score a goal, and the coin is returned to the start. The winner is the student with the most goals. The teacher should explain or elicit why sentences are incorrect at the end.

Student A

I must remember to call my mom tonight. It's her birthday.

I really regret getting married when I was so young.

Working for us will mean living abroad for at least three years.

As I was driving home I saw Joe walking down the street

After he finished college he went on to go to get a job in the city.

I hate to tell you, but your work is simply not up to our standards.

Student B

I was tired of driving, so I stopped to get a coffee.

I'll never forget seeing the pyramids for the first time.

As we stood there in the jungle, I could feel something crawling up my leg.

I dread to think what might have happened if I hadn't found him.

We're busy, but we will try to come to your party.

Activity Worksheets, pp. 140–143

Teaching Notes

Grammar 3

as . . . as; describing quantity

Procedure

Use after Lesson 3.

Divide the class into groups of two, three, or four. Ask each player to put their counter or small object on a letter. The object of the game is to get to the lettered square on the opposite side of the board. If you want to extend the activity, you can have students go all the way around the board and back to their original square.

Ask students to take turns moving one square at a time toward their goal. Tell them to make up a sentence using the prompts in that square. For example, Student B "*That lake is as large as a small ocean.*" If the sentence is accepted by the other players, Student B can stay there and then on his or her next turn moves to the next square. They don't need to make a sentence for the phrase in the starting square, just the squares that they are moving to and the final square. The winner is the first one to the other side or to return to his or her square.

Vocabulary

unit vocabulary

Procedure

Use after Lesson 3.

Have students work with a partner. Give each pair of students one handout. For each definition ask them to find the correct word by unscrambling the letters and writing them in the boxes. Another handout can be given to review so that everyone gets one.

Alternative activity: Divide students into groups of four (two pairs). Give definitions 1–8 to one pair and 9–16 to the other. Ask students to write the answers for their definitions and check answers with the teacher. Then have one pair read their definition to the other pair, who then guess the word being described.

Answers

1. mammals **2.** over-fishing **3.** the fur trade
4. predator **5.** carnivore **6.** natural habitat
7. animal rights **8.** cage **9.** breed **10.** exotic
11. hibernate **12.** sanctuary **13.** nature reserve
14. animal testing **15.** endangered **16.** reptile

Speaking

make a case

Procedure

Use after Lesson 4.

Tell the students that a new conservation organization has been set up but needs a species to represent it. Four species have been shortlisted as particularly needing to be saved, and a meeting is now being held to reach a decision as to which one should be the main focus of the organization's help. At the meeting there are four ecologists who will present facts about each species and reasons why they believe it is the right symbol for the organization. Have students work in groups of five, with four students assigned one species each, and one student acting as the chairperson who will ultimately make the final decision.

Give the species information cards to the students and have them read and remember as much information as they can. Then ask them to present the information about their species and justify why it would represent the organization perfectly. The chairperson should consider the following questions:

Which species will appeal most to the public and encourage them to support the organization? Is it better to save a mammal, insect, or bird? Which species can the new organization actually help? Can any of these species realistically be saved? Could an already extinct species maybe be a stronger symbol for the organization?

Extra Vocabulary

suffixes

Procedure

Use after Extra Vocabulary Study in ACTIVEBOOK.

Divide the class into pairs or fours. Give them a set of cards and a board. They will need two small counters or coins. The counters are placed at the start, and the cards are placed face down. The players take turns picking up a card and eliciting words from their partner. The title on the card should be read first to the listening player—for example, *Make verbs*. On each card are four cue words in bold. These are then read to the player, who has to say what, in this case, the correct verbs are. Players have a table of the suffixes they should use at the top of the board. Although it may be possible to add other suffixes to the cue words, only the suffixes in the boxes can be used. For every correct answer they give, they move one space around the board. Roles are then reversed, and the other player is now the one that reads and elicits the words. Incorrect answers can be corrected by the player eliciting the words. Cards are placed at the bottom of the pile and can be reused if the players run out of cards before they reach the end.

Grammar 1

reporting verbs

Procedure

Use after Lesson 1.

Divide the class into groups of four, with three students as players and one as the referee. Two of the players will be "hounds" and one is a "fox." The three players take turns moving by forming a correct sentence using the reporting verbs in the squares. For example, using *warn me,* the student could say, "*The teacher warned me that if I didn' t study hard, I wouldn' t pass the exam.*" The referee, who has a copy of the answers, checks the form. If the sentence is acceptable, the player can move to that square. If their answer is incorrect, the referee must not say what the correct form is, and the player doesn't move. Remind students that in some cases a preposition is needed too. Players cannot use the same sentence twice.

Have players use counters or coins. At the start, the two hounds have to place their counters on the top two dark squares and the fox on the one at the bottom. The object for the hounds is to catch the fox by moving across the board toward it and eventually moving onto the same square to catch it. The object for the fox is to escape from the hounds. Hounds and foxes can move one square at a time horizontally or vertically. When the fox is caught, the hound who caught it gets a point. The winner is the player with the most points, or the fox, if it manages to evade capture. It's possible for the fox who has just been caught to become the referee and for the former referee to become a player. It's advisable to make the strongest student the "fox" in the beginning.

Grammar 2

continuous forms

Procedure

Use after Lesson 2.

Divide the class into pairs and give each pair a handout. Tell them to work their way down the list of sentences and decide if they are grammatically correct or incorrect. Ask pairs to put a check or an X in the first column and then bet a sum of money between $1 and $5, depending on how confident they are about their answer. After all the bets have been placed, ask students to switch handouts with another pair. The teacher then gives the answers with explanations, if needed, and the third column is filled in with the amount won or lost. For example, if a pair bets $3 on a sentence, and they are correct, they win $3, but if they are incorrect, they lose that amount. Have students add up the figures, both plus and minus, and put a total figure at the bottom. The winners are the pair with the most money at the end.

Answers

1. ✗ (**verb** of the senses) **2.** ✗ (**verb** of thought) **3.** ✓ (repeated action) **4.** ✓ (**action** in process of change) **5.** ✗ (**verb** of personal feeling) **6.** ✓ (**temporary** action) **7.** ✗ (**verb** of the senses) **8.** ✓ (**action** in process of change) **9.** ✓ (**background** action in progress) **10.** ✓ (**background** action in progress) **11.** ✗ (**verb** of fixed situation) **12.** ✓ (**less** direct inquiry) **13.** ✗ (**verb** of personal feeling) **14.** ✗ (**verb** of fixed situation) **15.** ✓ (**incomplete** action) **16.** ✓ (**repeated** action) **17.** ✗ (**verb** of fixed situation) **18.** ✓ (**repeated** action) **19.** ✗ (**verb** of thought) **20.** ✓ (**action** in the process of changing) **21.** ✓ (**background** action) **22.** ✓ (**temporary** action) **23.** ✗ (**verb** of thought) **24.** ✓ (**action** in process of change) **25.** ✓ (**repeated** action)

Grammar 3

fronting

Procedure

Use after Lesson 3.

Divide the class into pairs and give them the appropriate handout. Ask them to take turns putting the scrambled words in the correct order to make sentences with fronting. They should start the sentence with the word or words in bold. Their partner will be able to elicit corrections and say whether or not they have done this correctly by looking at the answers at the bottom of the handout.

Activity Worksheets, pp. 147–149

Teaching Notes

Vocabulary

unit vocabulary

Procedure

Use after Lesson 3.

Divide the class into groups of three or four and give them one handout per group. Students then take turns winning squares by rolling the dice and making a sentence. For example, a student rolls a four and chooses a phrase from the two options in the "four box." They also choose a square—for example, "the automobile," from the board. Then they have to combine the two and say "*The automobile is a killer, because thousands of people die every year on the roads.*" If the other students agree that the sentence is correct and that the reason makes sense, then the player can initial that square and it cannot be used again. The activity gets progressively more difficult, and students may need to pass if they can't think of anything, but this should also push them to experiment more and think of more elaborate reasons. The winner is the person who has won the most squares at the end of the activity.

Speaking

offer solutions

Procedure

Use after Lesson 4.

Divide the class into groups of four and give each group a handout. There are two parts to the discussion. In the first part, ask students to discuss the questions. Review can be done with the whole class. In the second part, ask students to think of practical solutions. When enough ideas have been gathered and noted, the groups are rearranged so that students share their ideas with students from other groups. For example, in a class of 16 there are four groups of four (group A, B, C, and D); reorganize each new group so that it has one A, B, C, and D student in it. Ideas are exchanged, and the best solutions are presented to the class.

Answers

Possible consequences and effects include:

1. children playing computer games (lack of exercise, obesity, lack of social skills) **2.** soda machine (children's health, waste of energy) **3.** supermarkets in cities/towns (can undercut smaller stores and put them out of business, unfair competition, limits choice) **4.** cell phones (anti-social, disruptive to others, radiation) **5.** disabled access (political correctness, inconveniencing the majority)
6. large SUVs (dangerous for pedestrians, unnecessary for inner city driving, take up too much space and waste gas) **7.** litter (polluting, smells, look bad)
8. power lines in residential areas (inconclusive, but claims range from headaches to cancer) **9.** pigeons (disease, human wastefulness)

Extra Vocabulary

academic English

Procedure

Use after Extra Vocabulary Study in ActiveBook.

Divide the class into pairs and give them one crossword puzzle per pair. Draw their attention to the information in parentheses after each clue, which gives number of words and word form (either verb or adverbial phrase). Have pairs complete the puzzle together.

Answers

Across: 1. generate **3.** imply **6.** highlight **11** .underline **12.** on the other hand **15.** to be precise **16.** to sum up **17.** namely **18.** notably **19.** furthermore **20.** hint at

Down: 2. regarding **4.** point out **5.** evaluate **7.** in conclusion **8.** infer **9.** assess **10.** in particular **13.** what is more **14.** formulate

Activity Worksheets, pp. 150–152

Teaching Notes

Grammar 1

collocations with prepositions

Procedure

Use after Lesson 1.

To introduce the article, ask students when they think the computer was invented and by whom. Divide the class into pairs and give them the top half of the handout (Part One). Have them complete the article with the prepositions at the top of the page, deleting them as they go. When everyone has finished, ask the students to exchange the completed handout with another pair, and hand out the answer sheet for checking. The total number of correct prepositions needs to be entered at the bottom of the handout. The winners are the pair with the highest number correct. For part two, tell students to turn over the article and try to remember the prepositions from the five categories and fill in the chart. After this they can look at the article to check their answers and also to find other examples.

Answers

verb + preposition: excel **in,** conceive **of,** known **as,** begin **with**

verb + object + preposition: lend support **to,** take pleasure **in**

noun + preposition: contributions **to,** recognition **for,** rate **of,** kind **of,** characteristics **of,** failure **of**

adjective + preposition: disillusioned **with,** obsessed **with,** disappointed **in**

prepositional phrases: in particular, **in** the end, **in** Babbage's time, **on** completion, **in** his declining years, **at** home

Grammar 2

discourse markers

Procedure

Use after Lesson 2.

Divide the class into pairs and give them the appropriate handout. Ask students to read the scenario and then make small talk using the three conversation topics provided. Instruct them to slip the discourse markers into the conversation as naturally as possible. Explain to students that there are three separate conversations, and that they have to try to use as many of the discourse markers as they can in each one, and if possible in all the conversations. Start the activity and give the students about four or five minutes for each conversation topic, then tell them to change to the next topic. It's important that they don't do this until you tell them to. Encourage students to listen for the discourse markers their partner is trying to use, as well as using those listed on their own worksheet. After the activity, students can tell their partner which ones they noticed being used.

Grammar 3

unreal past forms

Procedure

Use after Lesson 3.

Divide the class into groups of three or four and give them one board, enlarged if possible, a die, and counters or coins. Ask students to take turns rolling the die and moving around the board. They must formulate an appropriate answer or response to the prompt they have landed on in order to stay there. The prompts elicit unreal past forms, all of which are shown at the bottom of the board to help students.

As students take turns, the other players should be encouraged to make sure that the most appropriate form is being used. Players must use **all** six forms before they reach the finish. When a particular form is used correctly, the box with the form is initialed by the student. In the case of *What if* and *Suppose*, because the students aren't going to produce them, they can initial the box after landing on a square with those forms in it. If students haven't used all forms as they approach the finish, they are allowed to move backward (and forward) until they have. The winner is the first player to reach the finish with all six boxes initialed.

Activity Worksheets, pp. 153–155

Teaching Notes

Vocabulary

unit vocabulary

Procedure

Use after Lesson 3.

Divide the class into pairs and give them "The gallery" to look at and the appropriate handout. Tell them to imagine that they are art critics at an art exhibition and are discussing their opinions about the pictures as they walk around the classroom. Ask students to look at the paintings one at a time and use the adjectives and phrases on their handout correctly and as naturally as possible. As explained, Student A likes the first and the third picture but not the second and the fourth, and vice versa for Student B. It's very important to encourage students to justify their opinions, as you might expect art critics to do. The teacher should make sure during the activity that the adjectives and phrases are being used correctly.

Speaking

make choices

Procedure

Use after Lesson 4.

To begin, cut up the squares and number the backs. Divide the class into groups of four and tell them that they have to find their way out of the maze by reading the situations and making collective decisions about what to do. Place the cards facedown, in order, in front of the students. Students can only turn over one card at a time, and as soon as they are directed to another card, they have to turn the first card back over. This makes cheating more difficult. Starting at square number one, have the students read the situation and discuss which option to take. The decisions must be unanimous, and students must not cheat by looking at the squares they are sent to before they make a decision. To prevent cheating, have one "neutral" student do the reading aloud. After students have finished, you can discuss which bad decisions they made and what, if any, lessons can be learned from this maze—for example, "Quit while you are ahead." Preteach "thriving," "crippling," "slump," and "flooding in."

Extra Vocabulary

confusing words

Procedure

Use after Extra Vocabulary Study in ActiveBook.

Divide the class into groups of three or four and give them one set of cut-up cards per group. Ask the players to take turns reading each other the prompts on the cards. The first player to correctly identify the word that the "BEEP" represents wins the card. The winner is the player with the most cards at the end of the activity.

Activity Worksheets, pp. 156–158

Teaching Notes

Grammar 1

modals (and verbs with similar meanings)

Procedure

Use after Lesson 1.

Divide the class into groups of four, with one student as the referee. They need one board, preferably enlarged, and one copy of the referee's answers. The three players take turns choosing squares and restating the sentence using the modal given at the bottom of the square. For example, a student chooses the first square, "I took my umbrella, but it didn't rain." They have to use *need* in the new sentence and if they say what is in the referee's answers, in this case "*I didn't need to take my umbrella,*" they win that square, and play moves to the next player. The referee should also accept answers that are similar to the expected answer and that are grammatically correct. The goal is to win three squares in a row either horizontally, vertically, or diagonally. Players may want to block each other and stop the other player from making a row. The winner is the player with the most rows at the end of the activity. It's possible for players to use squares that they have already won again in order to begin new rows. However, if there are four squares in a straight row, it does not count as two rows—there must be five. An example of how the board might look is below:

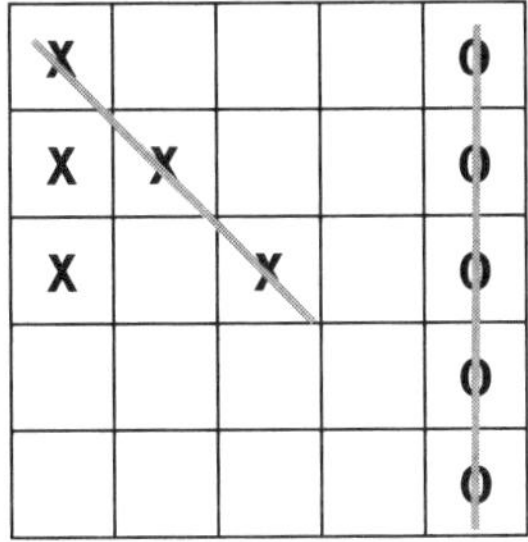

Grammar 2

modals of deduction (past)

Procedure

Use after Lesson 2.

Divide the class into groups of three or four. Ask them to use the pictures (in Part A), and then the headlines (in Part B), as prompts to make deductions about the past using past modals ("*He must have forgotten to send the invitations*"). Students should try to make at least three deductions for each prompt. Although it's often possible to make deductions about the present, they should be encouraged to speculate only about what happened before and not about a present situation. As an extra activity, have students change groups and compare their ideas with their new partners. Alternatively, ideas can be exchanged with the whole class at the end.

Grammar 3

uses of would

Procedure

Use after Lesson 3.

As a warm up, ask students if they have ever met someone interesting on a journey. Then tell them that the activity involves an encounter between two people traveling on a train through Italy. Divide the class into pairs and give them the appropriate handout each. Have them piece together the story by making complete sentences from the given prompts, then reading them to each other and putting the story in order. Each part of the story uses *would* in one of a variety of ways. Teachers can mention this to students or not, depending on the students' abilities. It's important that students don't show their handouts to each other and that they read them aloud clearly. The students can then, referring to the student book, identify how *would* is being used in each case.

Answers (in correct order)

1. Would you like to hear a story? I met a beautiful girl on a train in Italy last summer.
2. I saw her struggle with her luggage, so I asked her if she would like some help.
3. We ended up talking. I asked her if she'd give me her email address.
4. She agreed, and I took a photo so I wouldn't forget her.
5. When I returned home, we emailed every day for a while. I hoped I would see her again.
6. A year later, a new neighbor moved in. Would you believe it? It was the same girl from the train in Italy.
7. Just as I had got up the courage to talk to her, a tall man came over. Judging by the ring on her finger, I'd say it was her fiancé.
8. I wish I had asked her to meet a year ago. Maybe then she'd be moving into my house.

Activity Worksheets, pp. 159–161

Teaching Notes

Vocabulary

unit vocabulary

Procedure

Use after Lesson 3.

Divide the class into pairs or two pairs of two, and give them one handout, a die, and a counter each. Counters are placed in the appropriate places, and the first student or pair rolls the die and moves the required number of spaces. Once the game has begun, students don't have to just move in one direction; they can move up or down depending on where they want to go.

By using the number thrown, the student has to land on an adjective or adjective phrase that corresponds to the face on the left. For example, a student throws a six and the face on the left is the angry one, so they have to land on an angry adjective; for example, *livid* (by moving up and down as necessary). If they manage to do this, they have to complete the sentence, "I was livid because . . ." If the other student(s) accept the sentence, the word is won and the box initialed. If players can't reach the box they want, they have to choose another box related to their adjective.

If a word has already been won, students can still land on it en route to other adjectives or adjective phrases. The students soon realize that they always have a number of options in terms of which words they can land on, so with every move they are constantly thinking about the adjective and the kind of emotion or face on the left. When all the adjectives have been won, the winner is the student or pair with the most adjectives.

Answers

1. thrilled / ecstatic / pleased / delighted
2. miserable / upset / down in the dumps
3. indifferent / uninterested **4.** taken aback / flabbergasted / dumbstruck / surprised **5.** terrified / petrified **6.** furious / outraged / livid / at wits end / wound up

Speaking

discuss ideas

Procedure

Use after Lesson 4.

Divide the class into groups of three or four and give one worksheet to each group. If you are teaching a multilingual class, mix up the nationalities within each group as much as possible. Ask the students to discuss the following questions: *Which of the pictures show good luck, bad luck, or both? Do you know any reasons for these pictures being lucky or unlucky? If you don' t know, imagine why they are good or bad luck.*

Optional homework: Have students research the origin of the superstitions if they are not known. (These are easily found on the Internet). For example, walking under ladders, while appearing to be common sense, actually has more to do with the fact that when gallows were not available people were hung from ladders, and their souls were believed to linger there.

Extra Vocabulary

phrasal verbs and particles

Procedure

Use after Extra Vocabulary Study in ActiveBook.

Divide the class into pairs to complete the crossword puzzle. Have students find the incorrect word in each clue and correct it. The incorrect word could either be the verb or the particle of the phrasal verb. It's worth pointing out to students that more than one of the same particle can appear in the crossword puzzle; for example, there are three *arounds*.

Answers

Across: 3. back **5.** around **6.** around **10.** up **11.** went **12.** headed **14.** on **15.** out **17.** down **19.** up

Down: 1. down **2.** on **4.** carried **5.** around **7.** up **8.** down **9.** set **13.** down **14.** out **15.** out **16.** up **18.** out

***English in Common* ActiveTeach**
Installation Instructions

Windows

- Insert the *ActiveTeach* disc into the DVD-ROM drive of your computer. On most computers, the *ActiveTeach* program will open automatically. On most computers, the DVD video program will also open automatically (using your default DVD software player). Close the application you do not want to use.

If *ActiveTeach* does not begin automatically:

- Open "My Computer."
- Right-click on the DVD-ROM icon. Click on Open.
- Double-click on the "install" file to start the application.

Macintosh

- Insert the *ActiveTeach* disc into the DVD-ROM drive of your computer.
- Double-click on the DVD-ROM icon on your desktop.
- Double click on the "START_OSX" file to run the program.
- To install: Copy all files from the DVD-ROM to a folder on your hard drive.

Note:

- You must have administrator privileges on the computer to install the program.
- Do not remove the DVD-ROM from the DVD-ROM drive while using *ActiveTeach*.
- To watch the DVD video program on your computer, open the default DVD Player software installed on your computer.
- You can also watch the video program using a DVD player connected to a TV.

System Requirements

	PC Compatible	**Macintosh Compatible**
Operating System	Microsoft Windows® XP, Vista, Windows 7	Mac OSX v. (10.4 & 10.5)
Processor	Intel Pentium® IV 1000MHz or faster processor (or equivalent)	PowerPC & Intel processor 500MHz or faster processor (or equivalent)
RAM	512 MB RAM minimum or higher	512 MB RAM minimum or higher
Internet Browser	Microsoft Internet Explorer® 7.x or Mozilla Firefox™ 4.x, or higher	Safari® 3.x, Mozilla Firefox™ 4.x, or higher
Plug-ins	Adobe PDF 8, Adobe Flash 9, or higher	Adobe PDF 8, Adobe Flash 9, or higher
Hardware	Computer DVD-ROM drive, sound card and speakers or headphones. External DVD Player can also be used to watch available video.	Computer DVD-ROM drive, sound card and speakers or headphones. External DVD Player can also be used to watch available video.
Monitor Resolution	1024x768	1024x768
Internet Connection	DSL, cable/broadband, T1, or other high-speed connection required to download plug-ins	

TECHNICAL SUPPORT

For Technical Product Support, please visit our support website at www.PearsonLongmanSupport.com. You can search our *Knowledgebase* for frequently asked questions, instantly *Chat* with an available support representative, or *Submit a Ticket/Request* for assistance.